THE

For many Christians today the Old Testament remains a closed book belonging to a world with which they feel themselves unfamiliar. Yet it is impossible to read the New Testament without coming to recognise that a grasp of the history and theology especially of the opening books of the Bible is essential to making long-term progress in understanding the New Testament's message.

Recognising this need, Noel Weeks has written *Gateway to the Old Testament*. It will serve as an introduction to the literature and message of the Old Testament in general, but it also provides a more detailed study of the three foundational books – Genesis, Exodus and Deuteronomy – on which the rest of the Bible stands.

Those who are new to the study of the Bible will find that *Gateway to the Old Testament* will help to build a secure and lasting foundation for a life time of study, while others for whom the Old Testament is already a well-known companion will find insight which will help towards a deeper and even more rewarding grasp of the message of Scripture as a whole.

Gateway to The Old Testament

Noel Weeks

THE BANNER OF TRUTH TRUST

THE BANNER OF TRUTH TRUST
3 Murrayfield Road, Edinburgh EH12 6EL
P.O. Box 621, Carlisle, Pennsylvania 17013, USA

*

© Noel Weeks 1995
First Published 1995
ISBN 0 85151 690 4

*

*

*Typeset in 12/13pt Bulmer MT
Printed and bound in Finland by WSOY*

Contents

PART III: EXODUS

PART IV: DEUTERONOMY

Acknowledgements

The material included here began life mostly in several different series of sermons and studies. I therefore must thank in the first instance those groups of believers whose interest in the Scriptures encouraged me to prepare these studies:

> *The Progressive Message of the Old Testament* and *Genesis*
> – Revesby Congregational and Presbyterian Churches.
>
> *Exodus* – Sutherland Reformed Church.
>
> *Deuteronomy* – Emmanuel Chapel, South Philadelphia.

From the speaker's notes to a written manuscript that can actually be read with some measure of comprehension is a long road in which others are far more significant than the author. My wife, Jan, undertook the initial task of producing print from scrawl. The comprehensibility of the text is largely due to her.

Finally, I must record my thanks to the Banner of Truth Trust for the efficiency and unfailing courtesy and consideration through which the manuscript has become a publication.

NOEL WEEKS
Sydney, Australia

Introduction

For many Christians the Old Testament is virtually unknown territory. They read it only if they are using a particular reading plan which takes them through the whole Bible. They rarely hear expositions of it. If these generalisations are too sweeping, one will often find that the portions of the Old Testament to which believers are exposed are confined within narrow bands: the Psalms for devotional use or other passages relevant to some particular controversy. The riches of a large portion of the Word of God are largely untapped.

This volume aims to make a small contribution to the need of material which will open up the Old Testament to Christians. It is divided into four sections. One is a survey of the whole, the other three deal with specific books.

1.   It begins with a survey in eight short chapters of the whole Old Testament. These are organised historically so that the main truths revealed in each historical period can be seen in the context of the history of the time.

2.   Genesis is covered in eight episodes. Once more the objective is to combine together the historical events and the main truths which God was communicating to his people.

3. The section devoted to Exodus is not a survey. It is, rather, nine selections from various parts of the book. The aim of these is to bring out the relevance of each section in connection with New Testament teaching.

4. The treatment of Deuteronomy is similar to the treatment of Exodus. Eleven passages, or groups of passages, are related to New Testament teaching and applied.

After each section from Genesis, Exodus and Deuteronomy there are discussion questions. These are not aimed at mere reiteration of the material covered, but rather to stimulate further connection of the teaching of the passage to the rest of Scripture and application of it to the church and the Christian.

PART ONE

The Progressive Message of the Old Testament

1: *The Beginning of Revelation*

There are a number of different forms of overview of the Old Testament. One approach is to emphasise chronology and political history. Matters like the order and dates of kings would be prominent. It is possible to vary that approach a little with the addition of historical material from outside the Bible, such as what we know of the Assyrian and Babylonian kings mentioned in the Bible. The principle of organisation in this case is historical.

A second approach is the literary one. Who wrote the books? When did each author live? What was his literary style? The principle of organisation is thus literary. Where this procedure is followed, one tends to treat the book of Psalms separately from the books of Samuel, although both are closely connected with David.

Finally, there is the approach which deals with the development of ideas. This is historical in the sense that it follows the order of revelation, but it is more concerned with the ideas God revealed through men, than when they lived. The principle of organisation is theological.

I intend to follow largely the third approach, with some mixture of the other two. This brings books which are often separated, such as Psalms and Samuel, into a better and more natural connection to each another.

The Order of the Books

Many people learn, at some stage, the order of the books of the Bible. Learning the order helps to find a book. The order in which the books are placed reflects attempts to group the material of the Old Testament according to some logical principle. There are several means of arrangement. The order of the English Bible reflects that of the Greek translation of the Old Testament, which begins, as all arrangements must, with the books of Moses (the Pentateuch). From there, the principle of organisation seems to be first the historical books (Joshua through to the books of Kings, Chronicles, Ezra, Nehemiah, Esther), then the poetical books of Job, Psalms, Proverbs and so on, and finally the writing prophets (Isaiah through to Malachi). The defect of that order is to make us think of Kings in a separate category from Psalms, or Micah as separate from Chronicles.

The Hebrew Bible starts, as ours, with the Pentateuch. That is followed by the prophets, though not quite as we understand the prophets, as it adds Joshua, Judges, Samuel and Kings, and excludes Daniel from this category. The third division is called the Writings, and includes everything else. There is not much internal unity in the third section, with Psalms, Chronicles and Daniel, for instance, in the same section.

We must realise that we are influenced by the way we are used to having our Bible organised. I am not arguing for any particular arrangement of the books of the Bible, but want to raise the question: how would you arrange the books if you had to place them in historical order? It is a difficult question. Where, for instance, would you put Job? If Job is to be put in terms of the development of ideas, then where should it come? Which books are dependent upon and refer back to others?

The Role of the Pentateuch

Obviously the five books of Moses come first. For the moment I do not want to deal with the beginning of Genesis which, of course, deals with God and his work of creation. I would like to look rather at the first reference to the writing of Scripture. It is in Exodus. Of course there was a people of God long before Moses and there was revelation by God to man long before Moses. Yet we first read of written Scripture in the time of Moses and the history of Adam, Abraham and others was written for us by Moses. Is there something about that period which made the writing of Scripture appropriate at that time? Before we answer that question, let us look at the first cases which we have recorded of the writing down of God's words. (Note: 'recorded'. We are not told of the writing of God's word earlier, though it may well have taken place.) Our first instance is in Exodus 17:14 after Israel had been attacked by Amalek. The next instance would be the writing down of the ten commandments. From there on, we have the writing down of the other commands.

Even if we take just the two cases of the curse upon Amalek and the ten commandments, we have some interesting features. As you look back upon the cases of revelation in Genesis, we have there the giving of God's word direct to individuals. Abraham receives the message personally whether by the appearance of God to him, by visions or whatever. Now we have something new: a human agent, Moses, is involved in the recording and conveying of the message of God. Moses writes the curse

Amalek in a book and reads it in the ears of Joshua. Moses conveys the tablets to the people. Who is this Moses? He is the one sent to convey God's message *(Exod. 3:10)*. He speaks God's message to Pharaoh and to the people of Israel. There is nothing strange in the fact that God's word against Amalek should be conveyed through Moses. God's judgments on Egypt also came through Moses. Nor is it surprising that Moses should, on Sinai, be an instrument in conveying God's commands to Israel.

So we see that the directness of revelation that characterises the period of Genesis is complicated by a new factor. God's word comes via Moses, but that does not mean that it ceases to be God's word. God is very indignant when Moses suggests that his own lack of eloquence will limit God's ability to speak through him. Who made man's mouth? *(Exod. 4:10–12)*. The message will not be garbled by the transmitter, because God made the transmitter. Moses has another important function. He was sent to redeem Israel from bondage.

We could give all sorts of practical reasons for the advent of mediated revelation: God would have to appear not just to Abraham, but to each individual Israelite, but that is not the real issue. The combination we have here, of the one who conveys God's words to man and the one who delivers Israel, ultimately makes sense in the fact that Moses is an anticipation, a type, one conformed to the pattern of the Messiah.

Granted that, let us look once more at the activity of Moses. Then you see that the ministry of Moses, his work of delivering Israel, is a confirmation, a fulfilment of the promises God gave to Abraham, Isaac and Jacob. God's self-identification is that he is the God of the fathers (*Exod.*

3:16–17). This aspect comes out even in the first commandment to write Scripture (the curse upon Amalek), for it is a confirmation of God's word to Abraham: 'The one who curses you I will curse' (*Gen.* 12:3). The connection between Genesis and Exodus is thus the connection between promise and fulfilment.

The Structure of Genesis

Generally speaking, we are used to starting at the beginning and moving forward. What I have done is to start with Moses and his work and to move back. That takes us back to the patriarchs. What is the connection between the first of the patriarchs, Abraham, and what goes before in Genesis? That there is a connection is obvious, because Genesis 11 gives us a genealogy tracing the line of descent from Shem to Abraham, and so we can go back via the genealogy to Adam. There is also a very interesting point in terms of structure. Suppose we start with Genesis 4. We have the line of Cain: the line of men in defiance and rebellion against God. Certainly they do remarkable things like founding cities, and metallurgy, but they are the line that goes away from God. In chapter 5 we have the genealogy that leads from Adam to Noah and includes people such as Enoch. We do not know the beliefs of everyone in this line, but from what is mentioned of Enoch and Noah we know that God-fearers are in this line. So we have two ways, two peoples, placed in contrast: the way of Cain and his descendants, and that of Adam, Seth, Enoch and Noah. At the end stands one man who is chosen to escape the judgment: Noah. God makes a covenant with Noah and delivers him so that he becomes the head of a new humanity. Let us then take what happens after the flood. We read in Genesis 11 of men who build a city in defiance of God, as a memorial to human greatness. It is the same spirit as was in Lamech. We read later in the chapter of the line that leads to Abraham. One man is chosen to be the start of a new humanity: Abraham. What God does with Abraham changes the course of history but it also changes Abraham, as his change of name from Abram to Abraham symbolises. God enters into a covenant with him. So Abraham and Noah are similar figures, but while we are talking about heads of humanity, we should include one more: Adam. Adam has no genealogy to compare with Noah and Abraham, but Moses does give him a genealogy of a sort. In Genesis 2:4 the story of Adam begins: 'These are the generations of the heavens and the earth.' This section is about what comes from, what is generated from, the heavens and the earth: namely the garden and Adam. Compare Genesis 11:27, which begins a new section with the generations of Terah: what follows is not primarily about Terah, but about Abraham who came forth from Terah.

So Adam comes from the heavens and the earth. To know his background, we must go to Genesis 1 and the creation account. Let us recapitulate by going forward from creation. Adam and Eve came from the ground, or are made from the dust of the ground. When Adam sinned, mankind divided into two: the line of Cain and the line of Seth, leading to the judgment out of which Noah was saved, to become the head of a new humanity. Once more, mankind divided. The Babel builders were one expression of humanity, but there was also a new head chosen, Abraham, to begin a new people of God. God gives promises to Abraham which point us forward, to the birth of Isaac, but beyond also, to the deliverance of Israel from Egypt. The exodus was an important event, because it constituted the great Old Testament salvation. Redemption *par excellence* in the Old Testament is the deliverance from Egypt. (By that I do not mean that the Old Testament redemption was merely a political deliverance. Far from it, but the relationship of the political and the spiritual belongs to the next chapter.) As the great Old Testament redemption, the exodus carried with it some distinctive features. Moses was the man sent to deliver Israel, and to convey the word of God to Israel and to the Gentiles. With him therefore the writing of Scripture begins.

The Unity and Diversity of the Old Testament

The exodus is a climax, but it is far from the end; there were promises to Abraham yet to be fulfilled. There was a land to be won. The seed of Abraham was to be a blessing to all the earth. Further, we can go back to a promise given to Adam of a saviour who will bruise the head of the serpent. These points will be taken up in later chapters. Here we need to consider: what unifies the Old Testament? What connects one part to another? Our answer could refer to many things. We could trace history back to a common origin whether to creation or to Adam, Noah or Abraham. Promises also link the Bible together. We read what God promised Abraham, and the rest is concerned with the fulfilment of those promises.

What gives the Old Testament diversity? Genesis is very different in subject matter and style to the later books. In a sense it is these same things. Genesis as a book of promises is different from Exodus as fulfilment. These themes will be taken up later.

The Enigma of Job

In later chapters I would like to show how the books of the Old Testament fit into this structure. The process of promise and fulfilment does not stop with the exodus. After the exodus there are more promises to be fulfilled. To understand a book we must know where it stands in the pattern of promise and fulfilment.

Job is different in that it does not fit into the development of promise and fulfilment which we know in the Old Testament. We should not be surprised at this, as Job did not come from Israel. The book says that Job came from the land of Uz. That does not mean that there was no contact or possibility of contact with Israel. One of Job's friends was Eliphaz the Temanite, the Temanites being one of the tribes descended from Esau. However, there is scarcely anything in Job which could be related to the revelation that comes to Abraham and his descendants. Remember that it was not only from Abraham that God-fearers descended. We meet people such as Melchizedek, Jethro and perhaps Abimelech, king of Gerah, who served God. The tradition or teaching which stemmed back perhaps to Noah, perhaps to Enoch, perhaps to other godly men whose names are unrecorded, continued for a little while alongside of Israel. For how long it continued, we cannot say.

The book of Job is concerned with very basic problems. We treat Job as complex because some of the speeches are hard to follow, but the main points are clear. I think that Noah, for example, could have sat down and read, and understood, Job with no questions asked. However, I think that he may not have understood say, Isaiah, without being informed on the previous history of Israel. Thus whenever the book of Job was written, it makes sense to consider it with the earlier revelation.

The issue of the book of Job is the mystery of God's ways. How can the righteous suffer and God still be just? God's answer is, in effect, 'Yes, it is a mystery, together with a good deal else that I do. What are you complaining about?' It is an answer, and yet half an answer, because it is preparation for the central mystery of the New Testament: the suffering of the righteous Son of God. Job was not the only one whose suffering raised a problem!

2: The Promise and the Law

Exodus as Fulfilled Promise

I have already mentioned that there is a close connection between the promises to the patriarchs and the exodus (*Exod.* 2:23–25). God remembered the covenant. Two things need explanation here. One is remembrance; the other is covenant. In English, to 'remember' is the opposite of to 'forget', or at least when we say that we remember something now, it implies that it was previously out of our mind. Thus the verb 'remember' primarily focuses on the act of dragging something up from wherever in our mind forgotten thoughts lie. This gives us a problem when we speak of God as 'remembering'. Had he forgotten previously? I think that in Hebrew it is not the psychological process, but the result, that is primarily in view. The thing remembered stands in the forefront of one's mind with consequent action following. So at this juncture the covenant is what stands at the forefront of God's mind.

So we turn to covenant. One can define covenant in many different ways. I prefer to define it as an oath-bound relationship between two or more parties. This is a very broad definition, but it needs to be broad to include things as diverse as marriage, human covenants such as those between Abram and Mamre the Amorite and his brethren, and the covenant between God and man. Even among divine-human covenants we can observe great differences, which have led to various definitions of divine covenants. One thing we can say for certain is that a covenant is not always an arrangement between equals. God and man are not equal partners. Covenants are sovereignly imposed by God. Theologians define covenant differently, depending on whether they see covenants primarily as instruments of grace or primarily as law . This may be one of the differences which will remain unresolved because both are right. You can, however, find differences of emphasis in the various covenants recorded in the Bible. There are cases where the duties of man are fairly prominent (though grace is certainly not excluded), for example the covenant making at Sinai. Others can be found that have no mention of human obligation, though it may be implied, such as with the covenant God made with Abram in Genesis 15. They are primarily promissory covenants. God takes obligations upon himself. He makes promises.

We can make this distinction of emphasis, but we must not make a contrast nor imply that there is some contradiction in principle. Each particular covenant administration contributes to the developing relationship between God and his people. Paul gives an emphatic rejection to the suggestion that the law is contrary to the promises of God (*Gal.* 3:21). We can go further than just saying that the law and the promise are not contradictory aspects of the covenant. There is a sense in which covenant precedes law. Take the Sinai covenant in which the aspect of law is so prominent. How does it begin? 'I am the Lord your God, who brought you out of the land of Egypt, out of the house of slavery.' What is that but fulfilment of the promise given in Genesis 15:13–14? In the history of redemption, the great Old Testament example of the fulfilment of promise preceded the giving of the great Old Testament ethical system. It is people who have experienced the faithfulness of God who are themselves required to be faithful. The covenant keeping faithfulness of God prepares for the covenant keeping faithfulness of God's people.

Exodus as Redemption
There are a number of Hebrew words which we translate 'redeem'.

The basic idea of redemption is of acquiring, buying back what has passed into the possession and power of another. As so beautifully illustrated in the book of Ruth, family land which has passed into the hand of another must be redeemed by the next of kin. People as well as land can be redeemed. Leviticus 25:47–52 provides for the redemption of men forced to sell themselves into slavery. Once again it is the responsibility of the next of kin. When God is called the redeemer of Israel, then the Bible means that he is acting as kinsman redeemer.

The issue between God and Pharaoh is concisely stated in Exodus 4:22–23. God claims Israel as his. The covenant relation between God and Israel is that between a lord and servant. God demands that Israel be free to serve God alone. The relationship can also be put in family terms. Israel is God's son. As the father grieved by the bondage of his son, he has come to redeem him. There is a temptation, out of a desire to magnify the New Testament redemption in comparison to Old and out of the reali-sation that the exodus had little spiritual effect on those who took part in it, to play down the spiritual aspect of the exodus. It is sometimes described as a mere external political deliverance. Certainly the heart of Israel was hard and their response was wrong. Nevertheless, the idea of the son redeemed from slavery by the father in order that he might serve his covenant Lord is as spiritual as you could desire. There was a conflict for spiritual and physi-cal allegiance, with God on one side, and Pharaoh and the gods of Egypt on the other (*Exod.* 12:12).

So far as the Old Testament is concerned, the Exodus was the redemption of Israel from the bondage of a slave. That provides a clue to one of the most puzzling aspects of the exodus. The Israelites were commanded to ask for silver and gold and clothing from the Egyptians. (Let me warn against the translation 'borrow'. Borrowing implies responsibility to return, and if the Israelites were borrow-ing what they did not intend to return, they were guilty of deceit. There is nothing in the Hebrew text to imply they indicated they were going to return it. They simply asked.) Why did they do this? In the law concerning release of slaves in Deuteronomy 15:13–14 the slave must be furnished liberally upon his release. God is forcing Egypt to conform to this law. Of course there is, in the case of Egypt, an added element of judgment. Having wrongfully used the labour of Israel, they are forced to recompense the slave.

'The Law which was unto Life'

We have seen that there is no conflict between promise and law. We need to go further and explore the actual role which the law plays. The law was given to those who have experienced the mercy of God. It was given to a redeemed people. Israel did not enter into their special condition of privilege by keeping the law. They were in that position by the election of their fathers and by their redemption from bondage. As chosen and redeemed people, they were commanded to live according to the law.

Paul says something striking about the Sinai law in Romans 7:10, 'This commandment which was unto life'. In speaking of the very close connection between law and life, he is simply picking up a theme commonly expressed in Scripture, for example in Leviticus 18:5. In our concern over the danger of legalism, we must not contradict the clear scriptural testimony of a close connection between law and life. As Paul says in Romans, the problem is not that the law is at fault. The problem is that the human heart is at fault. Sin brings death through the good commandment.

We have already seen that a redeemed people, a people delivered from bondage, a people released to live and serve God, were brought out of Egypt to Sinai. The Passover signified that God in his mercy had provided a substitute for them that they might be granted life, while the judgment of death came upon Egypt. It is appropriate that the law be set forth as the way of life for those who have received life. It is an administration which takes note of the sinfulness of man. It is permeated by the provisions of the sacrificial system. There is forgiveness for sinners who have transgressed the law; but – and this is an important point – there can be no life for Israel in defiance of the law. If we remember our earlier discussion on the covenant, we can say that Israel had the law laid upon them as their covenant obligation, with penalties for covenant breaking. The penalty for covenant breaking is death, whereas the blessing upon covenant faithfulness is life. The atmosphere, the context in which we must place the law, is therefore that of grace and life: a people brought to life out of bondage are to keep the law whose keeping will maintain them in life.

The Presence of the Lord

When Israel were constituted as the people of God charged with serving their God, God himself came down to dwell in their midst. Exodus 25:8–9 shows that God's dwelling in the midst of Israel was according to the pattern which he himself set. The forty days and forty nights that Moses was on the mount are those in which he received the pattern for the tabernacle, its furnishings and its rites. To transgress these ordinances was to fail to treat God as holy. We note the sin of Nadab and Abihu who offered incense without explicit warrant. This invention in worship was severely punished (*Lev.* 10:1–3). God's holiness is his distinctive attribute, distinguishing and separating him from all else. It is closely connected to his glory and honour. God maintained his holiness by laying down the manner and form by which man may approach him in worship. God did not have to change into something else in order to dwell with Israel. He did not forego his holiness. Rather, by laying down in advance the manner of intercourse between himself and Israel, he preserved his holiness.

When God came to dwell in the midst of Israel, he fulfilled the promise of the covenant: 'I will be your God and you shall be my people.' This entailed consequent demands upon Israel; as God in their midst is holy so they must be holy.

The demand for holiness was not without consideration of the fact that Israel was sinful and sinful men in the presence of a holy God are liable to death. The elaborate ordinances which regulated the access of the Israelites to God, which set up barriers and which excluded certain people, also shielded the people from the anger of God (*Exod.* 19:20-24). This danger did not apply just to those places where God revealed himself. Merely to be numbered amongst Israel placed a man in danger. Thus those who were numbered had to pay atonement money to buy themselves out of their liability to judgment (*Exod.* 30:11-16). Surely this in itself should establish that belonging to Israel conveyed no automatic privilege. Carelessness about membership in Israel could lead only to death, for Israel stood in the presence of a holy God.

With the knowledge that these are merely external rites – knowing that the blood of bulls and goats or half a shekel cannot atone for sin – we wonder at the purpose of all this. Did there have to be all that detail: food laws, unclean animals, sacrifice, atonement money and so on? Yet we must realise that the dwelling of God in the midst of his people, from the biblical perspective, could not be accomplished if that people were defiled. Just as the exodus as the great Old Testament redemption foreshadowed the great New Testament redemption, so the establishment of the tabernacle foreshadows the great New Testament consummation, that is the heavenly city, new Jerusalem, in which God will dwell in the midst of his people. This explains the stress upon physical defilement in both cases. We look forward to the abolition of death, and therefore we should not be surprised that death and all associated with death had to be abolished if the camp of Israel was to be holy. Physical defilement was closely connected to death, the shedding of blood, decay and so on.

The Wanderings

All these themes that we have so far considered (promise, covenant, redemption, the presence of God), stand in sharp contrast to another refrain which runs through the account: the unbelief and rebellion of Israel. Let us put this rebellion into the context we have been considering. It instituted covenant breaking, most clearly evidenced in the making of the golden calf. Note the action of Moses. He broke the two tablets of the covenant. His action was appropriate. The covenant had already been broken by Israel, and Moses' action symbolised this fact. With the covenant broken, the anger of God and the curse of the covenant came upon Israel.

When the people refused to believe in God, after the spies had demoralised them, God threatened to annul the covenant (*Num.* 14:12). Note that Moses' prayer under these circumstances consists of an appeal to God's own self-imposed obligations under the covenant (*Num.* 14:14–16). God having taken these obligations upon himself, his glory was at stake.

God did fulfil his promise. He did not cast off Israel, but it was made clear that the unbelievers in Israel shall not enjoy the promises of the covenant (*Num.* 14:22–24). We see here a practical demonstration of the point made earlier. There can be no continuation in life unless there is obedience to the covenant. Lack of faith in the promise and power of God is a spurning of God's faithfulness and has death as the consequence. Being in the covenant community without faith does not entitle one to some lesser blessings. It destines one for death!

3: *Entering an Inheritance*

The division between the last section and this one is somewhat arbitrary. Inasmuch as biblical history is connected history, then all divisions can be somewhat arbitrary. In this section Deuteronomy and Joshua are together because they belong together, not so much from a literary historical point of view (where Deuteronomy belongs with the rest of the Pentateuch), but in terms of ideas. Deuteronomy prepared Israel to enter their inheritance, whilst Joshua tells of the possession of that inheritance. Of course we have to deal with the connections to the past of Deuteronomy and to the future in Joshua.

The Second Law – Renewing of the First Law

Deuteronomy means 'second law'. Even if you did not know that you might know that there are two versions of the ten commandments – one in Exodus 20 and one in Deuteronomy 5, and that there is an overlap in other legislation. Why is there this repetition?

Deuteronomy is connected to the earlier Sinai law. It tells us that these are the words which Moses spoke and when and where he spoke them. Moses took up his account at the departure from Sinai. We thus have a narrative of what has happened between Sinai where the first law was given and what we can call for convenience the second law. The historical scene is set but what is in that scene? It is largely the rebellion of Israel against the words of God and God's faithfulness to his own words. Israel refused to obey and go and take the land, and God's judgment came upon them, but God showed himself faithful. The children which they said would become a prey stand before Moses ready to go in and take possession of the land. His faithfulness in giving them victory over the Amorite kingdoms of Heshbon and Bashan is recounted.

It is against this background that God solemnly warns the people of the dangers of disobedience and gives them the law once more. It is the old law but there is a sharpness to the repetition of it. They belong to the generation who grew up under the curse, seeing in the wilderness wanderings the consequences of disobedience; therefore the warning and the insistence that they keep the law.

The Second Law – New Law for a New Situation

Having said this, it is also true that the new law is not merely a repetition. It does have some new features. There are commandments in Deuteronomy that are not in the earlier commands and, even more significant, there is a change in one specific commandment. Leviticus 17:3–6 makes it clear that as long as Israel are in the wilderness, any domestic animal killed for food had to be killed as a peace offering. That is, specific parts were offered to God and the rest was eaten by the offerer and his family. Thus it was killed at the doorway of the tent of meeting. This law was changed in Deuteronomy 12. When Israel came into the promised land and spread out it would be too far to travel one hundred miles to kill an animal for food. So in 12:20–22 God said they can eat where they like. The situation is different in that God by fulfilling his promises has created a new situation for his people. I would suggest that you can apply the same principle to other cases in Scripture of a change of law: when God as he fulfils his promises creates a new situation for his people there may be appropriate changes in the law. A very good example would be the changes in law connected to the work of Christ. It is important also that we distinguish the biblical view from what is called 'situation ethics'. In the biblical examples God is the one who creates a new situation as he fulfils his covenant promises. It is not that men's customs, situations or beliefs have changed in the course of changing styles.

The Blessing and the Curse
A significant portion of Deuteronomy is concerned with the blessings that will follow covenant obedience and the curses for disobedience. These blessings and curses also look forward to the new situation created, when Israel shall have taken possession of the land. Thus the blessings and the curses of Deuteronomy 28 concern the fortunes of Israel in the promised land (e.g. 28:11, 58-64). It is important to avoid the error which tries to make a clear separation between the physical and the spiritual blessings that God gave Israel under the Old Covenant. The impression is sometimes given that there was some sort of national blessing which came to Israel automatically, as distinguished from a spiritual blessing which came only to believers. That simply does not fit in with Deuteronomy. There cannot be continuation in the physical blessings of prosperity and possession of the land without obedience. True Israel must be faithful Israel.

We see once again that God has taken upon himself obligations, and man has responsibilities imposed upon him. God promised to bless obedience and punish disobedience. One of the major concerns of the later history writers – those who wrote books like Joshua, Judges, Samuel, Kings – is to record the faithfulness of God to what he promised to do here in Deuteronomy. Once God says he will do something then we want to know: did he do it? All history then becomes covenantal. It is a demonstration that what happened shows the faithfulness of God to his promise and the unfaithfulness or faithfulness of Israel. We must read the later history books with Deuteronomy in mind.

In the Footsteps of Moses

Against that background we can understand the frequent refrain in Joshua (e.g. Joshua 1:7–8) 'as Moses commanded'. A connected theme is the importance of the unified obedience of Israel. God, as judge, had the right to appropriate the Canaanites and their property. At Jericho, with the exception of metals which God devoted to the sanctuary, the property was devoted or offered up to God in fire. When Achan sinned in taking the devoted thing, he brought the curse upon Israel who then fled before their enemies. The faithfulness of one group in particular is mentioned. The two and a half trans-Jordan tribes (Reuben, Gad and the half tribe of Manasseh) had already been granted their inheritance to the east of the Jordan. They did not need to fight to receive land, yet they were given their inheritance only on the understanding that they join in the battle to secure an inheritance for their brethren. So Israel were to stand united in their obedience and in their concern for each other. The vision of the holy people was not restricted to the wilderness. Similarly, in Canaan, nothing which defiled was allowed in Israel. No part of Israel could divorce itself from the united struggle.

The Holy War

Here is not the place to deal in detail with the events of the conquest. Briefly summarised, we have first the destruction of Jericho. Then because of the sin of Achan, Israel was initially defeated at Ai, but subsequently destroyed it. Following this, Gibeon made peace with Israel (see below). A confederation of southern Palestinian cities, led by Jerusalem, attacked Gibeon. So Israel went to the aid of Gibeon and subsequently took the southern cities. Following that there was a campaign against the northern cities led by Hazor. They were defeated and Hazor was destroyed.

The strategy of Joshua is interesting. Jericho was taken. Its inhabitants and animals were killed. All metal objects were given to the sanctuary and the city was burnt. With Ai the same happened, except that the cattle and spoil (i.e. precious metal objects) could be taken by Israel. With the other cities, the inhabitants were killed and the spoil went to Israel, but only Hazor was burnt. The Israelites did not settle immediately in the cities thus captured.

The problem that is often raised is the destruction of the inhabitants. Is this not an unethical, barbaric massacre? Whenever we are asked this question we have to distinguish two possible sources of the question. Some will say this because they deny the right of God to judge the world. Suppose God had personally destroyed the inhabitants. Would that have been right? The person who says 'No' is attacking the justice of God. The Scripture makes it clear that the Canaanites deserved the judgment of God

(*Deut.* 9:45; 18:9–12). So the first issue is whether God is to be a righteous judge. The person who denies this does not have just an ethical problem. He has a problem with the biblical God. The second question is whether God can entrust his servants with the responsibility of carrying out his judgments. If it is right for God to punish, then why cannot God charge someone with executing that punishment? That is all that is happening: God tells Israel to administer and enforce his judgment. It is on the second point that one often finds confusion among Christians and this confusion shows itself also in opposition to the role of the state as an instrument of judgment, to church discipline and any other form of punishment administered by man. The problem troubling opponents of judgment administered by humans is: how do we know when we are charged by God and when our own desire to destroy our opponents comes in? Here the Bible is the only answer. Where there is confusion as to the certainty and sufficiency of Scripture then there must be uncertainty on this point because we cannot then be sure that God has delegated specific punishments to men.

Jericho formed a special case. Saying that the city belongs to God meant that all in it must die (*Josh.* 6:17–18). Once more we see that for sinful man to belong to God means judgment. The city was destroyed as a burnt offering. The fire of God's wrath destroyed what was unholy. For man to take anything was to steal from God. Hence the seriousness of the sin of Achan.

The Evangelistic Expectation of Israel

We often remember the story of Rahab the harlot as evidence that faith saved even from God's judgment on the

Canaanites, but we should raise also the question of Israel's attitude. The impression is often conveyed that Israel thought of themselves as completely cut off from all the peoples around – they erected high barriers and were quite indifferent to the nations. There was no concern for the nations. That is false. There were constant warnings that Israel should not be like the nations but that is not to say that Gentiles were unwelcome. On the contrary, the law was full of provisions for aliens who would live in the land of Israel desiring to worship God (*Num.* 15:14–16). The assembly of Israel contained aliens (*Josh.* 8:35). The attitude is shown best of all perhaps in the gullibility of Israel to the story told by the Gibeonites (9:6–27). Their story was believable!

Thus there was an expectation, an expectation that we find throughout the Old Testament that Gentiles will come and join themselves to Israel because they shall hear the fame of God's dealings with Israel. As a matter of fact one of the most prominent leaders of Israel at the time of the conquest was not a descendant of Israel. Only two men of the generation that came out of Egypt entered the promised land. One was Joshua. The other was Caleb, the son of Jephunneh. The latter was a Kenizzite (*Josh.* 14:6), one of the clans of Esau (*Gen.* 36:15). At some stage, his family has been absorbed into Israel and placed within the tribe of Judah. (He may be Caleb, the brother of Jerahmeel in 1 Chronicles 2:42. By the way, if you have ever tried reading the genealogies which begin the book of Chronicles and become completely lost even in trying to trace families, consider the possibility that many of the genealogies are those of foreigners who have come in at some stage and been adopted into Israel. For example, the Kenites of 1 Chronicles 2:55

belonged to Judah and yet obviously their genealogy cannot be traced back to Judah. It is significant for our understanding of Israel in Old Testament times to realise that aliens play a considerable part in the genealogies of Israel).

Dividing the Inheritance

Many chapters of Joshua are devoted to the apportioning of the land conquered. Exact bounds are given and we have the constant refrain that the tribe of Levi did not have an inheritance like the rest of Israel (*Deut.* 18:1-2).

No doubt the exact determination of borders prevented wars of conquest between the tribes, but there was another reason for giving these details. It showed that God had kept his promise. Not one of the tribes had been failed by God. The special case of Levi is not to be thought of as a failure since their inheritance was the Lord they served.

In this sense the time of Joshua was a period of fulfilment (*Josh.* 11:19-20, 23), yet the promise was not completely fulfilled. There was land yet to be possessed (*Josh.* 13).

Discipline in Israel

I have already touched several times upon the sin of Achan who took the thing which belonged to God. Once again we see that continuation in the blessings of the promise cannot go with disobedience. Israel are still required to be a holy people. This comes out very clearly also in the dispute about the altar built by the Trans-Jordanian tribes. The other tribes interpreted it as an attempt to establish a rival altar to the one in the central tabernacle. Their concern was that because sin defiles the whole body, the sin of the individual threatens the whole of Israel (*Josh.* 22:20). Hence the seriousness with which these sins were viewed. Thus the spreading out of Israel from the central shrine did not mean a lessening of God's requirements. All of Israel must be holy.

The Covenant Renewed

The death of Joshua marks the end of the first phase of the conquest. At this transition period there was a covenant ratification (*Josh.* 24) that pointed back and pointed forward just as Deuteronomy did just before the death of Moses. Joshua reiterated the past history laying emphasis on God's faithfulness and protection. He looked towards the future with the command that Israel should obey God, especially in the crucial matter of idolatry.

4: *A Promise Fulfilled*

There is a very great temptation which constantly faces the people of God, especially following a period of blessing and prosperity in which great leaders have been raised up by God. It is to rest content with the victories that have been won in the past and to fail to carry on the fight. The strategy of Joshua which had exterminated the Canaanites, but not destroyed the cities, required following up. If Israel did not take the fight to the enclaves and peripheral areas where Canaanites yet remained, there would be the possibility of their returning to their cities. Once that had happened, the temptation was then there to cut their losses and enslave the Canaanites rather than drive them out.

Judges – the Curses of the Covenant

After the death of Joshua and the generation of the conquest, a new generation arose that was not faithful. Judges 2:10–23 gives a summary of the period of the judges. Unbelief brought upon Israel the curses of the covenant. Once again we see that there can be no enjoyment of the physical blessings of the covenant apart from faith and obedience.

Consequently God delivered Israel into the hands of

oppressors. The oppressors were largely people on the borders of Israel who were allowed by God to extend their rule over Israel, or a portion of it. There was Cushan-rishathaim of Aram-naharaim (that is somewhere in Syria – Mesopotamia is not a good translation), then Eglon king of Moab. After that came Jabin king of Hazor (note that this city, once taken by Israel, has been repossessed by Canaanites); and then the raids of the Midianites and the Amalekites from across the Jordan. Those problems were followed by oppression from the Ammonites. Towards the end of the period of the judges a new enemy became prominent: the Philistines.

The problems of Israel were not limited to foreign oppressions. The book of Ruth tells us that in the days of the judges there was a famine in Israel so that Elimelech was forced to take his family to Moab to try to live there. We read also in Judges of a general decay of morals and unity. Judges includes the story of Abimelech who was made king of Shechem and killed his brothers in order to secure the throne. There was Micah who made household idols and consecrated a Levite to be his priest, only to have idols and priest stolen by the Danites. Finally and most tragically came the rape and murder of the Levite's concubine in Gibeah of Benjamin. The tribe of Benjamin refused to punish the murderers, thus making themselves all liable to punishment. As a result Benjamin was almost exterminated in a series of battles so that a tribe was almost lost in Israel. It was a time of rot and corruption. The enforcement of justice was weakening or lacking. 'In those days there was no king in Israel. Everyone did what was right in his own eyes' (*Judges* 21:25).

Judges – the Covenant Blessings Fulfilled

Deuteronomy 30 holds out a promise that, even though the curse has come upon Israel, there may still be blessing. That promise was fulfilled in the time of Judges. When the people, under chastening, repented of their sins and cried for God's help, he heard them. So he raised up a deliverer in the form of a judge. The narratives about the judges are largely concerned with their military exploits – their battles against oppressors – and yet they are primarily called 'judges'. This is because of the very close connection between internal order (suppression of sin and disputes) and Israel's ability to resist outside invaders.

The goodness of God is also shown in the book of Ruth. When Naomi returned from Moab, an impoverished widow who has lost her husband and two sons, with only an equally impoverished Moabite girl for company, she said, 'Do not call me Naomi (pleasant), call me Mara (bitter), for the Almighty has dealt very bitterly with me' (*Ruth* 1:20). Yet the story goes on to tell of the goodness of God to Naomi so that the women can say to her after Ruth gave birth to Obed: 'Blessed is the Lord who has not left you without a redeemer today' (4:14).

The Judges is surely one of the saddest times in the history of Israel, but in spite of sin and curse, God was still working to fulfil his promises and to demonstrate his goodness to Israel.

Samuel – Prophet, Priest and Judge

Towards the end of the period of the judges, the main enemy of Israel became the Philistines. This was probably connected with a great convulsion in the Eastern Mediterranean region around 1200 B.C. The remnant of the

Egyptian empire in Palestine was destroyed. The Hittite kingdom in Anatolia and many cities in Syria were destroyed. The arrival of these newcomers in Palestine seems to have substantially strengthened the Philistines. So the Philistines became the main oppressor of Israel.

The man who began the work of delivering Israel was Samson (*Judges* 13:5). Samson's own moral weakness was symptomatic of the age. The deliverance of Israel required more than he could do. He gave Israel respite, but not full deliverance. The work of Samuel was more lasting, for Samuel played an important role in calling Israel back to God, which Samson could not have done. Indeed there are few men in the history of Israel who rival him for breadth of calling. At a time when the word of the Lord was rare, he became a very important prophet. He functioned as a priest. He judged Israel. The ministry of Samuel was directed towards bringing repentance in Israel and a turning from idolatry (*1 Sam.* 7:3-4). As a result (*1 Sam.* 7:13), the Philistines were repulsed.

Saul: the Failure of Monarchy

What was the difference between a judge and a king? It would seem that kingship has about it a greater degree of permanence, stability and organisation. The judges were not a perpetual office. A judge was raised up as the need arose. He does not seem to have had an administrative apparatus. His influence was personal. On his death, there was no continuation of the office. Kingship has organisation and permanence on its side. Now, that very advantage can be a disadvantage. For example, organisation can be oppressive through demanding taxes and service. Its permanence may be of small consolation if the succeeding kings are corrupt. One of the points that is often made as a general historical rule is that revolutions never occur when things are at their worst in a country. Revolutions occur when things have started to improve. In a very significant revolution, Israel, towards the end of Samuel's life, rejected the institutions under which they had lived for hundreds of years and demanded a king. It is interesting that the revolution did not come during the worst of the Philistine oppression. It came after the ministry of Samuel had brought relief from that danger. Certainly one factor was the fear of what would happen when Samuel died. He had appointed his sons to judge Israel but they were very corrupt. Yet the most significant factor was the example of the surrounding nations (*1 Sam.* 8:5). Whenever the people of God desire to be like everybody else they have forsaken their holy and distinctive calling. So God says that it amounts to a rejection of his rule (8:7).

Kingship was not evil in itself. Deuteronomy 17:14–20 looked forward to the establishment of monarchy in Israel. What is significant is the attitude of heart. When Deuteronomy gave the rules for a king, it made clear that the kingship was to be a distinctive institution. The king was to be bound by the law. He was to read the law. That means a very different sort of kingship to that of the nations around Israel. Saul was the man caught and eventually destroyed by the conflict between a kingship limited by the law of God and a kingship on the pattern of the nations around. Saul lost the kingship for two offences. Both of them amount to an attempt to set kingship free from the restraints imposed upon it by the law. He offered sacrifice which was restricted to the priests. In all the other nations around, the king is high priest as well as king. Saul was conforming to that pattern. Second, he failed to carry out God's judgment against the Amalekites. In the previous section we saw that God was using Israel as his agent of judgment against the Canaanites. Saul's failure to do so against Amalek is not to be attributed to any compassion on the Amalekites (he saved only the king and the animals). It constitutes an attempt to free himself from the limited role the law allowed him.

David: the Rejected King of Israel

There is so much that one could say about David. Yet let us direct our attention to the aspects of David's life that receive prominent treatment in Scripture. 1 Samuel 16–17 tells us how he was anointed king and killed Goliath. Chapters 18–31 are concerned with David's career as the one hunted and persecuted by Saul. 2 Samuel 1–4 covers the war between David and Ish-bosheth son of Saul. Chapter 5 is about his defeat of the Philistines; 6 and 7 are concerned with the establishment of the tabernacle and David's plans for the temple and 8 and 10 with his further wars. Then begins the section which concerns David's adultery and what follows. A prominent part of that section is the rebellions of Absalom and Sheba (chs. 15–20). These rough figures show that a disproportionate amount of the account was devoted to David's life as the rightful but rejected king of Israel. Fourteen chapters are devoted to Saul's persecution; six to the rebellions of Absalom and Sheba. Compare that with one chapter devoted to his defeat of the Philistines after he became king and one to his victory over Aram (Syria). What does that tell us? Precisely that David as the model king of Israel – the later biblical text looks back upon him as the standard by which later kings are measured – was the rejected king. Certainly Saul was prominent in the rejection but it is very clear in the case of Absalom's rebellion that Absalom had the support of most of Israel and particularly of the tribe of Judah. Gentiles predominated in the people who supported David at that time: his bodyguards, who seemed to be the only men who supported him when he was forced to flee from Jerusalem, could best be described as Philistines; Hushai the Archite, who played the role of a double agent and deceived Absalom into a disastrous decision, was a Canaanite (*Gen.* 10:17); Shobi the son of Nahash, who brought David supplies at the critical stage of his flight, was an Ammonite (*2 Sam.* 17:27).

Every Christian should understand why the biblical text gives such prominent attention to the fact that the model king of Israel was rejected by his own people but supported by Gentiles. (Indications of ethnic origin are given in Scripture for a reason. Do not read over them.)

David – the Promise Fulfilled
In spite of the fact that there are no detailed descriptions of David's military victories, we should not ignore the importance of those victories. The conquest ends with David. Jerusalem would be the last major Canaanite city to fall. Conquest of the wider empire promised to Abraham from the river of Egypt (which is not the Nile but the wadi that marks the border between Egypt and Palestine) to the Euphrates (*Gen.* 15:18) was achieved with David's victory over the Arameans.

Thus the promise of the land found its final fulfilment in the time of David. That means that it was a period of transition in biblical history. Whereas the interest had been in the conquest, now there is a shift to following out the fulfilment of God's further promises.

David – Peace and the Temple

David was himself conscious of the fact that an important stage had been reached in the history of Israel. In Deuteronomy 12:5–14 there is a looking forward to the end of the conquest. Following rest from all their enemies and security in the land, then would come the establishment of the central place of worship as a place where Israel were to assemble to rejoice in all of God's blessings to them. David appreciated that this time had come (*2 Sam.* 7:1–3).

David's choice of Jerusalem as a capital is often ascribed to political considerations. While Jerusalem was well placed to be a political capital, to see its significance as solely political is to miss the vital connection between the end of the conquest and the establishment of the temple. In Psalm 68, God's march of conquest, which begins as Israel comes through the wilderness, ends at Jerusalem.

The New Song

There are a number of songs recorded in the historical books (besides of course those in the Psalms): the song of the sea (*Exod.* 15), the song which Deborah and Barak sang after the defeat of Jabin king of Hazor (*Judges* 5) and the song which David sang when the Lord delivered him from the hand of all his enemies and from the hand of Saul (*2 Sam.* 22). One thing links those three songs. They were sung to commemorate a great act of deliverance in which God had given his people salvation. The high points of God's redemption are celebrated in song. It is not surprising therefore that the period of David, which we have seen is the point where the promise of the land comes to fulfilment, is a period of song. David's songs, as in the example of 2 Samuel 22 (*Psalm* 18), are songs of how the Lord delivered him from the hand of all his enemies and hence the note of persecution is very prominent in David's songs. We should not be embarrassed by the constant reference to enemies in the Psalms. It fits in with David as the persecuted but rightful king of Israel and with the use of these psalms to describe the experience of the Lord Jesus.

5: *A Promise for Kings*

The House of David and the House of God

With the fulfilment of the promise of the land in the time of David new promises were given. In 2 Samuel 7 David realised that the time of peace had come. Hence it was appropriate to build the central place of worship. David's decision was in a way premature. David would fight other wars – expansionary wars rather than defensive wars – but wars nevertheless. The time of peace would not come until the next reign. There is another reason why David could not build God a house. In 2 Samuel 7:10–29 we see the fundamental principle of biblical piety: man's work is always a response, an imitation, of what God has already done. David cannot act before God acts. David can only build God a house when God has first built a house for David. David lived in a house of cedar and therefore thought he should build God a house. However God will build for David a different sort of house by establishing his dynasty on the throne.

This is the new promise which created a new focus for biblical history, now that the promise of the land had been fulfilled. God promised punishment for the descendants of David if they sinned, but the dynasty would never be brought to an end. God took his loving-kindness from Saul but would not take it from David.

This new focus is reflected in the early chapters of 1 Kings. Some historians take the approach: 'Now, this is real history: court conspiracy, scheming about the throne, political alliances between factions. The stories of victories in battle that we have earlier are too mythical – too fabulous. God is involved too often. The stories about the struggle for the throne between Solomon and Adonijah, they are secular power struggles.' Such historians do not understand the structure of biblical history. The Bible has not suddenly given up interest in the plan and purposes of God and become interested in secular political history. The importance of this section is that God is fulfilling his promises. He promised to David that his son would sit on his throne. The son to do this was a special son that the Lord loved and chose. The real story of Solomon and Adonijah is not about power plays. It is about the faithfulness of God to his promises.

Solomon – Peace and Prosperity

The name of the successor of David is a significant one. It means 'peace'. It is a name that sums up the new era into which Israel has entered. The reign of Solomon was one of peace and prosperity. Solomon enjoyed the fruits of what Samuel and David had accomplished. He built the house of God.

The judges had an important role in suppressing sin and solving internal disputes in Israel. That continued as an important responsibility of Solomon. Indeed, whereas with David the emphasis is on the military role of the king, with Solomon it has moved to being the role as judge. His wisdom (the thing which was his distinguishing virtue) was given that he might judge Israel (*1 Kings* 3:5-9).

Instructions for Kings

If the responsibility of the king in such a time of peace was largely judging, for which he needed wisdom, how was he to obtain it? Solomon was given a chance to ask for what he wanted from God. For his descendants, wisdom would be gained another way; hence books like Proverbs and Ecclesiastes. Just as Psalms fits the period of David, so Proverbs and Ecclesiastes fit the period of Solomon. Proverbs is an address to the son in order that the son may gain wisdom. Of course the aim was not merely to prepare the crown prince to rule. It was for the benefit of all of God's people – yet in places the royal emphasis is clear, for example the words of Lemuel which his mother taught him, which refer specifically to rulers, and the importance of being sober when making judgments (*Prov.* 31:3-4). Even though there is this royal emphasis, we should not forget that every believer is a prophet, priest and king. Proverbs is appropriate for all of us. Prosperity and peace in Israel were closely connected to the keeping of the covenant. So the law plays a very important part in the gaining of wisdom (*Prov.* 15:33). What then is the difference between the law of Moses and the wisdom of Solomon? Proverbs adds an extra component to the law – a knowledge of human nature. To be able to judge, one must know what is in man (note the story of the two harlots: 1 Kings 3:16-27). Here is where the instruction of parents is so vital. They are to warn of the sinful nature of the human heart and of its devious schemes.

The Legacy of Solomon

It is one of the great and sad mysteries of Scripture that Solomon failed to follow his own advice. He had the explicit warning of the law (*Deut.* 17:17), yet it was his foreign wives who turned his heart away (*1 Kings* 11:1-8). Hence the threats of two covenants come together – the Deuteronomic, that warns of the punishment for idolatry, and the Davidic, that says that the individual king who sins will be chastened. Yet there is also the promise of the Davidic covenant that the kingdom will not depart from the house of David (*1 Kings* 11:12-13). So adversaries were raised up to Solomon that were to result in the loss of Edom and Damascus from the kingdom.

The most significant adversary was Jeroboam the son of Nebat. He was the one chosen by God to receive a portion of the divided kingdom. The division of the kingdom on the death of Solomon did not put a stop to the royal patronage of idolatry. In Judah the decline continued in the reign of Rehoboam and Abijam (Abijah in Chronicles). The people turned to idolatry and the sexual perversions which accompany it. In punishment the Lord delivered Israel to Shishak king of Egypt, who took away the royal treasures. Thus the wealth of Solomon became a thing of the past.

In the northern nation Israel there was a sequence of idolatrous kings. Jeroboam set up idolatrous altars at Dan and Bethel to attract and divert the people who had been used to going up to Jerusalem for worship. Thus idolatry became even more rife in Israel than Judah. A compounding factor in Israel was that Jeroboam appointed his own priests and himself offered on the altar. So the pattern of the heathen nations around was being fully followed in

Israel. The places of worship were under the domain of the state. Hence we do not find faithful priests in Israel as we do in Judah, attempting to stem the tide of corruption. The independence of the priesthood in Judah plays a role in preserving it from corruption. In Israel the priesthood never played a role in resisting idolatry.

The corruption of the royal house in Israel brought punishment. The house of Jeroboam was destroyed in a bloody purge during the reign of his son Nadab. His successor Baasha followed in the ways of Jeroboam so his dynasty was ended in a very similar way during the reign of Elah his son. The conspirator who killed Elah, Zimri, perished as a result of an army rebellion which brought Omri to the throne.

To understand the future history of Israel, some factors must be understood. Israel was naturally more prosperous and more populous than Judah. Thus in war the ascendancy would tend to be with Israel. However, Israel was weakened by chronic instability of the throne and by the presence of a powerful enemy to the north in Damascus. Thus weak government and yet relative luxury were found at various times in Israel.

Covenant Renewal in Judah

After the reigns of Rehoboam and Abijam there was a change in Judah. Asa did good and right in the sight of the Lord. He put away the idols and the sodomites. He gathered all Judah and those from Israel who turned to him (*2 Chron.* 15:9–15). Thus the Lord gave them rest from their enemies. However, Asa himself was not a perfect king. When hard pressed in an attack by Baasha, he sent a bribe to Ben-hadad king of Damascus to make him attack

Israel. For this he was reproved by the prophet Hanani. To seek the aid of Syria was a reliance upon man and not on God (2 *Chron.* 16:7-9).

The good work of Asa was continued by his son Jehoshaphat. However, Jehoshaphat entered into an alliance with Israel and thus fought on the side of Ahab against Syria at Ramoth-gilead. For this he was strongly criticised by the prophet Jehu the son of Hanani (2 *Chron.* 19:2-3). As a result of the alliance, his son and successor Joram (or Jehoram in Chronicles) was married to Athaliah, daughter of Ahab of Israel. Joram walked in the idolatrous ways of Ahab. He murdered his brothers (2 *Chron.* 21:4). Consequently the curse came upon him and Israel. He was afflicted by a terrible disease and Judah was invaded by Philistines and Arabs who carried away his wives and his sons except for Jehoahaz (or Ahaziah) the youngest. So he died in great pain without anyone's regretting it. When Ahaziah became king he allowed himself to be guided by Athaliah the daughter of Ahab his mother and followed the idolatrous ways of Israel. Thus the reform initiated by Asa and Jehoshaphat was destroyed by Jehoshaphat's alliance with Israel.

The Troubler of Israel

The dynasty of Omri has been mentioned in dealing with Judah. We now turn to that dynasty and especially Ahab. One cannot deal with Ahab without his great opponent Elijah. Their attitude to each other is well summed up by 1 Kings 18:17-18. Omri established a powerful dynasty and the reign of Ahab was the one reign that saw Israel relatively successful against Damascus. Just as Judah was corrupted by alliance to Israel, so Israel, for her part, was corrupted by the influence of her neighbour to the north, the Phoenician city of Sidon. The Sidonian princess Jezebel was married to Ahab.

On the other side were the prophets, led by Elijah and Elisha. The prophet was first mentioned as a future office in Israel as an alternative to necromancy (*Deut.* 18:14–22). Rather than enquiring of the dead to know secret things, Israel must enquire of the prophet, for God will put his words in the prophet's mouth.

In situations where the priests, kings and people had become corrupt, it was the prophet who spoke God's word of rebuke and judgment to them. So the prophets played a prominent role in the various judgments which came upon Israel. It was a prophet, Ahijah the Shilonite, who prophesied to Jeroboam that he would receive part of the kingdom because of the sin of Solomon. The same Ahijah prophesied the destruction of Jeroboam's house (*1 Kings* 14:7–11). Hanani the seer rebuked Asa for seeking alliance with Damascus (*2 Chron.* 16:7ff.). Jehu the son of Hanani rebuked Jehoshaphat for alliance with Israel (*2 Chron.* 19:2ff) and there were many more.

However, the great prophet, particularly in the days of Ahab, was Elijah. He entered upon the scene to proclaim God's judgment on Israel (*1 Kings* 17:1). The role of the prophets in pronouncing judgments is well illustrated in 1 Kings 19:11–18. The significance of the fact that the Lord was not in the violent wind or the earthquake or fire was that the Lord will not show himself by these means of judgment. Rather he will judge through the prophets. In anointing Hazael and Jehu, they installed God's officers to execute judgment on Israel. Note how in 2 Kings 8:12, 13 Elisha weeps because he knows that Hazael is God's chosen instrument to bring God's judgment upon his own people.

Do not forget that along with the curses of the covenant, God also sends the blessings. Those blessings did not come to covenant breakers, but to those within Israel who loved the Lord and his servants. An example was the wife of one of the sons of the prophets who had oil miraculously provided to pay her debts (*2 Kings* 4:1-7). Another was the Shunammite woman who was granted a son and then had that son restored to life (*2 Kings* 4:8-37). Even more striking, when the blessing was taken from Israel it was given to those outside Israel, even to her enemies. Here the striking example was Naaman. By him the Lord had given victory to Syria. Whom were Syria fighting? Israel of course. So the blessing comes to the enemy. Note also the case of the widow of Zarephath. (In quoting that example in Luke 4:25-27 Jesus implied that Israel of his time was also under judgment.) So who were the troublers of Israel? In Ahab's view, the prophets were unsettling the country, but in reality, they were bringing the just judgments of God and his preserving blessings to the faithful remnant.

6: *The Kingdoms of this World*

The International Situation
The exodus of Israel from Egypt probably took place at the height of Egyptian power during the 18th dynasty (*c.*1400 B.C.). Egyptian power collapsed around 1200 B.C. (the latter part of the period of the judges) and for the period we have been considering since the time of the judges there were no great powers facing Israel. The greatest threat was posed by Damascus. In the period now to be considered, the rise of Assyria to a powerful nation threatened the very existence of the people of God. The Assyrian policy for hundreds of years had been to attempt to gain control across the Euphrates and then all the way to the Mediterranean. Once an Assyrian presence was established at the Mediterranean, Israel and Judah were caught between Assyria and Egypt. Assyrian policy was to attempt to conquer them to reduce possible Egyptian influence or threat. Egyptian policy was to stir rebellion and conflict with Assyria in these two countries in order to postpone any Assyrian attack on Egypt.

Assyria had many traits which would fit it to the modern world. Certainly there was a lot of polytheism and superstition there, but it was the country in which pride in human strength came particularly to the fore. An early Assyrian king directed the future king who should read his inscriptions, 'Let him read of my glorious deeds and praise my power.' On the reliefs that the Assyrians made to commemorate their victories, their god Assur floats above the scene but seems small and puny. What really stands out is the muscles of the men and the horses. Read the way Isaiah describes the pride of Assyria (10:5–14). Assyria was the land in which confidence in man had reached its height. So the Assyrian king thought he could do with the people of God as he liked. It is a recurrence of the spirit of Tubal-Cain or of the builders of Babel.

Note that Assyria is called the rod of God's anger (*Isa.* 10:5). Its king might attribute his victories to his own strength, but he was merely an instrument for furthering God's purposes. He was sent to exercise God's judgment upon Israel and Judah. In the period of the judges God used the nations to chastise Israel. In the time of Elijah and Elisha Damascus punished Israel. Assyria was another one in that group of nations raised up to chastise Israel. Yet Assyria did its work with such arrogance and brutal efficiency as to bring into danger the whole future of the people of God.

Stability, Prosperity and Decay in Palestine
In about 835 B.C., Ahab of Israel combined with many of the other states of Syria, including his old enemy Ben-hadad of Damascus, to inflict a great defeat upon Shalmaneser III of Assyria. It was not a lasting victory as the anti-Assyrian coalition fell apart but it gave Syria-Palestine breathing space until internal conflict put a temporary end to the Assyrian attacks.

In Israel, Jehu, who was anointed king by one of the prophets, led a bloody uprising that wiped out the family of Omri and those who worshipped the Baals. He also killed Ahaziah king of Judah. When Athaliah (the daughter of Ahab) heard of this she tried to exterminate the rest of the royal line in Judah and to reign herself. Joash son of Ahaziah was saved and raised in the temple until a revolt led by the priests killed Athaliah and placed Joash on the throne. Thus the house of Omri and Ahab was brought to its judgment.

However, Jehu failed to make a complete end of idolatry in Israel. He continued the idolatrous shrines at Dan and Bethel. So the Lord in punishment gave Israel into the hands of Hazael king of Syria. Syrian domination continued during the reign of Jehu's son Jehoahaz but in the next reign God had mercy on Israel for the sake of his promises and the ascendancy swung back to Israel.

In Judah, the dynasty established by Jehu was paralleled by kings who began well but ended sadly. Joash, who had been raised by Jehoiada the priest, turned to idolatry after the priest's death and killed Jehoiada's son when he rebuked him. So the Lord gave him into the hands of Hazael king of Syria. His son Amaziah also began well but turned to idolatry and pride after his defeat of Edom. He started war with Israel and was defeated. Both Joash and Amaziah were assassinated. Uzziah, the next king, was a faithful and victorious king until his pride got the better of him and he tried to offer incense as a priest. In punishment he was stricken with leprosy.

In spite of this lack of obedience and the complete dominance at one stage of Damascus under Hazael, there yet came a period of power and prosperity for Israel and

Judah. Damascus itself became weak and Israel under Jeroboam the son of Joash became strong (*2 Kings* 14:25–27). Put simply, Jeroboam restored a kingdom such as Solomon had enjoyed. Also Judah under the rule of Azariah (or Uzziah) became strong. They defeated the Philistines, Ammonites, Arabians and others. With power came prosperity. With power and prosperity came even more indifference to the truth of God and the demands of his law. We have seen already how success bred pride in the kings of Judah.

It is against that background that we must understand the first of the prophets in Israel and Judah whose writings have been gathered into books. Hezekiah began his ministry in the reign of Uzziah and Micah in the reign of Uzziah's successor, Jotham. Jonah's prophecy is not dated but we know he prophesied about the same period because he foretold the successes of Jeroboam (*2 Kings* 14:25).

Thus the prophets who foretold the judgment that must come upon Israel and Judah for their constant idolatry, corruption and covenant breaking began their message to prosperous and powerful states. Abraham had to believe the promises of God when everything seemed against them. There is also a trial of faith in believing the threat of judgment when power and prosperity are on every hand.

Ahaz: the Covenant Renounced

The times of stability and prosperity were not to last. With the death of Jeroboam came dynastic chaos in Israel. Within a year, Israel had three different rulers with assassinations and coups. In Judah, Uzziah was succeeded by Jotham, a good king who in turn was succeeded by Ahaz.

Ahaz was an idolater who made his sons pass through the fire and practised the abominations which the Canaanites had done.

Around 745 B.C. the Assyrian weakness ended with the coming to the throne of Tiglath-pileser III (also called by his name Pul in the Bible). He established effective Assyrian control of Syria. Menahem king of Israel capitulated to him and sent him tribute in return for Assyrian aid to help him keep his throne. The next usurper of the throne of Israel, Pekah, was involved in an attempt to form a great coalition similar to the one which had blocked Shalmaneser III. Pekah and Rezin king of Damascus led it. They invited Ahaz to join but he was unwilling. Rather than have an uncertain neutral in their rear, Israel and Damascus turned upon Judah. That is the background to the Immanuel prophecy in Isaiah 7. Ahaz at that time was contemplating what he is subsequently reported as doing in 2 Kings 16:7. He made himself a 'servant' and 'son' to Tiglath-pileser. Those terms, 'servant' and 'son', were covenant terms. Ahaz was placing Judah under covenant loyalty to Assyria, thus formally breaking the covenant with God. Whoever you look to for protection is your lord. You cannot have a human lord without violating the covenant. Ahaz' act was idolatrous. In chapter 7 Isaiah called upon him to look to God alone but Ahaz refused with a trifling excuse. It is in that context that the promise of Immanuel is given as the One who establishes and confirms the covenant between God and his people. Christ stands in clear contrast to the unfaithful house of David.

Ahaz, the unbeliever, sent to Assyria for Assyrian aid. Israel and Damascus were defeated, and Judah became an Assyrian vassal. One more attempt was made by the

Israelites to rebel. The result was the end of Israel. Its upper classes were deported by the Assyrians and replaced by exiles from other areas. The result was an ethnic mixture. The curse of the covenant was fulfilled (*2 Kings* 17:7–23).

Hezekiah: the Covenant Renewed

It was in those times that God brought to the throne the man the Bible calls the greatest king of Judah: Hezekiah (*2 Kings* 18:5). Hezekiah turned back to the covenant with God. In order to do that he had to renounce his allegiance to Assyria. This was classed by the Assyrians as rebellion and led to an attack during the reign of Sennacherib. There have been various interpretations of this attack because Hezekiah seems to surrender and to offer payment to Assyria and yet we read later of an Assyrian army preparing to attack Jerusalem. This has led some scholars to suggest two rebellions. The first one ended with Hezekiah surrendering but he later tried again. That thesis creates all sorts of historical problems and has to be rejected. A simpler and much more satisfactory suggestion is that Hezekiah tried to buy off Assyria. He paid his tribute but Assyria would not be bought off. They had determined to do to Judah as they did to Israel: to destroy it as a nation and to deport its people. Hezekiah refused total surrender.

So the Assyrians came, moving along the coast to take the fortified cities that guarded the way up into the highlands and to Jerusalem itself. While Sennacherib was doing this he sent an ambassador and propaganda agent to try to induce a rebellion against Hezekiah. Read the masterful piece of propaganda in Isaiah 36. Hezekiah stood firm in his trust in the Lord. Sennacherib was forced to return home by rumours of trouble. The army he left behind was destroyed by the angel of the Lord.

Even more significant was Hezekiah's action in purifying the worship of God. He did away with idolatry but went even further. Israel had looked forward to the time when God would give them rest from their enemies all around and then there would be the establishment of the central place of worship. That happened in the days of David and Solomon and yet the establishment of the true worship of God was never carried to its ultimate conclusion. The local shrines that had been used in the time of the judges continued in use. They were an anachronism. They did not belong in the time when God had fulfilled his promise and yet they remained. Good kings failed to do away with them. In the book of Kings there is a constant refrain noting the failure of kings to do away with the local shrines (e.g. 2 Kings 15:34–35). The failure to act was not a sin of the order of idolatry and yet it was held against the king.

Hezekiah removed the local shrines. In other words he was a reformer who saw the need of going beyond the achievements of those before him. Certainly he wanted to return to the example set by Solomon (note Proverbs 25:1) but he was not content with merely imitating the great deeds of the past. He went beyond Solomon in the consistency of his obedience.

He celebrated a great Passover festival in Jerusalem and sent messengers to the tribes of Israel to join together with Judah. As 2 Chronicles 30:26 tells us, there was nothing like this since the days of Solomon. Let us remember this about Hezekiah. The external threats to the people of God had never been greater. Assyria was intent upon crushing any remnants of independence. The spirit of Babel, of the kingdoms of this world, stood ready to destroy the people of God. At that time, Hezekiah pushed through his far-reaching, unprecedented reforms. We should not assume that there was no opposition. We learn that there was from a most interesting source: the speech of the Assyrian Rab-Shakeh before Jerusalem. The speech is somewhat illogical (as is all political propaganda). It was aimed at the fears and resentments harboured against Hezekiah (*Isa.* 36:7). The Rab-Shakeh said that God had ordered him to take Jerusalem in punishment against Hezekiah for destroying the local altars. He was attempting to pander to local resentment of Hezekiah's religious reforms.

Manasseh: the Day of Reckoning Draws Near

Hezekiah had made a great stand. It had been at great cost. The cities of Judah had been devastated by Assyria. Judah was standing alone against Assyria. Manasseh the son of Hezekiah reversed his father's policy (*2 Kings* 21) making Judah again a vassal of Assyria. Manasseh humbled himself in his later life and turned to the Lord (*2 Chron.* 23:10–13) but the damage was done. His son Amon continued the way of idolatry – until he was assassinated and replaced by Josiah.

Beyond the Judgment

One has to read prophets like Isaiah, Micah and Hosea against this background. Significantly they did see hope beyond the judgment. Israel and Judah will return to bondage because of their sin. In a statement of hope, Isaiah named his son Shear-jashub (a remnant shall return). If a remnant were to return, then God did not plan to make a complete end. If Israel were to return to Egyptian bondage so there would be a new exodus (*Mic.* 7:14-20). The prophet who gave considerable elaboration to this theme was Isaiah. He looked to a liberation from the bondage into which Israel entered. He looked even beyond that to a liberation from the sin that brought about that bondage. The liberation from captivity was not to stop with Israel. It was to be the beginning of a salvation that would reach to the ends of the earth (note Isaiah 48:20-22). Note also that the servant song in Isaiah 52:13ff. is also preceded by exodus allusions (verses 11-12). Remember that a new exodus must mean a new Moses. Moses was the pre-eminent 'servant' of the Old Testament (*Num.* 12:7; *Heb.* 3:5). Hence when Isaiah speaks of the Lord's servant after speaking of a new exodus it immediately reminds us of Moses. It raises the question of what is to be the new Passover. Isaiah 53 supplies the answer to that question also.

7: *Into Bondage Once More*

Woe to the Bloody City

Nahum prophesied the fall of Nineveh, the leading city of Assyria. The nation which had relied upon its gods and its magic, its chariots and warriors, was to be destroyed. As they destroyed cities, pillaged them and carried their inhabitants into bondage, so it was to be done to them.

The prophecy of Nahum was fulfilled in 612 B.C. A coalition of Babylonians and Medes gathered to besiege Nineveh. The Babylonians were now under the leadership of the Chaldeans, a tribe settled in the very south of Iraq. The Medes were a people settled to the east of Assyria, in Iran. Nineveh fell, but an Assyrian remnant fled to the west and tried to hold out in Syria. The Egyptians, who for so long had opposed the Assyrians, made an accurate assessment of the situation, realising that Assyria was no longer a danger and that the real enemy was Babylon. Hence, Egyptian help was given to Assyria. By the time the crucial battle came at Carchemish in Syria, in 605 B.C., it was essentially Egyptians versus Babylonians. There the Babylonian Nebuchadnezzar won a decisive victory and chased the defeated Egyptians back to the border of Egypt.

The Faithfulness of Josiah

During the period when Assyrian power was weakening, and Assyria's own problems prevented proper attention to the empire, a new king came to power in Judah. Josiah was a minor when he came to the throne following the assassination of his father. He was a worshipper of the true God. In the eighth year of his reign (at age sixteen), he began to seek the God of his father David (*2 Chron.* 34:3). In the twelfth year, he began to purge the land of idolatry. His work extended into the very north of what had once been Israel. It is an indication of the void created by the collapse of Assyrian power that Josiah was free to carry his activities that far north. In his eighteenth year, he began repairs on the house of the Lord. In the course of the repairs, the book of the law of the Lord, as delivered by Moses, was found in the temple. The reference is to the book which was placed beside the ark of the covenant (*Deut.* 31:26). Such was the apostasy in Israel that the complete law was apparently unknown in Judah, certainly in the royal court. How Josiah received his earlier knowledge, whether from the lips of men who had heard it from others, or prophets, or by written excerpts, we do not know. The finding and reading of the full book of the law had a dramatic effect.

The work of cleansing from idolatry was accelerated, the high places which Hezekiah had removed but which had been rebuilt were defiled, and the Levites who had officiated there were transferred to Jerusalem. A great Passover festival was celebrated. Since 2 Chronicles 35:18 speaks of all Judah and Israel who were present, it seems as though Josiah gathered believers out of Israel as well as Judah to come to the Passover.

There are thus many similarities between the work of Josiah and that of Hezekiah. They include the abolition of idolatry and of the high places, the endeavour to incorporate the faithful remnant left in Israel into Judah and the attempt to re-establish the old limits of the kingdom. Scripture has high praise for Josiah, as it has for Hezekiah. Yet, he did not succeed in turning away the judgment – the abominations of the reign of Manasseh had to be recompensed (2 Kings 23:26–27).

When Pharaoh Necho brought Egyptian armies north to try to bolster the failing Assyrians, Josiah opposed him. Scripture does not indicate Josiah's motives, but it makes clear that he was wrong (2 Chron. 35:21–22). Josiah was killed in that battle, tragically ending one of the greatest reigns in Judah.

Jehoahaz became king, but he did evil in the sight of the Lord. Necho deposed him, and made his brother Jehoiakim king. When Nebuchadnezzar defeated Egypt at Carchemish, Jehoiakim became Nebuchadnezzar's servant. He rebelled against Nebuchadnezzar, but died before the Babylonians arrived. His son Jehoiachin became king, but Nebuchadnezzar deported him and some of the leading men to Babylon. Zedekiah, another son of Josiah, was made king in his place by Nebuchadnezzar.

The Burden of Jeremiah

Jeremiah's ministry took place during the period from Josiah to the aftermath of the final destruction of Jerusalem by the Babylonians. He saw the decline from the faithfulness of Josiah to the corruption that followed and the slide to eventual destruction. That period marked his ministry. Before we rashly conclude that Jeremiah was a bit too pessimistic, we need to consider the situation he faced. In 14:19–22 he prayed fervently for Judah. God responded in 15:1–3 that he would not listen to prayer for the nation. Jeremiah was a priest, one of the priests of Anathoth. A priest's job was to pray, making intercession for his people. Jeremiah was being told by God that his priestly calling no longer had any place in a nation sentenced to destruction.

This prayer should dispense with any notion that Jeremiah lacked concern or compassion for his people. In chapter 28, after the false prophet Hananiah prophesied the return of Jehoiachin and the temple vessels that Nebuchadnezzar had carried off, Jeremiah expressed hope that Hananiah was right. Yet he knew that the prophets of the past have been characterised by the fact that they were willing to warn of the judgment to come, even against mighty empires. Jeremiah, for the sake of his people, hoped for peace and restoration, but was sceptical of the superficial optimism of Hananiah. According to Jeremiah's understanding of the previous prophets, the stern call to flee from the wrath to come is characteristic of true prophecy. It is instructive to compare the reaction of the officials when the princes, priests and prophets wanted to put Jeremiah to death for prophesying evil against Jerusalem. (The leader of those who supported and defended Jeremiah was Ahikam, the son of Shaphan (26:24) who had been a right hand man for Josiah. These were the men who still remained to represent the ideals of Josiah.) They argued (26:16–19) that Hezekiah listened to the words of Micah when he spoke of judgment.

The trend of the times was against such men, however. The royal family opposed Jeremiah and gave a lead to the people. Corruption won over godliness. That is not to say that corruption was restricted to the upper classes (5:1–5). Rather than encouraging civil righteousness, the king Jehoiakim was interested in display (22:13ff.). The corruption of the city and the leaders was well illustrated in an incident during the final Babylonian siege. The king and people entered into a covenant to obey the law of Moses and to release their slaves in the seventh year. They did so, but when the Babylonian army withdrew, they took them into slavery again. God therefore also proclaimed 'liberty' to them, that is, liberty to die via various means (34).

One form of judgment was drought, so that Jeremiah prayed for the land out of compassion for the animals and plants, dying because of the proud rebellion of man (12:4). Primarily, however, it was the Babylonians who were the instrument of judgment (27:1ff.), but it came also, most tragically, in the hardening of the people in sin and rebellion. Thus, even after the final destruction of Jerusalem, Jeremiah warns the refugee group in Egypt to turn from idolatry, and they answer that things were better for them while they were idolaters (44:16ff.). The unbeliever reaches the point where his answer to the misery and punishment brought by sin is to practise more sin. When his idols fail him, he decides to serve them all the more.

Did God therefore cast off his people? By no means! But salvation would not be seen by the generation who would perish in unbelief. Salvation lay in the future. God, in his anger against idolatry, would cast off Israel, but he would also perform a new exodus to redeem them from bondage, so that the nations would be induced to give up their idols. God's wrath upon Israel is a lesson to the nations. For the nations have also trusted in things which cannot save. God punishes Israel, then restores them purified and refined as a hope and incentive to the Gentiles. They too could be saved. We often use a completely false evangelistic strategy, thinking that we have to pretend that all is well with the church, in order to win unbelievers. The reverse is true. There is an anger of God against the church, for we have not obeyed the Word of God. Let the unbeliever take note, for he is in the same situation. If God may yet be merciful to the church, he may be merciful to the unbeliever also.

The anger of God, even against his own people, is not something we should hide in our evangelistic proclamation. God will manifest his own glory. He will manifest it against the false shepherds (23:1–4), who have scattered the flock. He will regather it. God's mercy and anger exist side by side. Both are proclaimed to the nations, and both are his vindication against the corrupt leaders of Judah. God has punished, therefore only God can restore. If God is in control, and it is he who has brought us low, then he can revive. If not, then what hope is there for restoration?

One of the things characteristic of the new salvation is an intensification of the personal element (31:31–34). The problem is in the human heart, so that is where it must be cured.

Jeremiah is a prophet of hope as well as doom. While the Babylonians were besieging the city, which, as Jeremiah knew must lead to its final destruction, Jeremiah was commanded to exercise his redemption right over a plot of land in Anathoth. Since Anathoth was outside Jerusalem, it would have been in the hands of the Babylonians. So Jeremiah did that, as a sign that commerce and agriculture would be restored in Israel (32:15). Certainly, he was commanded to take good care of the contract since it would be a while before it was of any practical use. Nevertheless, it was a tangible symbol of hope: beyond the destruction lay restoration.

The Babylonian Exile

Zedekiah, encouraged by promises of Egyptian aid that never materialised, rebelled against the Babylonians. Nebuchadnezzar sent his armies, and after a long siege, Jerusalem was taken, the temple burnt and the wall destroyed. Zedekiah was captured, his sons killed before his eyes, then he was blinded and taken in bonds to Babylon.

The upper classes were similarly deported, to join those already in Babylon. With the city and temple destroyed, and only the poorer people left in the land, Judah ceased to exist as an organised entity. Some people disobeyed God and fled to Egypt, but the real nucleus of the nation now lay neither in Judah or Egypt. It was amongst those who had been deported to Babylon.

8: *Prelude to a New Exodus*

Ezekiel – Prophet of the New Temple
The temple was burnt by the Babylonians. That mere fact creates all sorts of theological questions and problems, more profound than the question of what happened to the ark of the covenant and the tablets of the law. The temple was the visible symbol of the presence of God among his people. Moses' prayer, after the sin of the golden calf, was: 'If Thy presence does not go with us, do not lead us up from here. Is it not by Thy going with us that we, I and Thy people, may be distinguished from all the other people who are upon the face of the earth?' (*Exod.* 33:15–16). If God's people no longer have his presence, they cease to be his own distinct and peculiar people.

However the doctrine of God's presence had been paganised in Israel. God's holiness had been ignored. It was believed that God would look after them no matter what. There is a form of superstition which assumes that a church, no matter what is done or said, has the blessing and presence of God. This paganism is attacked by Jeremiah in 7:4. It expressed itself in the attitude of the inhabitants of Jerusalem to those involved in the earlier exiles. We speak of the Babylonian exile generally meaning the people who were exiled after the destruction of Jerusalem, but there were others. Daniel and his companions were exiled during the reign of Jehoiakim. Jehoiachin and others, including Ezekiel, were exiled after Jehoiakim's rebellion had failed. So there were the exiles in Babylon even while Zedekiah was still reigning in Jerusalem. Note the attitude of the inhabitants of Jerusalem to these exiles (*Ezek.* 11:14–15). They saw the exiles as those who had been sent away from the land of the Lord. They were out of his presence and favour. The land belonged to those who remained.

In opposition to this, God stated that he would be a 'sanctuary' for the exiles (*Ezek.* 11:16). I think this is why so much of Ezekiel is concerned with visions of God, surrounded by cherubim that Ezekiel saw near the river Chebar. For Ezekiel was amongst the exiles in Babylon when he saw that. The presence of God was not limited to Jerusalem. God came, in all his glory, to the exiles in Babylon. In contrast, in Ezekiel 11:22–23 the glory of God withdrew from Jerusalem.

Much of the latter part of Ezekiel is concerned with his vision of the new temple. We meet here something characteristic of the prophets of the exile. They look to the restoration. If God is once more to dwell in the midst of his people, there must be a new temple. But the prophecy also looks beyond the restoration after the exile to a more ideal and perfect state. It is an ideal picture, incorporating ideas drawn from the actual return. For example, in Ezekiel 43:1–4, the glory of God entered the renewed house by the east gate, which of course fits with the fact that God returned from the east where he had gone to be amongst the exiles. Yet, if you look at the dimensions given in chapter 45 for the holy portion of the land (which should be rods, not cubits), you will see that it is wider than the width of all Canaan. That is, the new Jerusalem would not fit on an ordinary map. In chapter 47, healing waters flow out from the temple to make the Dead Sea 'healed'. What we in effect have is the perfect holy city, in which sin shall be done away with and God will dwell in the midst of his people, described in figures and images drawn from the return of the exiles and the rebuilding of the temple.

Daniel – Prophet of Sealed Prophecy

If Ezekiel took up one problem, that of the presence of God in the midst of his people, Daniel took up another: the apparent victory of the kingdoms of man over the kingdom of God. Daniel was a unique prophet. Indeed the Jewish arrangement of the Bible did not classify him in the prophetic section. His ministry and message were directed to the great powers. Notice his involvement with Nebuchadnezzar king of Babylon and Darius the Mede. The refrain which recurs is the final victory of the kingdom of God over these kingdoms. At that time there was tribulation, in which human kings, inflated with their own power, attempted to lord it over the people of God, and to demand that obedience which belongs to God alone. God protected his faithful servants even in the furnace and the lions' den. Human empires fall. The statue representing the four kingdoms of Babylon, Medo-Persia, Macedonia and Rome would be broken to pieces by a stone cut out without hands, representing the kingdom of God under the King Jesus.

There was a time of war and conflict ahead for the people of God. The great tribulation of the Seleucid oppression of God's people still lay hundreds of years in the future, just as did the revelation of the true king. So Daniel was commanded (12:4) to seal up the prophecy. The time for it to come true lay in the future. Thus, Daniel performed a similar function to that of Isaiah, who wrote under the Assyrian kingdom, pointing forward to the Babylonian exile, and preparing the people for that ordeal and following deliverance. Daniel wrote during the Babylonian exile, when the people of God had before them centuries of Babylonian, Persian, Seleucid and Roman rule. By examples of faithfulness and by the promise of God that these human kingdoms would be smashed by God's kingdom, the book calls for perseverance and faith.

Cyrus – The Lord's Anointed

Isaiah, like Ezekiel, looked to the restoration, and even beyond. Isaiah gave specific details about the return from the exile, most striking of which is the prophecy of Cyrus (*Isa.* 45:1-13).

After Nebuchadnezzar's death, the Babylonian kingdom subsided into relative inactivity. There were no serious enemies. The Medes, their allies against the Assyrians, left them alone while they expanded their own kingdom before being halted by the kingdom of Lydia, which dominated what is today Turkey. One of the last rulers of Babylon, Nabonidus, was a very strange ruler. Due to internal conflicts within Babylonia he lived in virtual exile in Tema in Arabia while his son Belshazzar ruled in Babylon. During this period, the Medes had yielded control to the Persians. Cyrus king of Persia defeated the Lydians and then turned on Babylon. The Babylonian kingdom fell fairly easily into his hands.

Cyrus then set out to win support from the various

groups within his new empire, among whom were the Jews. He commanded that the exiles could return to Jerusalem to build the temple there. In acting this way, Cyrus was not aware that he was an instrument in the hand of God, for he issued similar decrees in the name of other gods. Yet he was chosen and raised up by God to allow the exiles to return to Jerusalem and to rebuild the temple.

The Builders

Cyrus gave the articles of the house of the Lord which the Babylonians had taken away to a prince of Judah, Sheshbazzar (*Ezra* 1:8), whom he made governor (*Ezra* 5:14). Sheshbazzar returned with some of the exiles and began work. It was later said that he laid the foundations of the temple. The men who seem to have been most actively engaged in the work of rebuilding the temple were Jeshua (Joshua in Zechariah) the high priest and Zerubbabel a descendant of the exiled king Jehoiachin. They faced opposition from the Samaritans, who at first wanted to be accepted on an equal footing in the rebuilding project. When the Jews rejected this, they tried to frustrate the work by complaining to the Persian authorities, causing the work to cease. The prophets Haggai and Zechariah stirred up the Jews to begin work again. By this time, Darius 1 (522–486 B.C.) was ruling Persia. He ordered a search, which turned up a copy of the original decree of Cyrus. Hence he ordered the Persian provincial officials to assist the Jews in their work. As a result, the temple was finished in the 6th year of Darius.

Later, in the reign of Artaxerxes (464–423 B.C.), Ezra the priest, the scribe, went from Babylon to Jerusalem, taking with him a number of the exiles, especially priests,

Levites and temple personnel. Thus the return did not take place at once, but as a series of returns, as more and more Jews made their way back to Palestine. Yet, there remained an important Jewish community in Babylon until it was dispersed in the Islamic period (a good 1,000 years later). Ezra took with him money, provided by Artaxerxes for sacrifices to be made in the temple, and gifts for the temple. Ezra's work when he came to Jerusalem was to attempt to secure obedience to the law of God. He was a priest skilled in the law. One of the abuses he set out to correct was marriage to foreign women. Whereas men like Zerubbabel had rebuilt the temple, Ezra's work was to attempt to rebuild the Jewish community. During the exile, there had been a natural tendency for surrounding peoples to press into the land. The restored community would have been small. Thus its existence as a distinct and separate community was precarious.

Ezra was assisted in his work by Nehemiah, who was cup-bearer to the king Artaxerxes and succeeded in getting the king's support for rebuilding the walls of the kingdom. For a very small and threatened community, that was a very important step.

Once again the peoples around were not sympathetic. (For example, Sanballat the governor of Samaria, Tobiah the Ammonite, Arabs and Ashdodites). They tried to frustrate the work, and had supporters even amongst the Jews. Nevertheless, Nehemiah succeeded in rebuilding the walls, after which they held a great assembly in which Nehemiah read the law. There was then an attempt to live by the law, and an attempt by Nehemiah to enforce the requirements of the law upon the people. Thus this period of the return from exile was a period of rebuilding not just the temple and the walls, but also the very idea of a covenant people. Ezra and Nehemiah had to contend against an indifference to the requirements of the law. They found within Israel men in high positions (even the high priest!) marrying foreign women, even in the family of Sanballat. In other words, Ezra and Nehemiah were struggling to make the lines and distinctions clear once again, for if there was no separation in life and marriage, Judah would have been destroyed. The work of Ezra and Nehemiah was vital if the covenant people were to survive.

Looking for the Day

We have already seen the tendency of the prophets to bring together the return from exile and a far greater deliverance yet in the future. The difficulties and discouragements of the return, such as the small size of the temple compared to that which Solomon had built, had its effects upon the returned exiles. So God comforted Zerubbabel and Joshua with the promise that this was but the beginning of a far greater work (*Hag.* 2:2–9). A similar theme is treated by Zechariah in 6:10–15. In a passage that reminds us of Ezekiel's vision of a holy city larger than Palestine, Zechariah looked forward to Jerusalem being a truly holy city. 'Holy to the Lord', once written on the forehead of the high priest, was to be written even on the bells of the horses (14:20). All of the city was to be holy, with the sanctuary taking in all of life.

Nonetheless, it was a hard struggle. Malachi attacked laxity and indifference among the priesthood. Lame and sick animals were being offered as sacrifices on the altar. Tithes were not being paid, resulting in impoverishment for the priests. Hence, Malachi closed with a stern warning to repent before the day of God's judgment comes. Elijah would be sent, as a last attempt as it were, to call rebellious Judah back to the law lest judgment and curse should come. The sending of the one who contended against Ahab and Jezebel indicated the seriousness of sin in Judah, and the need for a return to the covenant.

PART TWO

Genesis

1: *The Creation Week*

Translations of Genesis 1:1 show a significant variation. The alternatives offered by the Revised Standard Version are: 'In the beginning God created the heavens and the earth', or alternatively, 'When God began to create the heavens and the earth, the earth was without form and void, and darkness was moving over the face of the waters.' There is a very great difference in these two translations. The first teaches that it was the creative act of God that brought the first material into being. Matter did not exist before creation. The second says that pre-existing matter was already present when God began to create. It was not ordered matter, but something was there.

In one sense the translation question does not affect our doctrine. We have plenty of other passages which tell us that all things came into being through creation. With the second translation, we would still need to ask: 'Where did the matter that existed at the beginning come from?', and the answer would have to be that God created it. Nevertheless, it is important for our understanding of this passage. It also has significance when this passage is considered against passages from the polytheist myths of the time. The Bible alone teaches creation. All the surrounding cultures and, as far as I know, polytheisms in general begin with pre-existent matter out of which the gods come and, in turn, shape the pre-existent but unformed material into an ordered world. One of the arguments raised by some scholars for translating Genesis 1:1 as 'When God began . . .' is that it conforms to the view of everyone around. Of course, these scholars are rejecting the possibility that this is a revelation from God.

Which is the correct translation? Grammatically, either is possible. If it seems strange that the grammar is ambiguous, we could give many examples of similar cases from our own speech, where we do not feel the ambiguity because grammar is not the only clue to meaning. Context, syntax and words are also significant. In this case, the words used help us. The Hebrew word used for 'create' is used in Scripture of God alone. Both man and God are said to 'make' or form things, but God alone creates. When God and man 'make' things, then the material they use may be mentioned, but with the word 'create' there is no mention of any material (cf. Genesis 1:27 with 2:7). If you look at the contexts where 'create' is used, you will see that the emphasis is often on the new thing that comes into existence as a result of God's creation. In that sense, God's work is different from man's. Man reshapes what is; God brings new things into being. Hence it is quite contrary to the words used that we should expect to see a stress on the nature of the material when God began to create. When we see 'create', we expect to be told what happens as a result, not what was there before God's action.

This leaves the question of whether the first verse is a summary of the whole chapter, or just a beginning. I think it is a summary because it mentions the *heavens* and the earth. The heavens came into being later as the unformed original earth was shaped by the hand of God.

The Gap Theory

Some people want to translate verse 2 as 'the earth *became* waste and void'. They connect this becoming chaotic to Satan's rebellion. It is also a convenient way of explaining away fossils. One says that the fossils come from the previous creation which was destroyed when Satan fell. The translation 'became' is utterly indefensible. Some say that the same word in Hebrew can mean 'be' and 'become', but that is incorrect. Only when followed by the pre-position 'to' can 'to be' mean 'to become' (i.e. in Hebrew you say 'to be to' when you mean 'to become'). There is no preposition 'to' in Genesis 1:2.

The Purpose of Creation

Why then does the text tell us that the earth was waste and void? We must bring this into connection with a verse which is often used as a proof-text for the gap theory: Isaiah 45:18. The argument for the gap theory appeals to the fact that God says he did not create a wilderness; hence the chaos in Genesis 1:2 must be due to Satan's rebellion. Look however at the context in Isaiah. We are told that the alternative to chaos is that God formed it to be inhabited, and that is the conclusion you also reach from the natural reading of Genesis 1. Genesis 1 tells how a creation which was originally not suitable for man became inhabitable. God shaped the world so that man could dwell in it. Isaiah refers to the final end of creation, not to any stage in between. If the stages of creation that we read about in Genesis 1 are preparing for man's habitation, it follows that the return to an earlier stage will make the earth no longer habitable. It would be a judgment upon man, which is just how Jeremiah saw it in a clear allusion to this passage (4:23–26). There are many examples of the reversal of creation as judgment, for example the removal of light as judgment, the return of the waters to the earth as judgment and so on. (Jeremiah 4:23–26 is sometimes taken as a description of the result of Satan's rebellion, but in context it is a description of God's judgment on Judah.)

The last phrase of verse 2 is sometimes translated 'a mighty wind'. This translation has really nothing to commend it except that it makes Genesis 1 more like the pagan accounts. The verb means 'to hover', and is used in Deuteronomy 32:11 of the eagle fluttering or hovering protectively over its young as they learn to fly. 'Brooding', and all the suggestions that God is brooding or incubating life in the waters, are incorrect. An eagle does not brood over its young as they begin to leave the nest. It is the protective role of the Spirit which is described here.

The Meaning of 'Firmament' and the Character of the Passage

The second day raises questions about the 'scientific' nature of the account. We read of a firmament that divides the waters. In verse 8 that firmament is heaven. In verse 14 the sun, moon and stars are placed in it. So, what is this firmament? With any problem in Genesis 1, it is good to turn for help to Psalm 104, a poetic commentary on creation. Psalm 104 follows the order of creation days but with a different focus, especially at the beginning. Whereas Genesis 1 concentrates on the preparation of the creation for man, Psalm 104 sees it as the regalia and trappings of

God, the king. It begins with light as his garment. The canopy of heaven is his palace, which has its foundation on the waters. The clouds are his chariots, the winds and fire his messengers. Since the order follows the creation days, and Psalm 104:2a is concerned with day 1 and 104:5ff. with day 3, the description of 104:2b–4 must cover day 2. Whereas day 1 was described as creating light as a royal robe for God, day 2 is described as creating a tent which is also a palace. Thus it pictures a great royal tent which rests on the waters below but soars into the heavens. Winds and clouds act as the chariots and messengers of God's court. Where in this picture are the firmament and the upper waters? The closest equivalent in Psalm 104 would be the clouds. Could the firmament and the upper waters have something to do with the clouds? In favour of that possibility is the fact that judgment is a reversal of creation. With the flood, the waters of the seas returned to cover the earth. There was also rain, which fits in with seeing the return of the water of the clouds as a return of the upper waters, which were separated from the lower ones.

The stars and heavenly bodies are said, however, to be in the firmament! How can they be in the firmament if the firmament includes the water of clouds? We have this problem if we imagine that the purpose of the passage is to give us a spatial and mechanical model of the creation, as it might appear to an observer standing out in space. However the thrust is rather what God in his goodness has made for man. It is important to know that the waters are above the expanse because it is in God's goodness that the upper waters are kept from the earth. If the water all came back down, we would experience judgment. It is important to know that the sun, moon and stars are in the expanse because thus they give the light without which life would be impossible. They are for 'signs, seasons and years'; that is, they aid men by things like navigation signs and assist in calendrical regulation. Thus the primary thrust of Genesis 1 is not to make a spatial model of the universe. It is rather to teach man thankfulness for what God has created.

We are conditioned by influences which are basically pagan to think that a true understanding of the heavens involves a mechanical-spatial model. How far away is the sun? What goes around the sun, or what does the sun go around? When we come to the Bible, we put such questions expecting the Bible to speak in our terms. Instead it speaks of the goodness of God in shaping the creation. That is, it will not spell out the exact spatial relationship between parts of the creation unless that is relevant to the message. From our earthly point of view both the upper waters of clouds and the heavenly bodies are above us. They are both separated from us by the firmament and fixed in that firmament.

That is not to say that we have two separate and equally valid ways of looking at things: the 'religious' view such as we find in the Bible, and the 'mechanical' or 'scientific' which we inherit from the pagan Greeks. We should not think as Christians and then switch over to think as pagans. Such schizophrenia is a contradiction of the heart of biblical religion, which demands that we think and act christianly with all our minds and at all times. Rather Genesis 1 teaches man to see creation as what God has made in order that man may live. Whenever we deal with the creation, we must be reminded of that beneficence of God. If for some practical purpose, man needs to know how far away the sun is, then he must make the calculation with gratitude that the sun is there to allow him to make such practically useful calculations. He does not turn off his faith and say: 'Now I must think about a blob of matter in the sky and cease giving thanks. Now I see it in mechanical, atheistic terms.' When some say that Genesis 1 is not a 'scientific' account, they really mean that it is irrelevant to what they do as scientists, instead of seeing that they should learn from it what is the perspective of a real Christian scientist.

The Lord–Servant Structure
Note the description of the fourth day of creation. The sun and moon rule the day and night. They rule what was created on the first day. Light and darkness are their realm, that is the kingdom in which they exist and over which they have dominion. Let us look at the fifth day. What is created? The creatures of the waters and the heavens: fish and birds. What was the concern of the second day? It was the separation of the waters and the creation of the heavens. Do you see a pattern? What about other days? The sixth day tells of animals and man; the third of dry land and plants. So on the first three days we have creation of the environment, and on the second three days the creature who lives and sometimes rules in that environment.

Sometimes people point this out as proof that this parallelism proves Genesis 1 to be poetic. That is incorrect. The Psalms show the character of Hebrew poetic parallelism. There a line is immediately paralleled by another line. Rather the point of Genesis 1 is that the covenantal structure of a lord and a servant is built into the very structure of creation.

Man and the Animals

We should not assume that what the passage says about dominion is confined to this parallel structure. The lordship given man is specifically said to be over all the animate creation. There are other biblical passages which deal with what it means that man is created in the image of God, but a fair inference from this passage is that man's dominion is one aspect of his being in the image of God. We should also note that God speaks in terms of his own plurality: 'Let *us* make man in *our* image,' and speaks of man in his plurality as male and female. So being composite, being man and woman, is also one aspect of man's fitting the image of God. Note how Paul takes this up in 1 Corinthians 11:3, where he compares the relationship of God the Father to God the Son with the relationship of man to woman. So authority over the animals and authority of man over the woman are aspects of the image of God. We cannot understand chapter 3 without that perspective.

With regard to verse 28: 'Replenish the earth' gives the idea of filling it *again*. There is no 'again' in the Hebrew. It simply says 'fill'. 'Subdue it' can imply that there is an active opposition which needs to be overcome. 'Subdue' is a possible translation, but not the only possible translation. 'Hold in subjection' (cf. 2 Chronicles 28:10) is also possible. That is, man is to maintain the position of lordship which he has been given. He does not need to achieve it.

The Sabbath and the Meaning of 'Day'

There are three views as to the meaning of 'day' in this chapter:

1. The framework view sees the use of days, making up a week, as a literary device. God chose to explain things in a

sequence which was familiar to Israel but that did not correspond to the way things happened. We can make no inferences as to the sequence, order, duration or nature of the events of creation from the way it was described in Genesis 1.

2. The day-age view which sees every day as a long period of time.

3. A day means an ordinary day

A lot of the discussion is a little misleading because people are really trying to fit Genesis into the currently popular scientific theory. Total detachment is impossible, but it does seem wrong to begin by an attempt to make the Bible fit current theories. Let us find out what the Bible says and then worry about all the scientific theories.

The framework theory tends to undermine the very meaning of the passage. We see a clear order and progression as God shapes creation for man. The goodness of God is pre-eminent. To say: 'God did not really do things that way – he just chose to explain it that way' takes away from the fundamental thrust of the passage. Further it is a way of dealing with a passage which cannot be restricted to Genesis 1. As a means of explanation it undermines the certainty which we place in the Bible.

It is true that 'day' can be used metaphorically in Hebrew. We say: 'Every dog has his day,' and Hebrew also has that sort of use. However, numbering days as first, second, third day and so on; mention of morning and evening; and a connection to light and darkness, is far beyond metaphorical use.

Further, God's work sets the pattern for that of man.

God worked six days and rested one, and so must man. Some supporters of the framework view maintain that God is being described according to the human pattern of six days of work plus one of rest, but Scripture says the reverse. God is not described in terms of man, but rather, man is to conform to a pattern set by God.

On the face of the text, the most natural view is that a day means a day. I suspect that we all would have come to that conclusion but for the so-called problems of reconciliation of Genesis 1 and science.

There is one significant textual problem with the literal reading. What does it mean that God rested on the seventh day? Surely that seventh day continues until now in that God is not still engaged in creating. What then is the text saying?

The words which we translate as 'rested' in Genesis 2:2 and Exodus 20:11 have the same basic sense of 'desist', 'cease from activity' or, 'be quiet and inactive'. So the basic idea is lack of activity, but we must go a little further. That day had a special significance for God; a significance which led him to set it apart from other days. How could that be if that day is thought to be all the time from creation until now? We do have a verse which tells us more. Exodus 31:17 says: 'God ceased and *was refreshed.*' The latter is a striking verb since it means literally 'regained his breath', 'was enlivened' or 'his spirits revived'! We shrink from these translations because they seem so inappropriate for God if they convey the idea that God was wearied by creation (see Isaiah 40:28). Despite this problem there must be meaning in those words.

We are touching on the problem of passages of Scripture which describe God in terms which seem appropriate only for man. God is said to have eyes, ears, hands and so on. Generally people say that God is described in these terms to facilitate our understanding, but there is a better way of seeing these passages. Man was created according to the image of God. If there are in man the organs to perceive and know, to make and shape, then it is only because these capacities exist in God. Rather than saying, 'God really does not have eyes, he really does not see. It is just explained that way'; it is preferable to say, 'God really sees. It will be very hard for us to understand that, because our sight is so limited, so bound to the physical; but being in the image of God, we can have a dim comprehension of it.' (See Psalm 94:7–10).

We need now to apply this to our question. With man, ceasing after work, that is, resting, is bound up with our physical character, weakened as it is by sin and the curse. Nevertheless, there is an aspect of joy and satisfaction at the completion of work that is more than merely physical. To have a job done and done well creates its own refreshment. This fits the context in Genesis 1. The sabbath is a climax to the refrain: 'God saw, and it was very good.' At creation, the God who is not bounded or limited by time, acted within time. So his satisfaction at completion of what was within time also has a temporal character. We should not then think of the seventh day as an indefinite span from the sixth day to the indefinite future. To make sense, it has to be what immediately follows the cessation of labour. The sabbath pattern of six days plus one does not point to indefinite but rather to definite periods of time.

Questions for Discussion

1. Genesis 1 shows us an ordered creation. Using this passage or other passages of Scripture, determine the purpose of that order.

2. Psalm 104 begins with praise of God. In pointing out the reasons for that praise the author transforms Genesis 1 to focus more on the paraphernalia of a king. Would our response to God be slightly different if we focused on Genesis 1 as it stands, rather than on the transformation in Psalm 104?

3. Sun, moon and man are said to rule. Does that help us understand the sense in which man was to rule?

4. The aspects of the image of God described in Colossians 3:10 and Ephesians 4:14 are different from the aspects of the image that emerge in Genesis 1. How are these different aspects of the image of God appropriate to the different scriptural contexts in which they occur?

5. Over the years there has been a debate between those who see the sabbath primarily as a day of physical rest and those who see it is a day to be devoted to worship? How does the nature of God's sabbath relate to this debate?

2: *The Fall into Sin*

The Relation of Genesis Chapters 2 and 3 to Chapter 1
It is often said that the narrative in chapters 2 and 3 is a different account of creation from chapter 1. It is further claimed that it stems from a different author and is in conflict with chapter 1 at a number of points. The refutation of the broader theory which finds a number of authors or sources in the Pentateuch is not the issue here. Rather, it is whether, in the early chapters of Genesis, the same writer would write two accounts of the one thing and set them side by side. We would not write history that way because the way of writing history in our culture has been influenced by various intellectual fashions. Our objective is to create one grand synthesis which weaves every conceivable factor into a whole. That is partly why economic and sociological interpretations of history are so in vogue. By reducing everything to a few factors like economics and class struggle, the historian gives the impression that the great synthesis, which explains all, has been achieved.

In Scripture, on the other hand, there are a number of cases of duplicated descriptions of the same event where each description emphasises and brings out different aspects. People who believe that the biblical writers must have thought and written like modern historians ascribe these to separate authors or traditions.

It is clear, even at a superficial glance, that Genesis 1 and Genesis 2 do not cover the same ground. There is a difference of concentration, with points touched in one and not in the other. For example, 2:5–6 is concerned with the watering of creation. We read of a spring that provides water (see later). That is not dealt with in chapter 1. Of course we can ask where it fits within the framework of chapter 1, and then, once again, Psalm 104 comes to our aid. It inserts this aspect of creation where we would expect it; that is about day 3, between the creation of dry land and the creation of plants (*Psalm* 104:10–13). Just as we saw with the aspects of creation described in chapter 1, the removal of this act of goodness – drought – is judgment.

We should not see chapters 1 and 2 as completely divorced from chapter 1. The new section begins at 2:4 with 'These are the generations of the heavens and the earth'. The formula 'These are the generations of x' occurs a number of times in Genesis. It means 'these are what comes forth from x'; 'these are what are generated by x'. For example, the generations of Terah are described from Genesis 11:27 to 25:11, but only a few verses mention Terah since the real subject is what comes forth from Terah, that is Abraham. So Genesis 2:4 is not concerned with retelling the story of the heavens and the earth. It focuses on what comes forth from the heavens and the earth, namely plants, animals and man. It presupposes chapter 1. There is a certain overlap, but chapters 2 and 3 cannot be regarded as a creation account that could stand alone.

The Description of the Garden

The structure of chapter 2 is that of a brief introduction followed by a further elaboration. One issue, as mentioned above, is the provision of water for the world God had made. This is taken up in verse 6, dropped again while the creation of man is described, then returned to in connection with the garden in verse 10. The subject of man then comes back in verse 15.

For ease of discussion, we shall consider the garden and then man. In verse 6 we should translate not 'mist', which has been little more than a translator's guess, but 'spring' or 'river'. The word seems to come from the Sumerians, who were the earliest inhabitants of Mesopotamia known to us. The need for water for plants to live is met by a subterranean spring. This is then the natural source of the river mentioned in verse 10. Most attempts to identify the river ignore what the text says. One river breaks in four. Normally we expect four tributaries to flow into one. Two of these we know as the Tigris and Euphrates. Some people look for a stream that flows into the Tigris and Euphrates system, but that ignores what the text says about one stream breaking into four. Others point to the fact that the Tigris and Euphrates rise close to each other in Anatolia. The problem is then the description of the two other rivers. One is said to flow around the land of Cush, which is generally used for Nubia (south of Egypt). A way out of that problem is to connect Cush not with Nubia, but with a district in the Zagros Mountains (between Iraq and Iran) from whence the people whom the Babylonians called Kassites came. That still leaves a problem with the other river. Havilah seems to be Arabia, or a portion thereof. Thus the description does not seem to fit the present geography.

There seems no solution to the problem of the location of Eden if one accepts the current geography. A Sumerian story may place paradise on the island of Bahrain in the Persian Gulf. That to me looks closer to where Eden might have been, but we would have to assume major geographical and perhaps geological change.

Eden is probably a Sumerian word meaning plain or steppe country. The prominence of trees in the garden connects us back to 1:29, where seed and fruit are the foods God gave to man. The garden is provisioned with all that God has promised to man.

The Creation of Man

It is in accord with the emphasis of this section which tells of what comes forth from the heavens and the earth, that we learn of the material used in the construction of man. Being formed from the ground links all the animate creation. It is out of the ground that God causes trees to grow. It is out of the ground that God forms the beasts of the field. When God breathes into man's nostrils the breath of life, he comes to share with the animals the character of being a 'living creature'.

Yet, in all this, there are also distinctions. Man named the animals. There were none suited to him as a companion. He was to tend the garden and keep it. The similarity in physical composition says nothing against the pre-eminent position of man in the animate creation.

Similarly, in the creation of the woman, the stress is on her unity with the man. This is both a physical ('bone of my bone and flesh of my flesh') and psychological unity ('they were both naked and not ashamed').

Task and Temptation

The narrative of creation stresses the goodness of God to man in creation as well as man's lordship over creation. These emphases do not negate the fact that man is a servant of God. There were commands. Man was given a task. He may be a lord, but he is under a Lord. Only under the control of God did he exercise sway. That is to say, he was not a free and autonomous agent, able to do what he pleased. This comes to particular expression in the fact that there was a limitation placed upon him. He was not to eat of the tree of knowledge of good and evil. The name probably describes the function of the tree. To 'know' in the Scripture often means to 'experience'. When God is said to know good and evil, we must see good and evil not as separate but in contrast: good as distinct from evil. If man overcame the temptation, he would have had the experience of having chosen good in contrast to evil. If he did not, he would still know good and evil, but in the bitter experience of having chosen evil rather than good.

The temptation throws doubt on the goodness and veracity of God. What chapters 1 and 2 told us is that the creation had been prepared for man. Yet the tempter succeeded in implanting the suggestion that God had been withholding something good from man. Following that came a direct attack on the truth of God.

The Unnaturalness of Sin

Scripture often leaves out things in order not to confuse us with details. We learn elsewhere that Satan was behind the temptation. In this passage something different is highlighted. The created character of the serpent was such as to make it a fit vehicle for temptation but against a background of man's having named the animals, a speaking serpent is out of place. The Holy Spirit draws our attention to the character of the tempter as a beast of the field. The created order of authority places God over man. Within mankind, man has the authority over woman. Finally in the order of authority comes the animal. The sin of man reveals a complete reversal of this order. The animal taught the woman; she led the man and neither listened to God. Thus sin is unnatural, being a reversal, a negation of the natural created order.

This unnaturalness shows in the consequence of sin. With sin comes a sense of physical shame. The man and woman failed to play the roles of man and woman and in consequence there was shame in the physical concomitants of being man and woman. The unity between man and woman has been broken, along with the order of authority.

Curse and Restoration
When the order of authority between God and man is violated, so also is the unity. Man hides from God. The curses are also blessings in that they re-establish the created order, or promise its restoration. However, they re-establish it in a world already marred by sin.

God pursued as far as the serpent his enquiry into the instigation of the temptation and then pronounced the curse. The curse emphasises the lowly position of the serpent. Whereas the problem had been created by the woman listening to the serpent, God established enmity between them. This has nothing to do with anything so trivial as a woman's fear of snakes. For there shall come forth one of the seed of woman to crush evil finally. The image is that of a man who kills a serpent by stamping on its head, but in the process has his foot wounded. For the serpent, the blow shall be mortal, but for the seed of the woman, the blow shall not be fatal.

Next the woman is cursed. We see both with respect to the man and the woman that the curse falls upon their crucial roles in the creation. Curse comes upon what was their glory. The woman is cursed in her child-bearing function. Her pain and her conception are multiplied. The curse causes not just pain in labour, but frequency of conception as well, which has bearing on the ethics of contraception. If we have no problem with the use of anaesthetics in childbirth, why should we have problems with contraception as such (as distinct from the ethics of the various methods of contraception)? The created order of authority was also re-established. The woman's husband is to reign over her. In the sinful world into which we have now entered, that is curse, for the unity between man and woman is gone. Yet it is also blessing, for it is a restoration of the natural order.

As for the man, the curse impacts on his work. The unity between man and the ground has been broken. The ground rebels against him so that labour is toil until he dies. Yet the note of mercy is still here. The earth will yield him something. Death is not immediate.

There have been some interesting discussions on the question of whether hard work is a curse. It is quite rightly pointed out that we have many fat executives dying for want of good hard physical work. This merely points to the dilemma of man. He was created to work, and since he was created soul and body, that work should have a physical side. If he does not work then he is in trouble, and yet his work is toil, physically and mentally. Woman is in a similar situation. Whilst there are some whom God has gifted so that they do not need marriage, for most women the avoidance of conception and childbirth has a price. There is no method of contraception which will not carry with it its own problems. We may try by various means to avoid the rigours of the curse but we will never completely succeed.

So there is a mixed situation: curse, but nevertheless blessing and mercy, and our text draws that to our attention in verses 20 and 21. The immediately preceding context was one of death, but there is still hope. Man dies, but in the midst of pain and blood, children are born. Life continues until the one comes to bruise the head of the serpent. Adam shows his sense of this fact in that he gave his wife a name meaning 'living'. Life and hope are bound up with the woman and her seed. There is also an element of mercy in verse 21, as God takes action to lessen the shame which man's sin has brought upon him.

Expulsion
The words of God indicate that, as so often, deception feeds off truth. The deceiver said that they would be like God, and so they are. They know good and evil. Yet how unlike God! Their knowledge of good and evil is so different from his. To be like God is the height of piety and the essence of sin. The more man in his rebellion tries to replace God, the further he moves away from the divine perfection. The more he humbles himself in obedience, the closer he comes to his Lord.

So man was expelled. In the expulsion there is curse. The way to life is barred. Man goes to till the ground and faces consequent death. Yet is there also blessing? What would it have meant to have eaten of the tree of life in a sinful condition? Some suggest that it would have meant life continued and confirmed in that condition. It would have closed the door to real life. That view is attractive and, while the text might be read other ways, it would suit the tenor of the curses we have seen.

Fire and sword stand between man and paradise. What is the future to hold? We have seen already that it holds both curse and promise.

Questions for Discussion

1. Throughout history, drought and flood have afflicted the human race. How does the separation of the water from the dry land in Genesis 1 and the creation of a method of watering the earth in Genesis 2 help us to understand drought and flood?

2. Man names the animals and man names his wife. Is the similarity significant?

3. Some claim there was no order of authority between man and woman before the fall into sin. Does the passage make sense on that assumption?

4. In not naming Satan but rather focusing on the serpent, how does the passage influence our interpretation of the events?

5. God wraps together curse and blessing. How is that typical of God's dealings with sinful man?

3: *The Division of Mankind and the Flood*

The Trial of Faith Begins

We have seen earlier that, in the midst of the death that follows sin, there is a note of hope. Life continues, pre-eminently with the birth of children. From the descendants of Eve will come one to bruise the head of the serpent. In the midst of the pain of childbirth there is the joy that God gives life. Though Adam would labour until death, yet he can call his wife Eve as she was the mother of all living.

Hence the birth of a child was an extremely significant event, and that is particularly the case with the birth of the first child, Cain. Yet Cain was a murderer, killing his brother. We meet here already the hidden but recurring theme of Genesis: the conflict between the expectation that God's promise calls forth and what happens. It is what we may call 'the trial of faith', for it is the promise of God that generates faith and hope. How often that faith and hope seem disappointed!

When we look at the sin itself, we see some very interesting comparisons, but also some striking differences to the sin of Adam and Eve. In 4:7 God describes sin as being like an animal lying down at Cain's door (cf. the picture in

Genesis 49:14 of a donkey lying down). Cain has to rule over it just as Adam and Eve were required to rule the serpent. There are also significant changes: sin may be described as an animal but it is not a separate creature outside. It is inside. The temptation no longer comes from without, but from within. Man is called to exercise dominion not just over the animals, but also over himself.

The punishment is also very similar. The ground no longer yields bountifully. Man becomes a wanderer. Curse on the ground and banishment are the consequences. Scripture gives us very little on the nature of the difference between Cain and Abel. We are told very little here about the piety of Abel. Certainly, as Hebrews 11:4 tells us, it was by faith that he offered a more acceptable sacrifice. Yet the text in Genesis 4 is not concerned primarily with Abel. It focuses on Cain to show the spread and progress of sin. Cain succumbed to sin in himself, yet he remained under the protection of God. The long-suffering of God continued.

The Line of Cain

As we follow the description of the line of Cain, we see the further growth of human sin. The line of Cain was an illustrious line. Cain built a city. From his descendants came cultural progress and inventions. Yet, along with that came pride and arrogant self-confidence. Note the boastful song of Lamech. Lamech was saying that he can look after himself far better than God could. He was more severe than God. His judgment was greater than God's. Note also that he had two wives. Arrogance, brutality and polygamy were combined with great cultural achievement.

The Line of Seth

The text interrupts the tracing of the line of Cain and their achievements to turn to the second line: that of Seth. Compare what is said of this line with what is said of Cain and his line. If one were to take away the arrogance, there are things to be admired in the line of Cain. Herding, making musical instruments and cutting implements are not in themselves evil. These abilities and discoveries are the gift of God. As we read through Genesis, we discover a number of such genealogies where one line is compared to another. Generally, the line which is not faithful to God is narrated first, and it so often appears that God's blessing rested particularly upon them rather than upon the believing line. One would wonder, from the gifts God distributed to the line of Cain, whether God was blessing them more than the line of Seth.

The line of Seth offers us not human accomplishment but faith in God. It is with regard to the birth of Seth that we find a comparison between begetting children and God's creation of man. In begetting children, man is imitating his creator. As God made man in his own image, so man begets a son to resemble him. Here is a sort of being like God, which is very different from the arrogance of Lamech. Lamech's is an attempt to rule in the place of God.

The things that are told us of the line of Seth point to faith. Men began to call on the name of the Lord (4:26). Enoch walked with God (5:22–24). Lamech, in prophesying the future of his child, refers to the curse upon the ground and the hope that it will be lifted (5:29). Yet, there is another theme which also comes through: death. The refrain 'and he died' comes through to stress the certainty of the judgment, even upon the elect line. The stress on death makes the case of Enoch even more significant. Death is not inevitable. In this foretaste of the resurrection, we have hope that death will be overcome. That same hope shows in Lamech. The curse imposed labour and toil upon man. He looked for one who will bring rest from that. Noah was the head of a new creation.

The Culmination of the Line of Cain

The first few verses of chapter 6 are variously and, often falsely, interpreted. The period is described as being characterised by violence, which is precisely what we would expect, having read the song of Lamech in chapter 4. We have already been introduced to polygamy, and so we read in 6:2 that they took wives for themselves, whomever they chose. Who then are the sons of God? Any interpretation which sees them as angels, creatures from other planets or a remnant of pagan mythology in which gods married women, is to be rejected. The simple but conclusive objection to all these theories is the fact that the judgment falls upon men. The conclusion in verse 5 is that man's heart is wicked. The problem lies with man, and no other strange creature. The common explanation is that the sons of God are of the line of Seth who, as believers, are called 'sons of God'. If that interpretation is correct, then what is the problem? Those who hold this view say that it is the fact that they marry indiscriminately with unbelievers. Why were their offspring particular? It makes more sense to interpret the passage in accord with the biblical tendency to refer to rulers as gods. Note Psalm 82. (This apparently confusing reference to men as gods may derive from the fact that the Hebrew word in question has the sense of a 'great one'. While normally applied to a divine being, in certain, perhaps ironic contexts, it could be used of men.) What we have described in Genesis 6 is the arrogance, the violence, the pride and the polygamy (they married whom they chose) of a ruling military aristocracy. Imagine a period when the attitude of Lamech is dominant. Men may be out to do great feats, to prove themselves able to take care of themselves. Out of the harems came a host of arrogant young men, eager to establish strength and fame. These were the Nephilim: the warrior tyrants of antiquity. Since Nephilim elsewhere seems to convey the idea of giant stature (*Num.* 13:33), it may be that there was an aristocracy, physically set apart from the rest of the people. A parallel might be furnished by some African societies where different classes in the one society are distinguished by size with the ruling class being considerably taller.

So the picture we have is one of corruption throughout society, with the upper levels setting the example, and corruption rooted in the human heart. The very first inclinations of man's thoughts are evil, constantly evil.

The Flood – Judgment and Salvation
The flood has always been a subject about which there has been considerable interest and controversy. It is important to distinguish what the biblical text itself says from the various theories about the mechanism and the physical effects of the flood. The biblical text says that the whole earth was covered, which contradicts theories limiting it to Mesopotamia. There is some uncertainty as to the exact location of the mountains of Ararat, but they are some-where in the mountainous country that today would be

part of eastern Turkey or the Caucasus. There is no way that a flood merely in the Tigris–Euphrates system would carry an ark *upstream*. Furthermore, because water seeks its own level, a flood which covered the Caucasus would have to be world-wide. The flood lasted for a long time. It began in the second month, and the ark did not ground until the seventh month. The text speaks of the flood prevailing for 150 days, which would be about five months. There would be no way that water could cover the mountains of Turkey for even one month without it spreading out to cover the whole earth. It is therefore most unlikely that the biblical statement that the mountains were covered could refer to a local flood. The archaeologist Woolley, excavating the southern Mesopotamian city of Ur, claimed that he had found evidence of the flood. In reality he found evidence of a flood which did not cover all the area of Ur, let alone all of Mesopotamia.

The biblical text says that two factors were involved in the flood: the fountains of the great deep and the windows of the sky. The latter quite clearly refers to rain but imagination has had free rein with 'the fountains of the great deep'. For us, a 'fountain' means something which spurts out water, so the fountains have been imagined as eruptions of subterranean waters or as steam out of the molten centre of the earth. The Hebrew word does not give that sense, meaning, rather, a basin or reservoir of water. The fountains of the deep are no more dramatic than the seas. Note the description of creation in Proverbs 8:28–29. Here, the fixing of the fountains of the deep is connected with the setting of bounds to the sea. In the first chapter on Genesis, we noted that what God was doing was the preparation of the creation for man. Any return to

the earlier state of creation would make the world unin-
habitable, and thus amount to judgment. Here, therefore,
we have a reversion to the stage before the upper waters
were separated from the lower, and before the dry land was
distinguished from the sea. Let us be careful of speculative
theories about the cause of the flood (e.g. ice from outer
space!), which introduce things quite alien to the biblical
account.

We see that the judgment includes all the animals. In
returning to the earlier stage, the earth is no longer suitable
for man, but is also rendered unsuitable to birds and
animals. They need to be saved along with man.

The preservation of Noah is used in the New Testament
as an illustration of the New Testament salvation. It shows
the sovereign selectivity of God. Out of the mass of
sinful humanity he chooses one family to be saved and to
constitute a new humanity.

The Covenant with Noah

God spoke to Noah in Genesis 6 and established a covenant with him before the flood, and then God spoke to
him again in chapters 8 and 9. The covenant of Genesis 6
is largely concerned with the commands Noah had to obey
in preparing the ark. The covenant after the flood contains
a lot more detail. It is made not only with Noah, but with
every beast aboard the ark (9:9–10).

This shows that a covenant is not a contract dependent
upon consent of both parties, as the animals do not ratify
the covenant. God sovereignly established the covenant in
promising never to bring another flood upon the earth.
Once more, he took obligations upon himself, but in addition, he imposed obligations upon man. These obligations

were appropriate for Noah and his descendants as the beginners of a new creation. God again established man's authority over the animal creation (9:2). He renewed the command to be fruitful and multiply (9:7). There were, however, new commands which were not present at the first creation. Against the background of the violence we have already discussed, we have a special law concerning the sanctity of human life (9:5-6). This law is not really new. When Cain expressed his fear that everyone who came upon him would kill him, he was expressing his consciousness of this principle. Its statement here in Genesis 9, like much of the law, is a promulgation, a formal and authoritative statement, of what men know to be true, though they do not live according to it. Cain may have failed to be his brother's keeper, but he knew what he should have done and feared that other men, in killing him, might show loyalty to Abel.

The covenant had a sign attached to it, and a sign particularly connected with God's obligations under the covenant. The purpose was to place prominently before the mind and attention of God a reminder of the promises he had given.

Questions for Discussion

1. It has become fashionable in some Christian circles to emphasise the role of the devil in human sin. Does the way Cain's temptation is described give us a warning that sin has another origin as well?

2. The contrast of the line of Cain with that of the line of Seth shows us one marked by cultural discoveries and arrogant violence and the other by faith. Are there similarities today? How should we respond if there are similarities?

3. How does the flood prefigure the final judgment? (see also 1 Peter 3:20; 2 Peter 2:5).

4. What do we learn about the nature of a covenant from the two covenants made with Noah?

5. We normally see the rainbow as a reminder to us that there will not be another great flood. Scripture however depicts it as a reminder to God (*Gen.* 9:14–16). Why is the bow said to refer particularly to God? Is there a connection to other covenant signs?

4: *Mankind Divided Once More*

Here we take up one of the more difficult and technical passages in the book of Genesis. Especially when it comes to the names of all the people in Genesis 10, it is easy to become bogged down in detail. We must always ask the question as to why this detail was included in the biblical text. It is linked to the previous section in that the division of mankind is a primary theme in the early part of Genesis. We have seen that the division of mankind was the background out of which Noah was chosen to be the head of a new humanity. In a sense the same is true of Abram. The division of mankind into the many races and tongues of Genesis 10 is the background of the promise to Abram, that in his seed all the nations of the earth would be blessed.

The Sin of Ham

This is one of the passages in which we have a great temptation to add to the bare bones of the narrative. Let us make sure we have the basic sense before we begin to speculate. Noah became drunk and was uncovered in his tent. Ham saw the nakedness of his father and told his brothers. Shem and Japheth acted respectfully towards their father and covered his nakedness.

When Noah awoke, he uttered a curse and a blessing (9:25-27). The important point is that a division was introduced into the human race. There was a differentiation into those to be cursed and those to be blessed. Even within that differentiation there were further divisions. It was Canaan, one of the sons of Ham, who received particular curse. Amongst Shem and Japheth it was Shem who was particularly singled out for blessing. We see here that sovereign selectivity which we know as election. Why God chooses to bless some and not others; why some are particularly singled out for judgment, we do not know.

The blessing on Shem is interesting. To have God as one's God is the summit of divine favour. Japheth will enter into those blessings through joining with Shem, but the blessing is primarily to Shem.

We must reject the misinterpretation of this passage, in which it has been used to justify oppression of black peoples. The premise is apparently that black peoples descend from Ham and therefore should be made servants. Against that, we must point out first, that the curse falls on Canaan specifically and not Ham generally. Second, biblical evidence to derive all black peoples from Ham is lacking. The argument depends upon the fact that Cushites, who are black, come from Ham. However, that does not prove that all blacks come from Cush. All our historical evidence would indicate that the Canaanites who were particularly cursed were not black.

The Table of Nations

Genesis 10, at first sight, gives us a bewildering list of names. By combining information from elsewhere in the Bible and from literature of the surrounding peoples, we

can make some order within the apparent confusion, but
we must confess that some of the names mean practically
nothing to us. There are many ethnic groups which, as
far as we know, are not mentioned. The list is not a comprehensive list of all peoples of the world, but rather, a list
giving the origin of peoples known to Israel, even that
taking us far afield. Sometimes sons are named, and
sometimes whole ethnic groups. For example, in the
descendants of Canaan we have Sidon and Heth, but also
peoples like the Jebusites. The list is thus connecting the
Jebusites back to Canaan, but with no attempt to give
details of origin. There are some cases which point to
mixed origin, although details are not spelled out. An
example is Havilah and Sheba which occur amongst the
sons of Cush in verse 7 and amongst the sons of Joktan in
verses 28, 29. The Bible uses 'sons of' with reference to
grandsons or more distant descendants. So the probable
meaning of the double occurrence is that these peoples are
of mixed origin.

The sons of Japheth seem largely to include people
who settled in, or who had some connection with
Anatolia (= Turkey). The identifications which have some
plausibility are as follows: Gomer = Cimmerians, a
nomadic people who enter eastern Anatolia from the north
in the first millennium B.C. Ashkenaz = Scythians, who
enter Anatolia on the heels of the Cimmerians. They
spoke an Iranian language and so were, linguistically (not
necessarily ethnically) related to the Medes and Persians.
Madai = Medes, neighbours of the Persians, who seem to
come into Iran in the early second millennium. Javan =
Ionian Greeks, who particularly settled on the west coast
of Asia Minor. Tubal and Meshech are peoples mentioned

by the Assyrians in eastern Anatolia. Meshech has been equated with the Phrygians. Tiras are found in western Anatolia, and may be the ancestors of the Etruscans, who may have moved from Anatolia to Italy around 1200 B.C.

Amongst the sons of Javan: Elishah is probably Cyprus, though Cyprus received so many different peoples in the historical period that it is hard to know which group is referred to. Tarshish is particularly interesting. Ships sailed to Tarshish both from the Mediterranean coast of Israel (*Jonah* 1:3) and by sailing from Elath at the top of the Gulf of Aqaba (*1 Chron.* 20:36–37). We presume that in the latter case the ships were sailing around Africa. So Tarshish would seem to be in the western Mediterranean or even out in the Atlantic. Kittim has generally been associated with Kition = Larnaka, in Cyprus, but in Daniel 11:30, it refers to the Romans. Dodanim occurs in 1 Chronicles 1:7 as Rodanim, that is probably the island of Rhodes off the south-west coast of Asia Minor.

Cush is generally translated Ethiopia, but you must realise that what we today call Ethiopia is only part of what in ancient times was called Ethiopia. Then it included Nubia, that is the area of Egypt south of Aswan. Mizraim is Egypt. Put is probably Libya. The descendants of Cush are probably located in southern Arabia. Sheba in particular is probably in the Yemen. However, the descendants of Cush also included Nimrod, who established a kingdom in Mesopotamia. Babel (= Babylon), Erech and Accad are all important cities of southern Iraq (Calneh is not known today). Nineveh and Calah are well known as great cities of northern Mesopotamia, or Assyria. Rehoboth-Ir and Resen are not known today. Translations vary on verse 11, which can be translated 'He went forth to Assur' (= Assyria as name of country) or 'Assur (a personal name) went forth'. In favour of the first interpretation is the fact that Assyria is called the land of Nimrod in Micah 5:6.

Nimrod is called a mighty hunter before the Lord, which seems to indicate that his hunting was a service performed before God. The best explanation would seem to be that he was a hunter of man-eating animals (cf. Genesis 9:5).

We know little of the people descended from Mizraim, except possibly the Philistines, whose connection is not described in terms of descent. The Bible in one passage derives the Philistines from Caphtor (*Amos* 9:7) which we guess is Crete (note the presence of Caphtorim in Genesis 10:14). We know from Egyptian records that Philistines were amongst the Sea-Peoples, that is the people who attacked Egypt around 1200 B.C. The origin of these Philistines could have been Crete. However, Abraham encountered Philistines in Palestine long before 1200 B.C. It may be that Philistines or similar people were settled at a number of places around the eastern Mediterranean including southern Palestine.

Sidon, the first born of Canaan, is the name of an important Phoenician city. Heth is the father of the Hittites. Here, the situation is complicated by the fact that there are various possibilities. Abraham encountered the sons of Heth in Palestine. From outside of the Bible, we know of various groups of Hittites. In north central Anatolia there was a people called Hittites who spoke a poorly preserved language unrelated to any other known language. Around 1900 B.C. people speaking an Indo-European language moved into the area and took over the name.

Amongst the sons of Shem, Elam were a people in the

south of Iran, who lived there and periodically fought with the Babylonians before the coming of the Persians. They spoke a language which is not well known but some scholars have attempted to connect it to the Dravidian languages of the Indian sub-continent (e.g. Tamil). Asshur is Assyria; Aram is Syria.

Amongst the sons of Joktan we again meet Sheba and Havilah. The reference seems once more to be to Arabian people. Ophir however was the source of much of Solomon's riches. Various locations have been suggested, but somewhere in India seems the best suggestion.

This brief summary should be sufficient to establish the point that this list includes many peoples from a wide area. When the promise of blessing to the nations was given to Abraham, it is against this wide background. It is quite false to see the Old Testament as a narrowly nationalistic book. The table of nations is the backdrop for what goes on in the later books.

The Tower of Babel

There is an obvious parallel between the developments here and those we saw in the line of Cain. Remember that Cain built a city. They wanted to make themselves a 'name'. Compare also the 'men of the name' who lived in the period of violence before the flood (6:4). Here we have human progress and technical ability, but turned to the purpose of man's exaltation once more.

There is a connection between building the city and not being scattered abroad. Here was an attempt to unify the human race around one great enterprise. They were not after a landmark to guide their way home. They were after a technical accomplishment which would unite mankind in the making of it, and whose glory would serve to promote that unity. They wanted to establish a *name,* that is a reputation; fame; a unifying object and accomplishment. To catch something of the flavour, we can remember the way the moon landings were portrayed by some as a great human technological accomplishment in which all men could somehow join in praising the glory of man.

God frustrated that. The confusion of tongues was to obstruct the united attempt to build a kingdom to the glory of man.

The text is not clear as to who was involved in this project. 'They' is all that is mentioned. Were these all the descendants of Noah, who at that stage were still together? Note the statement in 10:25. Is this a reference to the division of tongues? If so it happened during the lifetime of Eber, who was at least the great grandson of Shem, if not further removed by generations being left out.

The Line of Shem
The line of Shem covers the period that saw the rise of the great Near Eastern civilisations: the Sumerian period in Mesopotamia, the Old Kingdom in Egypt with its pyramids. Nothing of that comes down to us in the Bible, because the important thing is the continuity of the line that God had chosen to bring forth the promised seed. The one figure who deserves mention is Eber, because 'Hebrew' means simply 'Eberite'. Obviously he was a significant individual.

The Homeland and Background of Abraham
In southern Mesopotamia is a city called Ur. It was one of the great Sumerian cities. The treasures recovered from

the royal graves of Ur are found illustrated in many books on ancient history. The discovery of Ur caused excitement amongst biblical scholars. Here, they said, was Abraham's home, in a great old city of the world's oldest civilisation. Therefore it could be expected that Abraham would bring ideas and traditions from Mesopotamia. Since there was a flood story from Mesopotamia, very like the biblical one, the search began to relate the Bible to Babylon, culminating in the Pan-Babylonian school who thought everything in the Bible was borrowed from Babylon.

All of this has a basic problem. The biblical Ur of the Chaldees is not in southern Mesopotamia. Ur is a common city name in the ancient Near East. There are at least two others beside the southern Mesopotamian Ur. The southern one was discovered first and people have latched onto this. The obvious reason that the biblical text says Ur *of the Chaldees* is to prevent confusion with other cities of the same name.

Two considerations point to northern Syria, perhaps falling within modern Turkey, for Ur of the Chaldees. Terah left Ur to settle in Canaan, reached as far as Haran and stopped there. Haran is in the north of the Euphrates system, definitely not on the road from the southern Ur to Canaan. Second, when Abraham sends his servant to find a wife for Isaac, he sent him to his country and family (24:4). Where did the servant go? To Aram-naharaim (24:10) which is in Syria or northern Mesopotamia.

If we are to find the 'background' for Abraham, we should find it up in the region of Haran, not down in southern Mesopotamia. This creates a further problem. We have many sources outside the Bible for southern Mesopotamia, but much less for the north in this period.

That may be partly helped by the discovery of thousands of texts at the north Syrian town of Ebla. What has so far emerged from those texts does not seem to have much relation to the Bible, despite some early sensationalist claims. We should not be surprised that the area of Abraham's homeland is less well known than some other countries of the time. We have already seen that cultural accomplishment does not necessarily coincide with the line of faith. It is not necessarily in the great rich urban centres which yield most of our early writings that God is working out his purpose.

Questions for Discussion

1. God says to Abraham: 'I will bless those who bless you and the one who curses you I will curse' (*Gen.* 12:3). Could the curse on Canaan and the blessing on Shem and Japheth be seen as a similar instance of blessing or curse flowing from one's relation to a particular individual? If so, what makes Noah and Abraham especially significant?

2. Some people are interested in tracing particular racial groups, especially their own, to individual sons of Noah. Does it matter?

3. Would it be desirable, in our age, if everybody spoke the same language?

4. Is it appropriate to refer to any human project today as a 'tower of Babel'?

5: *Abraham – The Recipient of the Promises*

In this section we focus upon one of the pivotal figures of God's plan: Abraham. To avoid confusion we must deal first with a matter of names. During the course of his life God changed his name from Abram to Abraham. Similarly his wife was changed from Sarai to Sarah (17:5, 15). To simplify matters I will refer to them as simply Abraham and Sarah.

The Promises
The prominent thing in the life of Abraham was the promises given him by God. There are several key elements of these promises. God promised Abraham a land, many descendants, and that his seed would be a blessing to the nations. The initial promises were given in Genesis 12:1-3, and are repeated in Genesis 15 with the very solemn ceremony in which God passed between the dismembered pieces, indicating his own willingness to undergo judgment if he failed to fulfil the promises to Abraham. In this ceremony God repeated the promise that he would give Abraham a son, with assurance that his seed would eventually possess the land. The ceremony added a visible element to the word of promise. In chapter 17, we again have the promise repeated and again a visible symbol

added to the word. The covenant sign of circumcision reminded Abraham of his position within the covenant, and of the promise God had made to him. The sign placed upon the organ of generation must have particular reference to the promise of the seed, but it is also a responsibility which Abraham had to keep. If he failed to obey the command to circumcise his offspring, he would have broken the covenant. As far as Abraham's descendants were concerned, they were within the covenant until by rebellion they refused to be circumcised, or broke the covenant in some other way (17:14).

The Trial of Faith

The details of Abraham's life are not given at random. They bring home to us the fact that almost everything that happened to Abraham made belief in the promises of God very difficult. The facts seemed explicitly contrary to the Word of God.

Famine

No sooner had Abraham entered the land than there was famine in it and he was forced to leave (12:10). What good was the land to Abraham when he was forced to leave it again to obtain food in Egypt?

The Crowded Land

The land was promised to Abraham, yet how could it be his? There were others living in it, with Canaanites yet in the land (12:6). This verse has been appealed to as proof that Moses could not have written the Pentateuch, or, specifically that the book of Genesis had to have been written long after Moses. Surely in Moses' day everybody knew that the Canaanites were living in Palestine. That argument ignores the whole point! We are not told this as a piece of casual information in case we are interested in the ethnic composition of Canaan, but to dramatise what we are told in the next verse. God said that he would give the land to Abraham's descendants. How can that be? The land is already full. What Abraham saw was contrary to the promise of God. It is this contradiction between what we see and what God has promised which produces the trial of faith. Faith is belief in the promise in spite of appearances.

The problem also has other ramifications, for the crowding produced problems between Abraham and Lot (13:6–9). Note that we are reminded that the Canaanite and the Perizzite are also in the land.

Barrenness

Perhaps the greatest trial was created by the barrenness of Sarah. It is to Abraham's descendants that the land was promised. It was his seed that was to be a blessing to the nations. Yet Sarah had no children. Worse than that, Abraham finds himself in situations in which it seemed that his wife herself would be lost. An example is 12:11ff. where Abraham found himself (as he saw it at least) in danger of losing his own life, and his wife. A very similar situation arose in chapter 20, where Abraham, to save his own life in the Philistine city of Gerah, again called Sarah his sister. It is sometimes objected that Abraham would not have done the same thing twice. Would it not be wonderful if we did not repeat our mistakes! Abraham found himself in situations where he had trouble trusting the goodness and mercy of God. The mistake Abraham made over and over was to try to achieve by human effort and strength what God himself had promised to do.

The other great example of this weakness in the life of Abraham occurs when he seeks a human means to solve the problem of Sarah's barrenness. To take Hagar as his wife was an acceptable legal means in the culture of his time for solving the problem of barrenness. Abraham was simply conforming to the culture and customs of his time. Conformity to this world is, however, very closely connected to doubt in God's faithfulness to his promises.

It may appear that Abraham, with all the promises given him, was a particularly favoured man, and he was! Yet the greater the promise, the greater the trial of faith, because the more it contradicts what we see around us.

Abraham the Redeemer

All this may give us a fairly low view of Abraham. The Scripture does not hide his failures. It is important that we consider also the triumphs of Abraham in order to reach a just view.

Chapter 14 describes an attack by a coalition of forces from outside of Palestine. The attack may have taken place in a confused time, after the fall of what we call the Third Dynasty of Ur, and before the rise of the dynasty of Hammurabi. The leader of the coalition was Chedorlaomer of Elam (southern Persia). Involved also were Shinar (= Babylon) and Arioch king of Elassar (possibly a city in Syria). A name like Tidal occurs amongst the Hittite royal names (Tudhaliyas), but this incident seems earlier than any of the attested Hittite kings of that name. In any case, a power which could exercise control from Elam to Palestine must have been the super-power of its day. The city of Sodom and the neighbouring cities were situated in the area now covered by the Dead Sea. They had been made vassals, but eventually rebelled. The armies of Chedorlaomer and his allies came down the east of the Jordan, avoiding the cities of the plain by sweeping to the south and west of them to deprive them of allies. They then turned on and defeated the kings of the cities of the plain.

Caught up in this squabble, which was not his own, was Lot, who was amongst those taken as prisoners of war to be made slaves. It was the responsibility of the next of kin to deliver his relatives from captivity. Abraham, in this case, was the next of kin. The war had left him untouched since the invaders did not cross the Jordan. Yet, Lot had been captured, so Abraham went to the rescue. He had with him his slaves and the forces of the Amorites, with whom he was allied. The magnitude of the task should be appreciated. Abraham took on a great power, the super-power of his day! The story does not dwell upon his faith in this instance, but it must have been there. He pursued the returning armies, surprised them in a night attack and recovered the people as well as the spoil.

It is in the light of this outstanding victory that we must understand the blessing of Melchizedek. The promise was that Abraham's name would be great, and it certainly would have been after that victory. The promise was that he would be a blessing to the nations, and he certainly was here a blessing to the cities of the plain, whose people he redeemed from captivity and to his own kinsman, Lot. Melchizedek traced the greatness back to its source: Abraham was blessed by God Most High, possessor of the heavens and the earth. He had accomplished all this because he had this great God as his God. There is a tremendous contrast between Abraham in Egypt and Abraham against the kings of the east. In one case we see the weakness of the believer struggling to trust in God. In another, the man of God as he stands in the strength of his God. That contradiction, those highs and lows, are part of the struggle of the individual believer.

There is one other significant point in the blessing of Melchizedek. Abraham gave Melchizedek a tenth of all. He blessed Abraham. As the writer of Hebrews saw, this placed him in a greater position even than Abraham. At the height of his glory, when he had shown what he could do by the strength of God, there was still one greater than Abraham. Melchizedek is a mysterious figure. He was a priest-king of Salem. Salem means 'peace' and is another name for Jerusalem. Melchizedek's name means 'king of righteousness'. We are told nothing of his genealogy or of his death (contrast what we know of Aaron). There is thus a priest-king greater than Abraham. Abraham, despite the promises he had received, needed a priest. The New Testament shows us the real significance of that fact.

Abraham and the Cities of the Plain

A second incident which shows the greatness of Abraham is the destruction of Sodom and Gomorrah. The greatness appears first by way of contrast: the contrast between Abraham's reception of the visitors (the three men who appeared to him) and the reception by the men of Sodom of the men who came to them and whom they tried to abuse. We are told that God had known (i.e. chosen) Abraham *in order that* he might command his children to keep the way of the Lord by doing righteousness and justice (18:19). The descendants of Abraham are to keep the way of the Lord. There is a special point to the requirement for righteousness and justice. Lack of these brought on Sodom the judgment of God. Lot distinguished himself from the men of Sodom by his reception of strangers and his attempt to protect them.

There was a vast difference between the purpose of the visit to Abraham and to Sodom. The visitors came to Abraham to announce that the birth of the promised child had drawn near. They came to Sodom as the two witnesses needed to testify against a man in order to put him to death (*Deut.* 17:6).

The greatness of Abraham shows also in that he was brought into the divine counsel over Sodom. He was brought in not because of what he was in himself, but because God had planned a great thing for him (18:17, 18). It was by his connection to Christ, in whom the nations shall be blessed, that he was brought in. Yet Abraham immediately justified his inclusion by his concerns. Abraham was concerned for God's own character: 'Shall not the judge of all the earth do right?' (18:25). He was concerned also for the people of the cities. Once again, Abraham was a blessing to Sodom. We saw how he delivered the prisoners of Sodom, and now how he attempted to save the city on behalf of the righteous few in it. There is therefore already in Abraham a partial and anticipatory fulfilment of the promise of God.

Questions for Discussion

1. How does Abraham's situation as a recipient of the promises compare with ours?

2. 'The problems of Sarah and Hagar are not due, as the Feminists would suggest, to a patriarchal society. They are due to Abraham's lack of faith and obedience.' Does that remark have contemporary relevance?

3. Abraham is portrayed to us as a coward in his unbelief and a hero in his faith. Why does there not appear to be an Abraham half-way between those extremes?

4. How did Lot show himself to be righteous?

5. Was it wrong that Abraham prayed for a city doomed to destruction?

6: *Abraham – The Father of the Faithful*

We have considered the promises given to Abraham, so let us now take a look at Abraham's response to those promises. In doing this, we shall see more of Abraham's success and triumph.

Faith by Hearing

It was remembered afterwards, indeed it is a very important point of Paul's theology, that Abraham made a certain response to the promise: he believed (*Gen.* 15:5ff.). Here is *the* biblical illustration of faith. The word used in Hebrew for 'he believed', *heamîn,* may sound familiar because of its close relationship to the Hebrew word known to us all: 'amen'. To say 'amen' to something is to agree and affirm the truth of what has been said. To believe is to affirm that what God has said is true. It has even been suggested that we should translate 'Abraham believed' as 'Abraham amened'. He said amen to the promise of God. Faith is believing, declaring that promise to be true. Faith rests on the Word of God. Faith is declaring that Word to be true. There is a great deal of loose and woolly thinking about faith. We have Christians charging off to do this, that and the other thing and saying that they are acting 'in faith', when really they are acting on hunch and wishful thinking. We cannot talk of faith unless we have a word of God on which it is based: 'Faith comes by hearing, hearing by the Word of God' (*Rom.* 10:17).

Abraham, as the recipient of the promise, is the great example of faith because he said amen to that promise.

The Promise Fulfilled (Isaac)

The stress of the earlier section on Abraham was upon all the promises he received. Now we see that those promises were fulfilled. The great fulfilment was the birth of Isaac, which came twenty-five years after the promise was first given! That was surely a sore test of Abraham's faith and patience. Having endured, he afterwards received what had been promised. The name of Isaac is in itself significant as it means 'he laughs'. Abraham laughed when told that he would have a son (17:17) and Sarah laughed in incredulity when she heard the promise (18:12) and in joy when the child was born (21:6), and Ishmael laughed at him (21:9). So the birth of Isaac was surrounded by laughter: of faith and unbelief, of joy and of scorn. As the child of the promise, there is something in the reaction to Isaac that is like the reaction to the promise. It provokes faith or unbelief, joy or scorn.

As the child of the promise, Isaac was circumcised. With Abraham, circumcision reminded him of the promise yet to be fulfilled. It pointed forward to the son yet to be born. It was a reminder to Abraham of the faith he had exercised in that promise. For Isaac himself it was a reminder that the promise had been fulfilled: for he was the promised seed. Yet it also pointed forward to the faith he had yet to exercise. Thus the covenant sign directs our attention to the complex of divine promise and human faith response.

A Tamarisk Tree in Beersheba

We should not think because one of the promises had been fulfilled, that all were fulfilled at that time, and that Abraham had no longer to endure the contradiction between the promise of God and what he experienced. There came to Abraham several reminders that he was in a land which was not his own. We read of one of these reminders in that same twenty-first chapter (verses 25–27, 31). Abraham's existence was not an untroubled one. The biblical text subsequently records that Abraham planted a tree at Beersheba. It is a small incident, but remember that a tree, even a tamarisk tree, is a long-term proposition. You do not plant a tree if you plan to leave town permanently the next day! Thus Abraham's action is recorded as an indication of his confidence that he and his family had a permanent presence in the land. It is not without significance, that Abraham calls upon the name of the Lord, the everlasting God. Here was Abraham's guarantee of permanence as he lived as a 'resident alien' in Beersheba. (The biblical word translated as 'sojourned' is better translated as 'resident alien'. He was not a visitor because he had no other home to return to, but he was not a citizen.)

Faith on Trial

Isaac: The fulfilment of the promise in the birth of Isaac did not mean the end of trials for Abraham. There is a little particle in Hebrew which seems to be added for politeness. It is often translated by words such as 'please', or 'I pray thee'. In Genesis man often said 'please'. When Abraham received the three men in Genesis 18:3–4, he said 'please' three times in two verses. When Abraham asked Sarah to pretend she was his sister in 12:13, he said 'please'. God himself said 'please' only once. That is in Genesis 22:2: 'Take, please'. It is a little point, but it stresses the uniqueness of the request made by God. That which God gave in mercy, he asks back. James takes up the point when he asks, 'Was not Abraham justified by works when he offered up Isaac?' (*James* 2:21). I think we have to bring that into connection with Hebrews 11:17–19. If we believe that the Word of God is true, we act as though it is true. Here we see Abraham doing just that. He acted on the basis that the Word of God was true. Since God has said that 'in Isaac your seed shall be called' (*Gen.* 21:12), that is, will come through Isaac, Abraham knew that he could sacrifice Isaac. Having faith, he could do the impossible; go the extra step in obedience to God. Note that James says that Abraham's offering of Isaac was a fulfilment of the earlier stage where he received righteousness through faith (2:23). Here, Abraham had faith, and because he had faith, he could be righteous in the sense of obeying God. Obedience follows faith in that it is consequent upon and dependent upon faith.

To put this another way: James had read Genesis, and one wonders whether many who quote him have done so. He knew the order of events: first the belief in the promise expressed in Genesis 15 long before Isaac was born and then the action of offering Isaac after his birth. One leads to the other. Those who want him to say that you have to have faith alongside of or at the same time as works, so that we are justified partly by works considered as a thing by itself, show that they have ignored the order of events in Genesis: faith first and then its fulfilment in action.

Similarly, Rahab said amen to the fact that God had promised the land to Israel, and therefore she hid the spies. Her
delivery from the judgment that came upon the Canaanites
through Israel came only because she acted on the basis of
her faith. James argues against the idea that a faith which
does not lead to action can be called faith.

It is because Abraham had faith that he took the action
of offering Isaac. God tested Abraham. The test cannot
itself substitute for faith as a way of righteousness. It can
only demonstrate the faith that is there. So, as Abraham
went to offer his son, he went with the conviction that
God's Word will be true, and that they (the two of them)
will return. The fact of faith does not abolish the agony, or
the tension of the trial. What a lot the biblical description
packs into the discourse between the two as they ascend
the mountain (22:7–8).

Yet, as we know, Isaac was not to be the sacrifice. That
was not just because God had promised children through
Isaac. He could have raised him from the dead. It was
because on the mount of God a substitute was provided.
Abraham had said to Isaac that God would provide the
offering, meaning something else. He found his own words
to be true when God provided the substitute offering. The
whole of the sacrificial system was built on the fact that
God provides a substitute. Sinful man cannot atone for sin,
so on the mount of God a substitute was provided.
Remember that 2 Chronicles 3:1 tells us that the temple
was built on Mount Moriah. On the mount of God, God
provides a substitute. This of course comes to its fulfilment
in the death of our Lord. God showed his love for us in
that he did not withhold his only son. We talk about the
sacrifice of Isaac, and yet we should remember that Isaac

was not sacrificed. Abraham was called the friend of God and God said 'please' to him, yet his demonstration of friendship to God was ultimately far short of God's demonstration of friendship to us!

The Death of Sarah: Even after this great and successful trial of faith, Abraham's trials were not at an end, and that was painfully brought home by Sarah's death. Abraham owned no ground on which to bury her. The biblical text describes her death in one verse, but takes a chapter to describe the purchase of a burial cave. That stresses the problem, the trial of Abraham. He had no land that he could call his own. Though he owned all of it by promise, he owned none of it legally. He must buy it. Behind the polite exchange with the Hittites lies the fact that they have him over a barrel. He asked for a burial plot, to which they replied: 'Why do you need it? We would be happy to share with you.' They knew, and Abraham knew that that would not secure the legal permanence and security which he required. He asked for a cave which was all he really needed, but the Hittite wanted a bigger sale, making him buy the field as well. Once again, Abraham showed faith. He was humble, as one can afford to be who knows that all this will be his. He politely approached the Hittites. When they drove a hard bargain, he went along with it. 'Blessed are the meek, for they shall inherit the earth.' How are we to act? As Abraham does here!

A Wife for Isaac: After Abraham returned from the mountains of Moriah, he received word concerning Nahor, his brother. Abraham had gone out to a land not his own in obedience to the command. He had been promised

[125]

numerous offspring. He had one son and had just been reminded that God had a claim even on that one son. His brother Nahor had eight sons and grandchildren. Wherever Abraham looked there was information which appeared to question the goodness and faithfulness of God.

Abraham's isolation becomes particularly evident when it came to a wife for Isaac. He thus made his servant swear that he would go back to his own country and people to find a wife for Isaac. Abraham was forced to place this most important undertaking in the hands of his senior servant, but the story illustrates two things. Abraham was not mistaken in his trust in God to guide the servant to the right wife. Nor was his confidence in his servant displaced. The servant feared the God of his master Abraham and asked God to show him the right wife. The test the servant chose was not without significance. Isaac's wife was to be the one who showed mercy and consideration to strangers (cf. Sodom and Gomorrah). He discovered that she had not only that proof of piety, but also the qualification of being of Abraham's family.

It is a fitting incident to close this account of Abraham. The trials of faith were so enormous that it seemed as though God had given Abraham an especially difficult time, when he could have made it so much easier for him. Yet, when it mattered, or when it was crucial, God made every piece to fit beautifully into place, and the servant's words of 24:27 are most appropriate. God did not forsake his loving-kindness and truth towards his master Abraham.

Questions for Discussion

1. How does the story of Abraham demonstrate the inter-relationship of God's covenant faithfulness and human faith?

2. The 'sacrifice' of Isaac has always exerted fascination upon Christians because so many biblical themes connect it with the death of Christ. How many connections can you find?

3. How does Abraham's situation of having great promises fulfilled and yet still waiting for others, parallel our own experience?

4. The servant prayed to the 'Lord, the God of my master Abraham' (24:12). Does this form of address betray a personal lack of familiarity with God or a rich understanding of God's character and purposes?

7: The Trial of Faith – Isaac, Jacob

Isaac Repeats Abraham's Trials

One of the arguments raised against the authenticity and truth of the Scriptures in the last few hundred years has been that Genesis is really a composite work, written by several different authors and put together by a later editor. One of the arguments for that position has been that there are repetitions in the account. For example both Abraham and Isaac lied about their wives, saying that they were their sisters. Surely it did not happen twice! So the claim is made that one source originally had Isaac doing this, whilst another had Abraham. When it was put together two persons were thus doing the same thing.

That theory is wrong on several grounds, but one of the most interesting reasons is that it ignores the extent of the parallel between Isaac and Abraham. It is not just in a few incidents that their experiences are parallel.

Let us mention a few such incidents. Isaac had a barren wife (25:21). Isaac faced famine in the land of Canaan (26:1ff.). He was afraid for his life amongst the people of the land and so lied about his wife (26:7). He was in conflict with the people of the land over living space (26:16ff.). All those incidents were amongst the trial of faith for Abraham, and we saw that they were amongst the trial of faith because they were things where the facts and realities of life seemed to contradict the promises of God.

Isaac goes through those same trials. It might seem good if we could simply take our fathers' hard-gained sanctification and start where they had left off. Against that we must recognise that we begin the Christian life with the same depraved hearts that our fathers started with, and so we all must learn by trials the necessity of patient faith.

The Struggle for the Birthright

We saw with Abraham the question of who was the promised seed: Ishmael or Isaac. In Abraham's case it was a case of who was the son of the real wife, the wife God had promised to bless with a seed though she seemed barren. With Jacob and Esau, the question could not be decided on those simple grounds, for both were children of the same mother. The fact which discriminated was not a human factor. Indeed it was against all human expectations, because normally the elder son would be chosen. It was God who made the choice (25:22–23).

At the beginning of the history of Israel stands the fact of election. Before Jacob and Esau were born, it was said that the older would serve the younger. This is the point taken up by Paul in Romans 9:10–12. It depends not upon man, but upon God's sovereign electing purpose.

We see in the story of Jacob and Esau more than just the election of God. We see also that other doctrine which Scripture is also concerned to stress: the moral responsibility of man. Esau despised his birthright. To Jacob, the birthright and the hope that went with it were valuable things, whilst to Esau they were not. Jacob's tactics remind us of those of Abraham in his attempt to secure the birth of an heir. Abraham clearly believed the promise before he sought to beget a son via Hagar, and yet he resorted to human methods to ensure its coming true. Jacob also valued the promise, whereas Esau did not, but he also resorted to human schemes. Clearly, both Esau and Jacob are wrong, but Jacob's sin is of a different sort from that of Esau.

We see the sovereignty of God and the responsibility of man, but we must add a third element. The sin of man cannot frustrate the purposes of God. That emerges very clearly in the account of the way by which Jacob obtained his father's blessing. The story reveals not just the sin of Jacob in his means of procuring his father's blessing, but also the sin of Isaac in his preference for Esau. He had seen in Esau's marriages (26:34-35) what sort of a man Esau was, and yet he preferred him. Though we are not directly told, it seems likely that Isaac knew of the prophecy to Rebekah. The division within the family, and the favouritism shown to each son by respective parents, is not a pretty picture. It is far from an ideal situation. The deception of Rebekah and Jacob, the desire of an old man for his favourite delicacy, and the influence of his appetite upon his choice of sons are hardly praiseworthy. Yet in this tangle of human weakness and sin, it is the will of God which is done. The sin of man cannot frustrate God: even sin accomplishes his purposes!

The blessing upon Jacob (27:27-29) takes up elements which come out of the original blessing and promise to Abraham. There is the promise of the land – a land blessed by God – and the promise of ascendancy over the nations and over his brethren (compare 'cursed be those who curse you' with Genesis 12:3).

The prophecy of Isaac to Esau reflects things said about Ishmael (16:12). Both are banished from the promised land and from the peaceful assembly of men. Esau was to live by the sword. Ishmael's hand was to be against every man. Both the line of the promise (Isaac and Jacob) and the rejected lines (Ishmael and Esau) are separated from other men. With the line of the promise, the separation is in order that they may be a distinctive and holy people. It is not total: the nations are to be blessed through the promised line which is to rule over them. The rejected lines are also separated, but it is a separation of hostility and antagonism. It is the separation of the sword.

The Deceiver Deceived

Jacob received the blessing, including the prophecy of peace and prosperity. Esau received the prophecy of banishment from the promised land. Yet, who is forced to flee from the land? Jacob! Once again, the facts appear to contradict the promise. Jacob's trial of faith, his discipline, was about to begin. He faced banishment from the land. Yet, before he went, God was gracious to him by reaffirming the promise (28:12–15). Remember that Abraham promised his servant who went to find a wife for Isaac that God's angel would go before him (24:7). The servant went away from the promised land, away from Abraham; but God's messenger went before him. The assurance to Jacob as he left the promised land was similar. The agents and messengers of God are in constant communication between God and the earth.

It seems that the experience of the servant was to be repeated with Jacob. God led him to the household of his father's brother, where he found a wife. There is a significant variation however. Jacob had his specialties: hard bargains driven with a man in no real position to bargain; deception and disguise. He found himself delivered into the hand of a man with similar specialties. Laban also drove hard bargains. Laban deceived him in giving him Leah. It has been claimed that there is a low moral level in the story of Jacob's deception of Isaac. His lies and deceit are not rebuked. Perhaps this criticism misses the point of the story. It is not so much Moses, the story teller, who had the job of rebuking Jacob. It is God who corrects Jacob in the hard school: 'Do unto others as you would have them do unto you.' Jacob learned what it is like to be on the receiving end.

In the story of the patriarchs, the weakness of men is clearly displayed. One of the outstanding features of this weakness is the tendency for the problems of the parents to recur in the families of the sons. We see that in the deceitfulness of Abraham and Isaac about their wives, and the deceitfulness of Jacob. We see that also in the family lives of Isaac and Jacob, which were troubled with the same problem: favouritism. Isaac had his favourite son; Jacob his favourite wife (and as we are to see, his favourite son). They are divided families. Yet God delights to reject the judgments and values of men. Isaac preferred the older, manly, hunter son, which is a common human reaction of a father. Jacob preferred the beautiful wife, a very common human reaction for a man. God shows his favour according to different rules. It is Jacob who was chosen by God to receive the blessing, and Leah to whom God gave children (29:31). Rachel herself had to learn patience and looking to God through her tribulation, though God was eventually merciful to her (30:22–24).

The time came eventually for Jacob to return to his own land. Once again, the deceitfulness and hard bargaining of Laban came to the fore. Yet God was merciful to Jacob. His presence and direction were with Jacob, so that Laban's wealth became his. When Jacob fled, it was God who intervened to save him from any punishment on the part of Laban. Jacob was concerned lest he lose his wives and children, but just as God had protected the wives of Abraham and Isaac, so he did the wives of Jacob.

A False Fulfilment

Jacob returned to face Esau. In his preparations, and in his fear of Esau, we see all the weakness of the flesh, but it is hard to be confident in the mercy of God when you have a guilty conscience before man. So Jacob feared the indignation of Esau.

Just as God had come to Jacob at Bethel to prepare him for the trials in Mesopotamia, so God appeared to him before he met Esau face to face (32:24–30). The point of the encounter was change in the status of Jacob. Previously, Jacob had been concerned with his conflict with men. He was given the name 'Jacob' from the fact that he had hold of his brother's heel at birth. As with a number of biblical names the meaning and significance of the name is not simple. On one level it is a pun on the Hebrew word for 'heel'. Yet the same root has connotations of acting deceitfully and of being in contention. His struggle with Esau in the womb was symbolic of his later life. He was in constant conflict with men. The new name, Israel, points to his relationship to God. He came as a sinful man to enter into the holy land of the promise, and to stand before the man Esau, who, in that he had a rightful grievance, executed the righteous judgment of God. Yet God, for his covenant mercies, may chastise Jacob, but he cannot destroy him. Jacob wrestled with Esau in the womb and in life, and he wrestled with God, and survived! The new name reflects that. (Note however, that the name of Jacob continues in use in later chapters. Jacob's conflict with men was not at an end.)

God gave Jacob mercy in the sight of Esau. It does not appear that Jacob had yet learned his lesson as he seems once again to deceive Esau (33:12–17. Seir is down to the south-east of the Dead Sea. Succoth is still to the east of the Jordan and hence could be on the way to Seir, but he stayed there, rather than going on to Seir and later crossed the Jordan to Shechem.)

Thus Jacob came in peace to Shechem. His trials with Laban and Esau were over. The people of Shechem were peaceful and friendly. He bought land. Although he did not buy much land, it was land in the land of promise. Was this the fulfilment of the promise? It soon emerged that Jacob's trials were not over, and his conflicts had not ceased. Jacob was probably in greater danger than ever before. One of the saddest things in church history is the way, after great conflict in the church, when men have contended for the purity of the church and for orthodoxy, the church can so quickly lapse into error and worldliness. Jacob was soon to find that the world looks friendly, especially compared to the attitude and threats of his relatives. The world is in reality just as much a threat.

An incident brought the danger to focus. The son of the prince raped Dinah, the daughter of Jacob. He wanted to marry her. The men of the city offered Jacob an alliance: 'You can have our daughters for your wives, you can acquire property. Intermarry with us.' The bribe was women and property. The price was the destruction of Israel as a distinct people. Jacob could inherit the land by becoming unified with its present owners. He could own the land – as a Hivite. It was the trial again: whether to wait until God gave the land, or whether to take the land as offered by the world. Note also the motivation of the Shechemites in verse 23.

Why did Jacob fail to provide the necessary leadership? His silence seems to indicate indecision and weakness. The response of the sons of Jacob was deceit. They persuaded the men of Shechem to be circumcised and attacked them whilst they were still weak. Note carefully what they then did. They took their property and their wives. What is the difference between the covetousness of Shechem and that of Israel? When they took the wives of the Shechemites, was the consequence and the danger any less than that which would have followed agreement with the terms of the Shechemites?

Jacob the Fugitive

Jacob appeared concerned, largely because of the external threat. He feared retaliation which would wipe him out. God came to the salvation of Israel – again! He ordered first of all repentance. He ordered that the idols, which would have been brought in by the foreign women, be put away.

He intervened to protect Jacob from reprisals. There was to be no settling down for Jacob. The time to inherit the land had not come. Jacob went to Bethel, but did not stay there. He went on, to finish his life eventually as an exile in Egypt. There was for Jacob no abiding city here.

Questions for Discussion

1. Both particular sin and the trial that induces faith tend to recur in the family of Abraham. Why would that be so?

2. When God by-passes the manly Esau and chooses the sneaky Jacob, does it create a problem for his holiness?

3. What is the message to be gained for the modern Christian from the parallel between the deceitfulness of Jacob and Laban and that between the covetousness of the sons of Jacob and that of Shechem?

4. How has the church been harmed by a premature expectation that the promises have been fulfilled?

8: *The Trial of Faith – Joseph*

Egypt at the Time

We conventionally divide the history of Egypt into a number of periods of strength and some periods of weakness when foreigners entered the country. The Old Kingdom in about the mid-third millennium B.C. saw the building of the Great Pyramids. There followed a period of weakness we call the First Intermediate Period, around the late third or early second millennium. Then came the Middle Kingdom, stretching to about 1750 B.C. The Second Intermediate Period came next reaching down to around 1500 B.C.

Many books place the entry of Israel into Egypt in the Second Intermediate Period, because at that time a group of foreigners, called the Hyksos, were ruling Egypt. It is thought that these people came from Palestine and spoke the Canaanite language and thus it is argued that they would be sympathetic to the Israelites, allowing them to settle.

That, however, ignores what the text says about Joseph's dream interpretation. Saying that the Israelites were allowed to settle because the Hyksos were favourable to them is an attempt to make the story plausible without requiring the power of God. However the whole point of the story is the reality of God's power.

Given the uncertainties there are in dating, it would seem likely that Israel entered Egypt in the late Middle Kingdom (around 1780). There is no Egyptian reference to their arrival, the sojourn or the exodus. That is not surprising. Popularisers of recent discoveries in Bible lands forget to point out how incomplete is our knowledge of those lands. During the reign of Sesostris III who, if our chronology of Egypt is correct, reigned about the time of the entry into Egypt, there was an apparent decline of the wealth and position of the provincial governors. Maybe this was a result of the sale of land by the Egyptians to the Pharaoh, in order to stay alive during the famine. If so it would be the only reflection in Egyptian sources of the events described in the Bible.

The Trial of Faith Resumed

The story of Joseph is simple enough for a child, yet profound enough for any adult. In order for the Scripture to be fresh and new to us, we must hear not familiar recollections, but the details of what the text actually says. Take for example the fact that the Bible introduces the story not as that of Joseph, but as 'the generations of Jacob' (37:2). We should not take that to mean 'the story of Jacob'. 'Generations' means what issues forth from Jacob. In that sense it is the story of the sons of Jacob, particularly Joseph. Nevertheless, it is instructive to watch the story unfold from what would have been Jacob's perspective.

The fact that the generations of Jacob begin at this point is significant. They begin here because Isaac died at the end of chapter 35. In chapter 36 we have the generations of Esau, who has gone away from the promised land. His was not the line of the promise. Isaac was dead. Esau was removed from Canaan. Jacob and his family now stood alone. They were the promised line, the ones to receive the Lord's blessings. They were the heirs of the promises which God had given to Abraham and Isaac. What was the outcome? Were they to see the fulfilment of the promises?

If you ask those questions of chapter 37, you receive an unexpected answer. For the story of Joseph merely continued that theme which had already typified the life of Jacob: family fights. Do you remember Isaac's favouritism of Esau, Rebekah's of Jacob, and the trouble over the birthright so that his brother sought to kill him and he fled? Remember also Jacob's favouritism of Rachel and the contention between his two wives, Rachel and Leah. Rachel, the favourite wife, had only two children and she died in childbirth, calling her son 'son of my sorrow'. The strife continued. Joseph was favoured by his father, and hated for that reason by his brothers.

The promise was for a multitude of offspring. Jacob had twelve, and sorrow and trouble with them. Joseph had dreams which confirmed that his position was to be one of pre-eminence amongst his brothers. This caused them to hate him all the more.

Though we may wonder about the wisdom of Jacob's obvious favouritism of Joseph, whom amongst his brothers could he pick? Reuben, the first-born, lay with his father's concubine. The next two eldest, Simeon and Levi, were ruthless, treacherous men who massacred the city of Shechem. The fourth son of Leah, Judah, was a man whose sons were evil in the sight of God; a man who did not keep his word; who resorted to a harlot, yet commanded that an unfaithful daughter-in-law be burnt.

Perhaps we might now sympathise with Jacob. One son showed promise, a son who was the first-born of a beloved wife. One son's dreams marked him out as pre-eminent. Then word came in the blood-stained coat. Joseph was dead, and Jacob wept for the light which had gone out of his life. He wept for him and expected to live in sorrow until the day he would die. What next? *Famine!* What good the promise of the land? Death stalked the promised land. They could not even stay alive in it. Only in Egypt was there life. Only Egypt had supplies. So, ten sons went to buy grain. Benjamin stayed at home lest something should happen to him. The sons returned without Simeon, who remained a captive in Egypt and they brought back the money that they should have paid. The harsh ruler of Egypt demanded Benjamin.

Joseph was gone. Simeon was gone. Benjamin was in danger. What would this Egyptian care for a poor resident of Canaan? Egypt's commercial and cultural presence dominated Palestine. Egypt alone had grain to sell and could dictate the terms.

Jacob had no choice. If they did not act, they would all die of starvation. What good were the promises of God now? Jacob's family and happiness lay in the hands of a callous Egyptian. 'May God Almighty overrule and make this man merciful. If I lose all my children, then I lose them!' So Jacob waited all alone with only his hope in God as comfort – that same hope which had been so cruelly treated by the death of Joseph and the imprisonment of Simeon.

The sons returned and said, 'Joseph is alive and rules all

the land of Egypt.' What did Jacob say? 'Yes, I always knew that it would turn out well in the end. I just kept on praying and never gave up hope.'? No! He went into shock. He could not believe it until he saw what Joseph had sent.

You may think that I have been hard on Jacob. I do not mean to imply that he was without faith. He was a man of great faith, but faith cannot guess what God will do. 'Things which eye has not seen and ear has not heard, and which have not entered the heart of man, all that God has prepared for those who love Him.'

Or shall we consider the story of Joseph as his brothers saw it? In hatred, malice and envy they had sought to kill Joseph, and had done the next best thing by selling him into slavery. How hypocritical their attempt to comfort their father must have been! They were in a position to tell him that Joseph was alive, yet they could not do that without admitting their own sin. Guilt is hard to live with at any time. It is even harder to live with when there is something to remind us of it, and yet we can make no confession. So they lived with their father's sorrow as a constant reminder of their sin – like a murderer living with the corpse of his victim in the same house, always knowing that it is there, yet never able to bring things into the open.

It is when adversity strikes that our sins rise up before us. We know that we deserve judgment, and so we relate the calamity to our own sin, fearing the judgment of God. So the brothers saw the hand of God in what happened to them. When Benjamin's life was threatened, the pressure was really upon them. They knew that it would be too much for their father if Benjamin also was lost. In their imprisonment, they saw the hand of God bringing upon them what they deserved. They had seized their brother and ignored his pleas. Now they were put in the power of one who ignored their pleas.

Finally, when Benjamin was caught as a thief, the irony became crushing. The brothers wanted to become slaves. They could not bear the prospect this time of having to return to their father with the news that Benjamin was a slave in Egypt. In contrast the Egyptian lord was a righteous man. He would not think of making slaves of innocent men! Judah tried a last desperate plea: to become a slave instead of Benjamin, because he would prefer that to seeing his father die under the extra load of grief.

At this, the stern, impassive Egyptian, who spoke to them through an interpreter, was strangely moved. He ordered the Egyptians to leave, and in their own language, revealed himself to them. The brothers were speechless. Their stern Egyptian lord whom they had feared was someone they had even more cause to fear: Joseph!

God is merciful to sinners. Joseph bore no grudge. He could see the providence of God behind it all: 'You meant it for evil, but God meant it for good' (50:20). Even the sin of man is used by God in our salvation. The greatest example, of course, is the crucifixion of Jesus. Men in their evil ways tried to defeat God's plan, but they only aided it. So it was also in this story. The brothers sold Joseph into Egypt so that what God had predicted in the dreams might not come true, but they were merely the instruments for fulfilling God's plan. They still came to bow before the Egyptian Joseph. God was merciful! Not only did they escape the just punishment of their sin, but it was turned into the means of their salvation. They had condemned Joseph to the living death of slavery, but God sent him before them to be the means of saving their own lives.

What of Joseph himself? There were no surprises for him, were there? When his brothers sold him into Egypt, he could look ahead and know that he had to become a slave in order to be lord of Egypt. When his early prosperity in his master's household was turned into imprisonment, he could rejoice because he knew that it would put him into contact with the servants of the Pharaoh. When the cup-bearer forgot him, he could wait patiently because he knew that his appearance before Pharaoh was to be strategically timed. There was no point in his being released to return home to Canaan. Of course, Joseph could not have foreseen any of these things. The path was one of misery and disappointment. Whenever things seemed to be going well, they went badly. A high position in the house of Potiphah was followed by prison. It was two years before contact with the cup-bearer bore fruit.

It is in retrospect that Joseph saw God's hand. The plan was beautiful, once you knew it, and there was no possibility of knowing it beforehand. All Joseph could know was that God does what he promises.

If we read the story of Joseph, not as those who know the end before the beginning, but through the eyes of those who were seeing the story unfold, or suddenly and unexpectedly break upon them, we would see something far closer to our own experience. Man cannot see how events will turn out so as to fulfil God's promises. Jesus could see the plan and purpose behind his betrayal and crucifixion. The disciples were more like Jacob. Their hopes crashed, thinking that Jesus was the one to deliver Israel. It was only when the stranger on the Emmaus road showed that the Christ must suffer and rise again that they saw the plan, and were amazed when the final piece went into place to reveal the stranger as Jesus

Men cannot see the end from the beginning. We can see the evil that other men do. It lies beyond our comprehension to see how this may be used by God for their salvation. We believe that God is merciful and good to his people. We know all that he has promised. And yet everything that happens does not seem to fit our expectation of God's mercy.

As we watch the details of our lives unfold, and the significant events, we find ourselves trying to play God: 'Things will work out wonderfully if only this or that happens.' We know how things should work out in order for God's promise of mercy to be fulfilled, but it does not work that way. Indeed we find real tragedy in our lives. We expect the best from God's mercy and it seems the worst. Simply remember that it is not given to us to know the end from the beginning. We cannot see how God will bring good out of evil; all we know is that he will! True faith is not the ability to predict the future, but the sure confidence that God controls the future for our good.

Dying in Hope

The book of Genesis ends with the deaths of Jacob and Joseph. They died in a foreign land without having received the promised land, yet they still looked forward to it. In a number of passages in the final blessing of Jacob, the future presence of Israel in Canaan was assumed. Jacob commanded his sons to bury him with his fathers in the cave of Machpelah. Joseph commanded his sons to take his bones with them when they left Egypt. Thus whilst entry into a land of their own seemed just as remote as ever, they died in hope, looking for the fulfilment of the promise.

Questions for Discussion

1. 'The story of the other patriarchs shows us that faith is believing in the specific promise of God. The story of Joseph makes us realise that we not only have to wait to see the promise fulfilled. We also have to be prepared for it to be fulfilled in most unexpected ways.' Discuss this statement.

2. Jealousy, conflict and sexual sin are recurrent phenomena in the history of Jacob and his children. Are we lacking the realism of the Bible when we do not recognise the evidence of the same problems amongst the people of God today?

3. What does Genesis 50:19–20 tell us about dealing with the animosities which we harbour?

4. Do you know what it means to be a foreigner looking forward to God's land?

PART THREE

Exodus

1: *The Exile of Moses: Exodus 2:11-25*

In this passage our attention is directed to the preparation for the exodus, and specifically to the exile of Moses. The role of Moses as the man to bring redemption to the people of God is closely related to his previous exile and rejection. Hence, since Christ as our redeemer follows the pattern set forth by Moses, we learn about Christ's rejection. Finally, we learn what we must also endure – if Christ is rejected, his followers must also expect rejection.

First we look at what caused Moses to flee for his life. Though he had grown up in the Egyptian court, he took the side of Israel. He tried to act as the redeemer of Israel. This action of Moses is approved elsewhere in Scripture, the clearest endorsement being in Hebrews 11:24-26. Moses had made his choice, a choice which cost him riches, ease, position and glory in this world. Late last century in England, novels about orphans were very popular. The hero would live his early life abandoned and unwanted in an orphanage. He would be mistreated and have to struggle against opposition and contempt until he was finally revealed not as the child of some impoverished family but of some rich and noble family; able to enter finally into the wealth and position which was rightfully his. You can understand why such novels would be popular. They represented the unexpressed wishes of many ordinary people. Would it not be great if wealth and position suddenly dropped into my lap? I feel in a way that I deserve it. Am I not a noble chap as worthy of riches and fame as any other?

Moses had it, and he gave it up! If you hunger for money and fame, and could not imagine yourself giving them up, then pay close attention to the story of Moses, because Moses had found something far more worth while. The real heirs of riches and fame were not the royal families of Egypt. They were a collection of poor, despised slaves, for to them would come one day the Lord of all riches and the source of all power and authority

It was a choice which appeared to lead nowhere but to banishment and the meagre, unimportant life of a wilderness shepherd. Who could have predicted that this Moses would again stand in the court of Egypt, as an opponent of Pharaoh, and come out victorious?

I warn you, as you also have to make that decision: which road leads to success, wealth and fame? Which will you take? Look beyond the apparently obvious. Look beyond the surface and the here-and-now. You will get no riches now by being a Christian. You will get no fame and honour here and now. Yet the riches you will ultimately receive will far exceed the riches any man can offer, for they include the treasures of the Lord of the world.

It seemed that Moses had made the wrong choice. Power lay neither with him nor with Israel, but rather, with Pharaoh. The moment the king heard, Moses had to leave Egypt very fast. He had not the power to resist. Even more serious however, was the fact that Israel would not unite behind him. Surely with his royal upbringing and training,

Moses was uniquely suited to be the man to give Israel the leadership it needed. However Moses stood for righteousness, and there were many in Israel who found the unrighteousness of Egypt more to their liking than the righteousness of Moses. Their own corruptions would go undetected in an unjust Egypt.

Often, people use the corruption of the church and its internal conflicts as excuse for siding with the world and not with the church. In case you are doing that, may I point out that the problem is a very old one. Moses faced the same situation. There were those who rejected his leadership because they were really no different from the Egyptians. It is not that there is something wrong with Christians that is not wrong with the non-Christian world. The attitudes and corruptions of the non-Christian world are all too evident in the church, leading to rejection of true righteousness.

So Moses became a fugitive and a failure. Before looking at the positive purpose for the exile of Moses, I would make just one point. Moses did not give up what mattered most: the life of faith and obedience to God. An exile – away from home, people and everything – what do we find him doing? He helped some other oppressed people. The sign of the true man of God is that failure and rejection do not build in him that self-centred bitterness which prevents his ever trying again. I have met people who claimed to have had a bad experience of rejection from fellow Christians. How do you know whether that is genuine or merely an excuse to abandon the faith? The genuine believer acts like Moses. Rejection by one group of oppressed people does not stop him trying to help the next.

Now let us turn to the positive purpose of Moses' exile. All things are in the hand of God. If it was not God's purpose for Moses to fail and be rejected, it would not have happened. What can we learn from Scripture about the purpose of God in Moses' rejection?

A redeemer has to share the experiences of the people he redeems. Remember that Christ also suffered as we suffer; was tempted as we are tempted; was baptised like us to fulfil all righteousness. Note the experiences of Moses. Most dramatically, he was delivered from the threat of death by water, just as Israel were. Compare his being cast into the Nile with the Israelites' crossing of the Red Sea. There was another way Moses was delivered. As he returned to Egypt to deliver Israel, God met him and tried to kill him (*Exod.* 4:24-26). After all, if we are comparing Moses with Christ, and see Moses as the great Old Testament redeemer, we would expect the redeemer to die in order to redeem his people. Moses was saved from death because his wife circumcised their son and touched Moses with the blood. It was the blood that sheltered Moses. Similarly, when the angel of death passed through Egypt, to destroy all the first-born, Israel were preserved by the blood. In the part of the story that immediately concerns us, Moses' leaving Egypt to spend forty years in the wilderness was the forerunner of Israel's forty years in the wilderness. Moses' meeting with God at Mount Sinai was the foreshadowing of Israel's later meeting with God there to receive his law.

We may say that Moses' exile was preparing him to be the redeemer of Israel. Yet, that could be interpreted as a psychological or spiritual preparation. That is not what I mean. Moses, as the redeemer of Israel, had to conform to the pattern which would be followed by Christ. As Christ is the Forerunner of his people, experiencing beforehand all their trials and deliverances, so Moses experienced beforehand the trials and deliverances of Israel, and that experience equipped him to be a redeemer.

There was another way in which Moses was following the pattern of Christ, and that is in his rejection. When he tried to deliver them, they said: 'Who made you a ruler and judge over us?' And it was not just the once. All through his life, even after he had led Israel out of Egypt, they constantly rebelled against his leadership. When we read the book of Exodus, we are at first struck by the foolishness and ingratitude of Israel after all Moses had done for them. Yet, is the rebellion against Moses any different from the rebellion against Christ? The Word of Christ says one thing, but the world says: 'Who says I have to do that or believe that?' Moses was the deliverer that Israel did not want, just as Christ was. Are we able to point the finger at Israel? Look at the church. How often has there been a rebellion against the leadership of Christ? The Bible is the book that transmits Christ's commands and leadership to us. How often has that book and what it says been ignored when those who supposedly belong to God's people wanted to go their own ways?

Moses was also setting a pattern for God's people. In Revelation 12 we have the picture of the church being persecuted by Satan. How does she escape? She flees into the wilderness. That picture, like so many of Revelation's pictures, is taken from the Old Testament, and partly from the flight of Moses. Note what Revelation 12:14 says. In the wilderness, the church is nourished by God. When Elijah hid from Ahab, God appointed ravens to bring him food. When Moses fled from Egypt it was with a believing Midianite that he found refuge and livelihood. The life of a wilderness shepherd did not have the luxury of the courts of Egypt, but still it was life, and life with a good conscience. So often God's people have had to choose that sort of life as they have been forced to flee from persecution.

If I were to put it all in a nutshell, why did Moses have to flee? Why could he not have done early in life what he did forty years later when he led Israel from Egypt? The basic answer is that Moses holds a very important position in the history of God's work of salvation. He was a saviour of God's people. As such, he followed the same pattern as Christ who, as Saviour, had to experience the trials of the people he came to save. Moses had to be rejected because, in the sinful world, God's people are rejected. If you claim to belong to that people of God, then you must also be willing to face hostility and rejection. There is no dodging this issue. If you are a believer, you must side with believers and accept the hostility which comes with that. Moses did it, and it cost him a lot. Jesus did it, and it cost him far more. None who claim to stand with Moses and Christ can avoid the rejection of the world.

Questions for Discussion

1. Some say that believers should expect to be rich and prosperous in this life. Do you think Moses believed that?

2. In Exodus 2:14 Moses was accused of pride and presumption. What details of the story of Moses refute that allegation? Is that of any use to you in determining whether the opposition you encounter is an opposition to righteousness as distinct from opposition to your very real pride and arrogance?

3. Moses had final success in spite of his initial rejection; Jesus has acceptance with the Father and his people in spite of those who reject him. Where do you look for the acceptance and success that compensates for the rejection of men?

4. When should a believer conclude that it is time to flee persecution?

5. What preparation should we, who now have relatively abundant material possessions, make for persecution?

2: *The Name of God: Exodus 3:1–17; 5:22–6:8*

If you were in Moses' situation when God called him to be
the one to speak to Pharaoh and to deliver Israel out of
Egypt, I wonder what you would have wanted to know.
What would you expect to be the main topic of conver-
sation between you and God? As with Moses, all the
reasons why you were not the right choice might be high
on the list. Would you expect the name of God to be a
major issue?

The name seems to be a major item of what God had to
reveal to Moses. It is often suggested that Moses' question
reflected the extent to which Israel had been influenced by
Egyptian paganism; that they would no longer be sure who
the God of their ancestors was. Israel may well have been
influenced by Egyptian beliefs, but there is more than that
in it. There is more here than the question of what name
you apply to God. The passage which makes that clear is
the difficult passage in 6:3. There is a problem on the
surface of this verse, as it seems to say that the patriarchs
did not know the name which we translate as 'the Lord'.
Yet it is clear from the Bible that they did know it. For
example, Abraham sometimes spoke to God by that name.

If Abraham did know that name, how can God say
that it was not known? Some of you may have heard the

explanation common amongst scholars who study the Bible without believing it. They say that Genesis was put together from a number of contradictory sources. One author believed Abraham did not know this name, and another author believed he did. So sometimes God is called God in Genesis and sometimes Lord. I will not go into a detailed refutation of this view which really holds Scripture to be divided and contradictory.

There is a much simpler solution, in accord with the context of Exodus 6:3. God announced this name in a context where he says he is going to fulfil his promise. That promise was made, but not fulfilled, to the patriarchs. Now God is to fulfil it. There is a sense in which God will be better known because he will show more of his faithfulness to his covenant promises. It is along this line that we must seek to understand 6:3.

There are a number of passages in the Old Testament, where a 'not' does not make sense in translation into English without further qualification. For example, Ezekiel 16:47, in modern English translations, is rendered as 'not only' or 'not merely', yet the Hebrew has simply 'not'. As a language, Hebrew uses very few adverbs. It may be that there was a reliance on people inferring from context that an adverb is needed to complete the sense. In Exodus 6:3, I suggest we read, 'I did not fully reveal myself.' Then the passage makes sense in the broader context. God will make himself known more completely when he fulfils his word.

That leads to the next question raised by these passages. What does this name mean? We translate it as 'the Lord' because that is what the New Testament authors did. We are not sure how it was pronounced. The Jews stopped pronouncing it because they thought it too holy to use. We are therefore left with guesses. An old guess is Jehovah, but we can say that is wrong. A more modern guess is Yahweh. We cannot be sure whether that is correct or not.

What is probably more important is that it is based upon the Hebrew verb 'to be'. That is why, in 3:14, God calls himself 'I am'. It seems another way of saying the same name.

Israel have been a long time in Egypt. They have endured oppression. Where was God? Had he ceased to exist? Had he changed? The name is an answer to these questions. Biblical Hebrew does not have past, present and future tenses like English. It has rather a tense in which the action is viewed as completed and another in which the action is viewed as in process. When God says, 'I am', he uses the second tense: 'I am and I continue to be, without prospect of change, what I am'. That is the answer to the doubts of Israel.

As well as a name having a meaning, it has connotations derived from its past usage. So this name does not have just a meaning. It has a history. That is what God goes on to say in 3:15. The name 'Lord' (or whatever the Hebrew was behind it), was associated with Abraham, Isaac and Jacob. Which God is this? It is the God Abraham, Isaac and Jacob worshipped and the God who made the promises to them.

To summarise what I have said so far: God was coming to save Israel. The one who was coming was the unchanging one and yet the one who will not really be known until he has fulfilled the promise made long ago. God would make himself better known by coming to save Israel.

We often hear people depreciate the Old Testament,

saying that we do not have a full knowledge of God from it. To know God truly we have to see him revealed through Jesus. Sometimes when people say that, they have a hidden agenda. For example, they may want to say that the God of the Old Testament is the God of hate, and the God of the New Testament is the God of love in order to eliminate the element of judgment in the New Testament. We are often uncertain as to how to respond since there is an apparent element of truth in what they are saying. We do have a fuller revelation of God in Jesus, but it is important to realise that the same progressively fuller revelation was already going on in the Old Testament. God was revealing more of himself as he fulfilled his promises. The New Testament is not something different, but a part of that process of the fuller revelation of God. We must also realise that the New Testament is not the end. When God's Word comes true and Jesus returns, we will know even more about God. We will no longer see in a glass darkly!

We can go on from here to see what this means for our own knowledge of God. People often say: 'I feel I need to know God better.' Sometimes they are not sure how they will come to know him better. The first thing you should do if you want to know him better, is to pray: 'Come quickly, Lord Jesus.' Very often people, when they talk about knowing God better, do not think of that, for in spite of the fact that they talk about knowing God, they focus on themselves. What set of devotional exercises, what meditative practices shall I take up in order to bring God to me? That is putting things backwards! We do not discover God, but God reveals himself to us. If we want to know God better, then let us pray that he will reveal himself in power and grace. I singled out the return of Christ, but I would not stop there, for there are many other ways by which God intervenes to show his power and grace before Christ's return. It is by those ways that we come to know God more: a friend converted, a sinful habit broken, a threat averted, somebody healed. There should thus be no conflict between the activist Christian and the contemplative or meditative Christian. The concern of us all should be that God display himself!

There are implications also for our study of Scripture. Why do we read the Scripture? Some people read it for some feeling and fall into the danger of continually trying to excite themselves: unless they have the feeling, they have had no blessing. Scripture is the record of the progressively greater revelation of God. It is the wonder, the excitement, as that light shines brighter and brighter that is the true blessing of Scripture. Read it not for the feeling but for its disclosure of God. If your knowledge of God grows, then the feelings will follow.

With that background, I would like to look back at the passages we have read. Moses might be called the original 'yuppie'. He had great ideas of saving his nation – once. Those ideas had unexpected consequences, and Moses became an exile with the routine life of a shepherd. Then God broke in. In chapter 6, it was on the heels of a much more recent reverse that God spoke. Moses' attempt had not led to liberty, but to more grievous bondage. It is in this discouraging context that God revealed himself. In chapter 3 the bush burning but not consumed is more than just an attention-getting device. Generally God is described as a consuming fire (e.g. Deuteronomy 4:24). If he shows a different character here then it is significant. God has not come to consume; he has come to save.

God never engages in small talk. He goes to the point. The failure and the disappointment of Moses were quite irrelevant. God had a purpose which he would fulfil. Against this background, Moses' complaint in 3:11 lost its point. God had a promise to fulfil. He repeatedly identified himself as the God of Abraham, Isaac and Jacob because it was to them that he made the promise. He is under a self-imposed obligation. Moses' inability was really irrelevant. God is. He must fulfil the obligation.

There is another detail that I might point out. I said that the 'I am' of verse 14 is related to the name we translate as Lord. 'I am' comes in a passage before verse 14, occurring also in verse 12, and could be translated as 'I am with you'. 'I am' is the same word in verses 12 and 14. God's answer to Moses' uncertainty was to say, 'I continue unchanged, and I am with you and will continue to be with you.' The God who had already made a promise and came to fulfil it now made another promise. His relationship to his people consisted of one fulfilled promise leading to the next.

When Jesus departed from his disciples, having finished all the work God had given him to do, he made a promise: 'I am with you always, even to the end of the age' (*Matt.* 28:20). I think the relationship between this promise and the promise to Moses is more than merely verbal. It is rather the pattern of one fulfilment leading to another promise. Remember how distressed the disciples were at the prospect of Jesus' leaving them. When he told them that he must go to the Father, they found that very hard to accept. Jesus constantly said that it was better that he should go away. He made it clear that he did not just mean that it was the plan of God, but rather, that it was for the disciples' advantage. They were better off if he returned to the Father and the Spirit were sent forth. Of course, before Pentecost, the disciples could not imagine how that could be true. Yet, with Christ present with them through his Spirit, they were far better and stronger men than they had previously been.

I read recently an analysis of why people want to see pictures of disaster and calamities on the evening television news. It is to reassure them that they themselves are not so badly off after all. It is comforting to see the pictures of the bomb and famine victims, and to know that our world is nice and secure. After they have watched that reminder of their security, they must then watch some thriller where they go to the edge of death with the hero, for their lives are too dull. They need a little synthetic excitement which is provided by 'the box'. Thus, we find security in others' misfortunes, and excitement in men pretending to be in danger.

God has a name which emphasises his unchangeability. It is in that name that he makes a covenant relationship to people and makes promises. In that name is our security. It is not in a relative peace or prosperity. Those things are very unreliable. That name guarantees all the promises of God, and hence our own future.

However, with God, dependability does not mean dullness or boredom, for this dependable God makes promises. He has purposes. Indeed, it ensures a life of unpredictability in our experience here. It leads to surprises as unsettling as that received by Moses when he learned that he had been chosen for God's work. Very often we recoil against the earthly unpredictability of that life. It does not have for us the stability, even the dullness, that we would prefer. Consider Moses. An idealistic phase, in which he so wanted to deliver his people, was followed by a secure, danger-free existence and yet one which accomplished nothing of great moment. Then God said 'Go', and he said, 'Please, not me.' We prefer the dullness of failure to the thrill of danger and trial.

God has a name. There is something relentless in the name of the one who does not change, but relentlessly presses on to the goal. If God has placed his hand upon you, and there is a task for you to do, it will not do any good arguing. It is not in his nature to give up. Moses was wasting his breath. Let us not waste ours.

Questions for Discussion

1. Can you relate this discussion of the name of God to other references to God's name in Scripture?

2. There is a sect which has taken a guess at the Hebrew word behind 'Lord' into their official title. Scholars have disputed whether the correct pronunciation is 'Yahweh' or not. Do such concerns about pronunciation approach what it is to know the name of God?

3. Even though Scripture records people who received visions, it is singularly uninterested in techniques for mystical meditation and stimulating visions. How does this lack of interest relate to the biblical teaching on the knowledge of God?

4. What is the difference between Abraham's prayer for Sodom and Gomorrah in Genesis 18:23–32 and Moses' argument with God in Exodus 4:10–16?

3: *Sent to Serve: Exodus 4:19–23; 12:29–36*

A lot can depend on the impressions conveyed by translations. Some phrases can even become so impressed upon the Christian consciousness that any other translation sounds unacceptable. 'Let my people go' is such a phrase. It became part of the words of a Negro spiritual, and from there, as Negro Christianity became secularised and politicised, it passed into a slogan of the American civil rights movement: 'Let my people go'. The only problem is that that is not quite what God, via Moses, said to Pharaoh. A more literal and accurate translation is 'Send my people from your land that they may serve me.' What is the difference? 'Let go' is permission: 'Yes, Israel, you may go'. 'Send' is command: 'Israel, get out!', and that is what did happen in the end. Pharaoh and Egypt urged the Israelites to go. They did not say 'Oh, well, if you really want to, I guess you can go.' They forced them out.

With that in mind, turn back to the passage in question. Israel have been working for Pharaoh as slaves. God steps in and says, 'Pharaoh, that is *my* son, not yours. Send him out of your land that he may serve me.' Pharaoh is directed to make Israel go and serve the Lord. Pharaoh, the god-king, the manifestation of the gods of Egypt, is told to send his slaves to serve another god.

Can you imagine? You turn on the television to watch your favourite soap opera, cops and robbers or whatever. Just before it, there is a special announcement: 'For all Christians we have a special announcement. This program will keep you from serving the Lord. It is time-wasting junk! Its values are distorted and perverted. Christians, you have better ways to spend your time. Turn off the T.V.'

The youth club enters the skating rink. The manager spots them. 'Get out! What are you doing, you Christians, making me rich and wasting your time entertaining yourselves? There are people in need out there. Get out and serve the Lord and not yourselves or my bank balance.'

Can you imagine that happening? Well, that is what God said Pharaoh had to do. God was making even god-less, proud Pharaoh to serve him. Just as he used envious Jewish priests, a self-serving Roman governor and a corrupt disciple to save his people through the death of Jesus, so he used Pharaoh. Pharaoh was to send Israel to serve him.

The reason given is also very interesting. It was because Israel was God's first-born son. God had special claim on his service. To be a son of God is to serve him. Hence, God could say to Pharaoh, 'I claim Israel's service. You have no right to it. I am telling you that you must send Israel to serve me.' As we know, Pharaoh was not too keen on the idea. Can you understand why? The basic question, as it has always been, is 'Whom do you serve?' The battle between the church and the state that tries to take the place of God as Pharaoh did, has always revolved around this question: 'Whom do you serve?' the state, or Jesus?

What does it mean to serve God? It means first of all, to worship. The first request which Moses put to Pharaoh was seemingly innocuous: to go three days journey into the wilderness to hold a feast to the Lord. The first demand was not that Israel be entirely free from the service of Pharaoh, but that they also serve the Lord. Pharaoh would not hear of it, for he was trying to take the place of God. Why do Communist and other godless governments try to close churches? It is because they claim complete lordship. To worship even one day per week is a repudiation of that complete lordship. We tend to emphasise the danger in our culture of nominal worship: when people worship on Sundays but do not serve the Lord during the rest of the week. We should indeed be aware of that danger, but let us not forget the significance of worship. It is not nothing to gather with God's people to worship him. Have you really wrestled with the pull of the world; with non-Christian relatives who want to discourage your Christianity; with a whole system whose entertainment, sporting activities, industrial and business activities all have the same end: to prevent your worshipping God with his people? If you have faced that pressure from the world, then you know that Pharaoh was no fool. He could not have complete allegiance from Israel if he were to allow them to go to worship God. The world knows that too. If you do not know it, then you merely show that the world is wiser than you.

Ultimately, however, Pharaoh had to concede that point also, and ultimately, in opposing the freedom of Israel to worship, he was to lose all their service. The point comes where he literally throws them out of Egypt. Egypt's opposition led to their eventual freedom and release:

freedom that is, to serve. Unless you serve the Lord Jesus, you are still in bondage to other masters. If there is anything that the modern church, with its addiction to the self-pleasing, entertaining lifestyle of the world, needs to learn, it is that freedom is freedom to serve!

The consequences for Egypt in refusing to send Israel to serve the Lord are clear. They are judgment. It has frequently been pointed out that some of the plagues have reference to Egyptian religious beliefs. The Nile was a god. The sun was a god. Thus God's use of them to punish Egypt was a manifestation of his power over the impotence of what Egypt worshipped. Yet, the climactic and final plague has another explanation. Pharaoh had said to God: 'You cannot have your son. He will serve me.' 'Right,' said God, 'I will take your son. Your son will die.' The bondage in Egypt foreshadows the bondage of God's people in our age, preceding the return of the Lord. It is what the world does to God's people that brings the final judgment (*Rev.* 6:9,10). The contest is between God and the powers of this world for control over God's people. There is a sense in which we can take calmly the world's attempt to control God's people. Certainly if we encourage that attempt, if we want to serve the powers of this world rather than God, God will not be pleased with us; but I refer to those attempts by the world to restrict the freedom of God's people, to dominate them and make them serve the world. God says, 'Israel is my son.' God has that prior claim on the allegiance of his people. The world will be judged when it disputes God's lordship. Do not be on the side of the world. The world that opposes God's people will be judged.

What, though, was to be the ultimate consequence for

the people of God? They were not only sent out of Egypt, but they were sent out with great riches. Once again, a translation problem has somewhat obscured this point as I mentioned earlier. The wording of the Authorised Version in Exodus 11:2, says that Israel were to 'borrow' from the Egyptians and in 12:35-36, it speaks of the Israelites borrowing and the Egyptians lending. That is a problem, because you are expected to return what is borrowed, and Israel clearly had no intention of returning what they took from the Egyptians. The newer translations have corrected the problem. While the Hebrew word can mean 'borrow', it more commonly means simply 'ask', which makes a lot more sense here. The Hebrews had no intention of returning the goods, and the Egyptians knew that.

Why were Israel to ask for these things? There are two answers. God made Pharaoh do the right thing in sending Israel from his land and service. He also made Egypt do the right thing with respect to Israel. The law has rules for what to do when a slave is sent out (*Deut.* 15:12-15). A slave was to be sent away with gifts. Egypt had to obey the law of God in sending away its slaves. At the time of judgment, men have to obey God. They have no choice about it, but must submit to him and do what he says. Yet, that obedience is to their own ruin. The Egyptians are plundered.

The second aspect of this is that the gifts represent the wages of Israel. They had been made to serve Egypt, but now God made Egypt pay so that the slaves were made rich! The masters for whom they had worked became poor.

Once more we may make comparison to the final judgment. All the riches of the world are to be taken from the unbelievers, and all the riches of the new world will be given to believers. Since materialism is one of the greatest temptations of our day, that point needs emphasis. Present wealth will offer no protection or comfort when the Lord comes. All the wealth will be gathered from unbelievers and given to God's people. Wealth and the desire for it are, therefore, delusions. It was for money that Judas joined those who killed Christ. And it is for wealth that many have forsaken the ways of the Lord. If your heart is set upon money and possessions, you will end up poor. If you serve the Lord, you will be rich. Redemption brings reversal of the world's way of seeing things. Slaves become rich and masters become poor. There is a choice. You may seek to accumulate money here, and place your security in that. If you do that, you will find yourself forced onto the side of those who oppress and oppose the people of God. If you make that decision, you will be poor. All that you have will be taken away, and you will have nothing. If you make the second decision, you will be rich. Make your choice!

Questions for Discussion

1. Is it only in times of judgment that God makes unbelievers to do his will by encouraging believers to serve him or do we find that happening constantly?

2. In response to the failure of human fathers in today's society, people are being encouraged to know God as a Father. According to this passage what should such knowledge imply?

3. Are we too reluctant to warn society, entertainment and business of the judgment they are preparing for themselves by impeding God's people in their service and especially in their worship?

4. Would it be legitimate for us today, in anticipation of the final judgment, to demand the riches of unbelievers?

5. 'When it comes to attempts to impede the church there is very little to choose between Communist and Democratic countries.' Would you agree?

4: *Persecution and Judgment: Exodus 6:28–7:6*

Israel's experience in Egypt, and their deliverance out of Egypt is often referred to in the New Testament Scripture because the exodus was the Old Testament redemption: the great Old Testament example of the way God redeems, delivers and saves his people. Hence, when the New Testament wants to explain, by Old Testament examples, the redemption achieved by Christ, it goes back to the exodus. When it wants to picture the bondage of the people of God as they await the return of the Lord to set them free, it pictures them as being in Egypt. There is much, therefore, of importance and relevance to our situation, which can be learned by a study of Israel's deliverance from Egypt.

Israel were in bondage, and a bondage which was a part of the plan of God, and which he predicted to Abraham. It was not something which God was unable to prevent; something the Egyptians did whilst his back was turned. Rather, God himself led them into Egypt, knowing that imprisonment and harsh service awaited them.

The parallel with our own day is pretty clear: the church is now in bondage awaiting the coming of the Lord to deliver her. We may not feel that so much now, but what of our brethren in Communist or Muslim countries? Why does God allow them to be held in prisons and labour camps? If we ever have to face persecution in this land, we will have to answer that question. It is not merely a theoretical question. How do you know that God has not turned against you, or even, that God is still in control?

We learn several answers to that question from the Scripture:

1.   The time for judgment has not yet arrived. God could not give Israel a land without dispossessing those already there, and the time for that had not yet come (*Gen.* 15:16). The non-Christian commonly looks upon the destruction of the Canaanites as evidence of the injustice of God; that God commanded Israel to massacre an innocent population. On the contrary, we have evidence here of the mercy and long-suffering of God. Surely God has the right to punish man for his sins and the right to delegate that punishment to others. Yet, in spite of the sins of the Canaanites: idolatry, child-sacrifice and sexual perversion, God did not immediately condemn them, but waited four hundred years! Furthermore, he waited and delayed the punishment even though the sins of the Canaanites were not sins in ignorance. As Romans 1 teaches, those sins are unnatural, against the evidence of the created world around and man's own created nature. Yet, God postponed the judgment until those sins had become clear, crystallised and confirmed.

If we try to relate this to our situation, then the parallel to the judgment of the Canaanites is the final judgment. God's people will not receive an inheritance in the new heavens and the new earth until the final judgment. Thus, once again, there is a connection between judgment of the unbeliever and an inheritance for God's people. That connection is to be stressed because the most unbiblical idea of universalism is being promoted in many churches today: that is, the idea that everybody will be saved in the end and that the only difference between believers and unbelievers is that believers know that they will be saved whereas unbelievers do not. To that idea, one simply asks: if the Canaanites were to be saved in the end, why did God have Israel kill them? The clear biblical teaching is that God separates those who will be judged and condemned to eternal destruction from those whom he will save and bless.

We see the delay of the judgment not only with the Canaanites, but also with the Egyptians. God did not deliver Israel with great judgments the moment Egypt began to oppress them. Since Moses was forty years in the wilderness before he returned to lead Israel out of Egypt, and since he had already grown up before he was forced to flee Egypt, there would have been at least fifty to sixty years and maybe quite a bit longer, between the beginnings of the oppression and the deliverance. With Egypt also, God was patient.

Is it then surprising that God continues to show patience in our day, waiting for the sin of oppressive nations to reach the point where judgment, and full judgment, is called for? We might wish that God were less patient, but if he were, then he might also be less patient with us. We who receive so much because of that patience are in no position to complain against it!

2. A second reason for the bondage of God's people applies particularly to Egypt. God, in judgment, hardens

people in their sin. This is quite clearly taught in Exodus 7:3 but also in Romans 1. When men refuse the truth, and harden their hearts against what is natural and loving, then God removes his restraints and gives them over to what is cruel and unnatural. God's hardening of Pharaoh's heart gives many people problems. Let me point out first of all, that the Scriptures say it very clearly many times in Exodus as well as in Romans 9:17. Why would God harden in sin? Here, Romans 1 is again very clear. It is a judgment. God is not making people sin when they do not want to. On the contrary, he is removing the restraints that he has formerly placed on their going their own way. That is judgment, because the more people go their own way, the more they end up in misery.

When there is an outbreak of fierce persecution, people are inclined to see Satan as being on the rampage and almost as the key figure, rather than God. I would not deny for a moment that Satan is involved, but I think we have to remember that what we have said about evil men applies also to Satan. I will not here go into a study on the book of Revelation, but would draw attention to chapter 16; to the bowls of wrath that the angels empty upon the earth. The sixth bowl is very interesting. The consequence of the pouring out of the bowl is that evil spirits go out to gather men to the great last battle against God – the battle of Har-Mageddon. What is conveyed by this picture? One of the results of God's judgment is that men gather for their futile attempt to fight against God. It is just another way of saying that God, in his judgment, hardens men in their opposition to what is right and good, that they might be judged. Who are the instruments he uses? They are the evil spirits. Satan is not in control. God is! The more implacable men's hatred of God, and in consequence the persecution of the church, the more you can be certain that God is there and is at work.

In Exodus, we do not have these things spelled out, but we do have some interesting hints. Note Exodus 12:12. God's judgment is to be upon the gods of Egypt. As Scripture tells us elsewhere, the sacrifices that the Gentiles offer are really being offered to demons (*1 Cor.* 10:20). Here we have just a hint of the battle behind the scenes: the battle involving the demons. That hardening of the Egyptians against Israel involved demons, and so the demons also share in the judgment.

We do not simply stop with the judicial anger of God that hardens men in sin, nor with the role of demons in inciting men to defiance of God. That opposition to God has an outcome, which is God's spectacular victory. It was the very determination of Egypt to keep Israel oppressed, that opened the way for the great and public judgment of Egypt and the display of God's might and power. One never succeeds in diminishing God's glory by opposing him. His glory is only enhanced! He gains fame by destroying all who seek to oppose him. To put it another way: God's salvation of his people is magnified by the fact that they are in bondage and that their enemies are determined to keep them in bondage. It can never be said that God won over Egypt because the Egyptians really did not care whether Israel left or not. God won over all that Egypt could do. Egypt, the greatest power of the age; Egypt, whose king had been regarded as god, the Great God, for more than 1,500 years, set herself to keep Israel in bondage. Yet Egypt was broken in the attempt.

There is one further consequence of this. People are made to acknowledge that God is God. Men will be made to bow the knee. Even those who oppose God will finally have to give him the glory. Pharaoh asked in contempt, 'Who is the Lord?' – 'Who is this God? Never heard of him. Why should I take any notice of him?' Egypt did not have to ask that question when it was all over. Then it was too late. There is a knowledge of God that is not a saving knowledge. Everybody who on the last day is made to bow the knee to Christ will know him, but that is not going to save them. They will know him as their victor and judge.

On that day, it will be too late, but there are other judgments before that day. Nations which have tried to hold the people of God in captivity will suffer for it, and that in itself is a testimony to the power of God. Indeed the lack of success of the many attempts to destroy the church is one of the great testimonies to the power of God.

The other nations knew of what God had done to the Egyptians, and yet for very few did that become a saving knowledge. Rahab and the Gibeonites are examples of people where it did have that impact, but the rest of the Canaanites only redoubled their efforts to fight against Israel. Look at the situation of our age. Men can even look back upon many, many unsuccessful attempts to destroy the church, yet the reaction of the unbeliever does not change. Does he cease his opposition to God? Sadly, he does not. When you look through the history in the Bible, or through church history, you find that relatively few people are converted because of God's deliverance of his people. It is not that it never happens, but it is rare. God has ordained that the major way by which people are converted is through the preaching of the gospel. God's deliverance of his people, without the gospel, will not have a great converting impact. Why then is God concerned that the Egyptians come to know him as the Lord? I think it is a part of God's own glory. It was a test of power between Egypt and God, and in the end, Egypt had to acknowledge that God was the stronger one.

So every unbeliever will be forced to acknowledge failure. What good will that do you on the last day? Take the lesson from history. His people have always been victorious through his power. Put yourself on their side!

Questions for Discussion

1. Why do people ask how God could allow earthquakes and such calamities when they ignore the even greater problem of the persecution of Christians?

2. How does the case of Pharaoh fit into Paul's argument in Romans 9:17?

3. Is it a comfort under persecution to know that God plays a role in hardening the rage and hate of demons and men?

4. If so few people are stimulated to turn to God by the way he delivers his people why does God make a point of the nations knowing? How can it be that God's 'evangelism' is relatively indifferent to results?

5: *Becoming an Israelite: Exodus 12:40–51*

If you were asked how people under the Old Testament became Israelites, you would probably answer a silly question by saying: 'By being born an Israelite.' Yet, this would not be completely right, for there was provision in the law for a foreigner to become an Israelite.

It was not just a theoretical possibility, for we know of people who actually did become Israelites. One of these persons is a very well-known Old Testament character, Caleb the son of Jephunneh, who was one of the two spies sent by Moses to spy out the land of Palestine, who trusted in the Lord and urged Israel to attack. The Bible consistently calls him a Kenizite (*Josh.* 14:6) and we know they were one of the clans of Edom (*Gen.* 36:11). We also read passages like 1 Chronicles 2:55 (The Kenites were a Midianite tribe [*Num.* 10:29; *Judges* 1:16]). The significant thing about Caleb and these Kenites is that they were connected to tribes of Israel. Caleb was even a leader of a tribe. Hence, they had fully joined Israel, even to the point of being placed in a particular tribe.

Further, Israel had specific policies which would encourage aliens to come to them. Note particularly Deuteronomy 23:15, 16. (Harbouring refugees is a good biblical practice.) So Israel, rather than being closed to evangelism or to outsiders, as is often the impression, had an open door to those who came to Israel for refuge or who wanted to become Israelites.

We are also told what anybody who wanted to become an Israelite had to do, and the intriguing thing is that the whole matter comes up in the discussion of the Passover. It is not in Leviticus or Deuteronomy, where, after Israel have left Egypt and are looking forward to Canaan, they receive all sorts of detailed instructions. Rather, it comes up in the first Passover. When the Scripture is saying that this is the crucial feast for Israel; when Israel will remember its roots, the most significant event in the whole history of Israel as a nation; at that time you think about those from outside who will want to participate in it.

This is a significant point of debate. What is the connection between our own re-education of those within, and our bringing in the outsider? The whole point of the Passover was to remind Israel of their roots. Remember the emphasis: 'Your son will ask: Why are we doing these things? And you will say: Because something special happened to us. We are the people whom the Lord redeemed by sacrificing the blood of the Passover lamb, when all the first-born of Egypt were killed.'

This was a covenant ceremony, emphasising the faithfulness of God to his covenant promises. It was about the redemption which established a distinctive covenant community. It was a means to instruct the youth in what the covenant was all about.

It is anticipated the alien will want to partake in this very ceremony. Notice that each individual household partakes. It was a very home-based ceremony, even prohibited from being taken outside. It was not like a parade or a letterbox drop, or a public performance which would attract attention. With everyone in Israel doing this, the alien would surely discover what was going on. Yet it is not as though they would all be lined up in some public place where the aliens might feel out of place because they would be the only ones wearing blue shirts instead of green shirts. It was a private ceremony.

Why then would the alien want to partake? I think that there is one obvious answer: in order to be part of that people who had the privilege of being singled out for redemption by God. David puts that sense of unique privilege so well in 2 Samuel 7:22–24. Israel, and Israel alone, are the nation that God went to redeem. Who would not want part of that if he were in his right mind? If the other side of your street were singled out by the local shopkeepers and they were told they could have as many gift vouchers as they liked to come to get anything they liked any time they liked, wouldn't you try to become an honorary member of the other side of your street?

I would like to use this clear and close connection that we see here to quash some fallacies commonly found amongst Christians:

1. There is no conflict between covenant consciousness and evangelism. Sometimes people will say: 'We are busy training our covenant youth. That is our emphasis and it does not fit with evangelism. The two emphases cannot be mixed.' Rubbish! Nonsense and rubbish!

2. Some say we can only attract the world if we become like the world – 'Nobody will join us if we are somehow different; we must be like them to attract them.' Rubbish

again! Unless we are different, with something distinct to offer, there is no point in joining. Would you join a club if all that club offered was to sit and watch television just as you do at home? Being different and unique will not necessarily bring people to us in droves. What I would say is that uniqueness is the prerequisite to bring people to us.

Well, you may ask: 'We put emphasis on the covenant training of our youth. We reindoctrinate in the foundations. Why are people not coming and saying: "How can we join you?"' We are the people God came to redeem. Who else can say that? The Humanist cannot say it. The Marxist cannot say it. The Muslim cannot say it. The Buddhist cannot say it. The Aboriginal witch doctor cannot say it! We are the people the Lord Jesus came specifically to make his people. Does the sense of that wonder and privilege shine out of us? I suspect it does not, otherwise we would not have people arguing that we have to be like the world to attract unbelievers. Those who say that do not believe we have something unique. If I believed that I was marketing a soap powder which cleaned better than all the others put together, then would I say to my packet designers: 'Let's see if we can design a packet that looks like Fab or Cold Power. Maybe they will purchase some of ours by mistake and we might get some sales after all'? No! I would want a distinctive box.

What are Christians really saying in such words as: 'We have to show that Christians can have fun too'? The same kind of comment can be heard with many variations: 'We must have a rock band to attract them', or, 'Well, people aren't likely to become Christians in our church because we're too rigid. We make them come to church. They can't play sport on Sundays.' People who speak like that are really saying that they envy the world. They see the world as having something they are missing. Will that attitude attract the outsider? It is a denial that the believer is the one with unique privileges.

Note the emphasis placed in this passage on the fact that the same standard is to be applied to foreigners as to Israelites. Obviously there would be a temptation to say that if a foreigner wanted to keep the Passover, then he could do that without conforming to all that was required of Israel. That is not the position of Scripture however, because it really runs contrary to God's holiness. The foreigner cannot come into relationship to God on an easier basis, because the demands upon Israel are the demands of a holy God, not arbitrary demands made for no real reason. They are connected to God's very character.

Perhaps we should go back a step before that and note that the same standard can be applied to both. To apply the same standard is not seen as a problem. People, though not born Israelite, could become fully Israelite under the law of God. Indeed, as the example of Caleb shows, they may be even more Israelite than most of Israel, because being Israelite was a matter of faith and obedience.

A romantic view of race and nationality has been very strong in the modern world. Nationality is seen as something you acquire with your mother's milk. You cannot really feel and appreciate the culture of a country unless you are born into it. That same thinking has infected the church. If you are born into a Christian family, and especially a Reformed one, then you will appreciate what it is to be a Christian to a degree that no foreigner ever could. That is not biblical. Though there may be examples which seem to prove it, there are also many which could be used to disprove it. It is wrong, because to be a faithful Christian is a matter of faith and obedience to the revelation of God, and not something like accent which unless you learn as a child you may have trouble ever learning.

We may need to exercise patience with new converts, but we can never say that because they did not have a Christian background we can never expect them to reach our standard. That would really be a form of pride: we have it, they will never have it.

Conversely, Scripture forbids the hypocrisy of having a lower standard for the insider than for the outsider. To put it another way: you cannot tolerate something in a member of the church which you would use as an argument against accepting somebody into church membership. This is something which should really make us search our own consciences, because we may often fall into this hypocrisy. Let me give a few examples to drive the point home. Suppose somebody began attending our church from outside, and eventually wanted to join, but that they said either of the following: 'We do not agree with the teaching of the church (e.g. we do not believe in election or creation)', or, 'We do not see why any more involvement in church activity is required other than a formal attendance on Sunday mornings', or, 'We are in the process of obtaining a divorce.' Would we say 'Yes, we will accept you into membership'? I suspect that we would not. Are we not then caught in hypocrisy if we tolerate such attitudes amongst our members? I do not say that the answers to these problems are simple. I am saying that we are in great danger of hypocrisy, and an hypocrisy displeasing to God and inhibiting to evangelism because people will see the double standard. I am convinced that weak churches, tolerant of sin in their midst, often have two levels of approach to a new convert. Officially they are in favour of evangelism, but unofficially and personally they do everything they can to discourage the new converts because they find their zeal an embarrassment.

This may be why internal reformation and revival is closely connected to evangelism. Any church with double standards must avoid having the double standards exposed: it must avoid evangelism. If we take a look around, we will see that this is the tendency. Is this the real explanation why Reformed congregations can die?

Finally, what was required of the man who wished to keep the Passover? He and his household had to be circumcised. He had to take on the external badge of an Israelite. You could not be an Israelite without open identification with Israel. The abolition of circumcision has not changed that in any respect. To be a Christian and to join the church go together. These are the redeemed people. The whole point is to become one of them.

Questions for Discussion

1. Does our approach to evangelism reveal that we think our church has nothing to offer to the unbeliever?

2. 'The church which is without enthusiasm in its evangelism will, barring a special intervention of God's mercy, lose its covenant youth. If it has nothing special to offer the outsider, then it has nothing special to offer its own children.' Evaluate your education programme for your own children in the light of that statement.

3. Is the standard you apply to people joining the church higher than what you expect of long-standing members?

4. An ethnic church expects that only people of a certain sort would ever want to join their church. On that definition was Israel an ethnic church? Is your own church an ethnic church?

5. How do the privileges of our Passover as Christians exceed those of Israel?

6:   *The Blessing and Curse of the Firstborn:*
Exodus 13:1–16

I recently visited a church with an unusual custom. There were two ministers, each of whom preached a separate sermon on the same text each Sunday. This was not by accident, but clearly discussed between them. The experience impressed upon me that when one believer finds a text difficult, then two are likely to have the same trouble. The text with which they struggled was Psalm 137:9. How can we say that there will be blessing upon anybody who kills little children?

The problem does not stop with this psalm or this verse. Israel were commanded to kill all the Canaanites, and that included children. When Christ returns to judge all those who have not believed, that will include children. Does not our passage in Exodus tell us that the judgment of God came specifically upon children, the first-born of Egypt only, but certainly children?

Obviously this will be the sort of thing used by many to attack the love and justice of God. However, I want to consider the topic for more than that reason because there is another side. Just as the first-born of Egypt experience a particular judgment and curse, so the first-born of Israel experience a particular position of importance. In general it might be true that God destroyed children along with adults, but so also, on other occasions, he has blessed children along with adults. As in many matters, we find that those who object to the justice of God must also logically object to the mercy of God. If we can say it is wrong for God to bring children under judgment – for what have they done wrong? – or that they do not have a chance, and other such arguments; then we must also say that it is wrong for God to bless children – for what have they done right? People do not like to be so logical or consistent. They accuse God of inconsistency and injustice, yet they do not want him to be consistent.

Let us move on from this, however. If any man has doubts or charges against the justice of God, then it is easy to show that it is a case of man being unfair to God, not God being unfair to man. Why is it that we have what I have described: children as the particular object of the curse in Egypt, and children as the particular object of God's blessing in Israel?

It is part of the very way God has created. Anything that is his order will lead to greater blessing and happiness if it is used properly within the sphere of his mercy, but that same thing will lead to greater misery and curse if misused. Take the whole institution of marriage, which was ordained by God, not invented by man. What greater device for the joy, contentment, satisfaction and peace of man? Yet, at the same time, what greater device for the misery, degradation and destruction of man? It is not a matter of blessing or neutral. It is blessing or curse! Take government: that also is a case of blessing or curse. Take rain, or sunshine: it is the same thing. Let us return to children. The judgment of God on Egypt falls particularly upon the first-born whereas the mercy of God to Israel is shown in the special privilege of the first-born. If Adam had obeyed, then in God's order, there would have been special and extra happiness for all his children. Because Adam disobeyed, there came curse upon all his children. Egypt's hardness means curse on the children of Egypt. The mercy of God shown to Israel will continue as a mercy on their children.

God institutes in Israel a reminder of that fact. He institutes a setting apart, a consecration, of the first-born. The connection is made clear. It was a reminder that Israel were redeemed from Egypt. Redemption is built into the reminder because all the children have to be redeemed. What otherwise would be their fate? They would be killed and offered up as sacrifice to God, just as the Egyptian children were. Remember that on the night of the coming out from Egypt, the children of Israel also had to be redeemed; redeemed by the blood of the lamb of the Passover so that they were passed over by the angel of death. Both in Egypt and later in the land of Canaan, every child of Israel would deserve to die just as much as every Egyptian child. The choosing out of the first-born for curse or mercy is a reminder of what all deserve.

The whole institution of the first-born in Israel points backwards, as a reminder of God's mercy to Israel. It also points forward. We read in Luke's Gospel (2:22–24) that Christ was redeemed as the first-born of Mary. He also was a first-born who belonged particularly to God. Yet his redemption was not the same as the redemption of the other first-born in Israel, for in his case, God chose to apply the curse, to single him out for death and judgment.

There are those, as I have said, who object to God's

condemning the first-born of Egypt to death for the hardness of Egypt. What then would they say to God's condemnation to death of his own first-born? Surely that is far less just. Egypt deserved it. The sin of Adam deserved it. Jesus did not deserve it. It was not for his own hardness that God's Son died, but for the hardness of heart of Israel and for the sin of Adam. I again return to my earlier point which I want to stress. We cannot object to the justice of God and still approve the mercy of God. So the man in the church who raises objections to God's justice, and perseveres in thinking himself more righteous than God, must be led, eventually, to abandoning the gospel.

The consecration of Jesus was also to be a consecration of one for the whole. Just as the death of the first-born or the redemption of the first-born is a symbol of God's judgment or mercy on all, so Jesus was consecrated to that special role of the first-born, not this time as a symbol or reminder of God's mercy upon all, but as the actual means of God's mercy to all his brothers and sisters. As Simeon said, a man's attitude to that first-born would determine whether he rose or fell. If you reject Jesus as your redeemer, then you must be like an Israelite household who refused the lamb of the Passover, or an Israelite first-born who would refuse the lamb for the redemption of the first-born. You have chosen to receive the judgment that justly comes to you and your household. Conversely, if you receive Jesus as your redeemer, then, like the household of Israel on the night of the Passover, you are redeemed, and like the first-born you are redeemed. Simeon goes on: 'that the thoughts from many hearts may be revealed'. How do you really know what is in people's hearts? Man is so good at acting. There are things where even those good at acting find it more difficult to pretend. One of these is one's attitude to Jesus. What is really deep down, hidden in your heart, comes out in your attitude to Jesus. Do not pretend to be good when there is indifference to Jesus. Jesus is the test that reveals what you are.

There is another role played by these ceremonies, which bring to Israel's attention the redemption or the judgment of the first-born. They are a reminder of what God has done for Israel, and as such they serve as a means of reminding Israel and giving an occasion to instruct their children.

As we look at the reminder let us keep in mind the Lord's Supper which has come in place of the Passover for Christians (see Exodus 13:9). Remember that Israel were commanded to keep the words of God always before their eyes (*Deut.* 6:6–9). I am not sure that this command was to be taken literally in the way later Jews did, in having little scrolls or portions of Scripture on their wrists or fore-heads. It may just be a picturesque way of describing how they should remind themselves and each other constantly of the law of the Lord. Make sure it is constantly kept before your attention. The commandment that it is first to be in the heart shows that this was not a command to do merely formal and external things. It was a command to fill the heart to overflowing with the truth of God. So, these various ceremonies, the Passover and the redemption of the first-born, were to have that function in Israel. They were a reminder of what God had done for Israel, in order that Israel might then be stimulated to obedience. That is not just the nice feeling of being redeemed, but an obedience to God which results from the knowledge that we are redeemed. So also with the Lord's Supper. I am sure that Paul had the Lord's Supper in mind when he wrote 1 Corinthians 5:6-8.

There is also a teaching function, an opportunity to explain to children how God had redeemed them from bondage. Notice in passing that though the redemption is made for a baby, yet the children are still going to ask, whether for themselves or others, 'Why?'. The answer is not: 'Well, that is just the way we do things, for no special reason, just an old Israelite custom.' No! The answer is: 'It is because the Lord did something.' It is easy for us to look at the ceremonies of Israel and to think: Why did they do this and that? – what a lot of rigmarole Israel went through. Yet it had purpose in directing them and reminding them. It had teaching value for their children. It kept God and what he had done for them before their minds.

Naturally, thinking about this makes us ask what we have in the church which does something similar. We have already mentioned the Lord's Supper, and baptism could also be mentioned. Compared to the Passover, however, we have little in the way of ceremonies. Some churches invent all kinds of extras, but Jesus did not. What fills the reminder/teaching role of these Old Testament ceremonies in the church? Read Hebrews 3:12, 13; 10:24, 25; 2 Peter 1:12, 13; 3:1, 2; Romans 15:14, 15. It is obvious! In the church, the emphasis has shifted from the ceremonies to the words of Christian people admonishing and reminding each other. Reviving the ceremonies is going backwards from the fulness of the New Testament to the Old Testament. What if there is not mutual admonition and encouragement, that directing of the mind and attention of each other to the things God has done for us, for which we should love and obey him? Well, we are like Israel without ceremonies. There is nothing to remind us, nothing to provoke our children to wonder and to ask questions.

I am convinced that many of the activities in which churches indulge, whether for adults or children, are our substitute for our lack of what really matters. We have formal teaching and social activities, but are our children in our homes hearing us reminding and encouraging each other with the things the Lord has done? Are they being provoked to wonder at what we say, and to ask, 'Why did you say that?' We cannot get that reaction out of a whole lot of activities which we invent, because all we can say about them is that they are the custom of our church. It is the truths of God of which we remind ourselves, that stand out as monuments and beacons, pointing back to God.

I know from myself and from others how easily we fall into the secular habits of our companions to whom God is irrelevant and remote, and even in the circle of our homes and Christian friends, God can often be the unmentioned. Then we say: 'Well, talking that way is not normal to us.' If we do not do it, then of course it is not normal to us. It is not our natural instinct, any more than it was instinctive for Israel to redeem the first-born without the command to do so. We do it because God commanded. We need to encourage one another to talk of what the Lord has done, just as we need to encourage one another in any other forms of obedience; for it is the Lord Jesus himself, who had all that privilege of the first-born Son of the true God, and exchanged it for the curse, who tells us to do it.

Questions for Discussion

1. In the redemption from Egypt, God's deliverance could not occur without God's judgment. Describe the ways in which that is also true with the death of Christ and the final judgment.

2. 'The man who claims that children should not receive what they do not deserve is really saying that children have no right to be born.' Do you agree? Does this completely solve the problem of judgment upon children or do we need to consider also the way God in blessing and curse deals with people in groups?

3. It is being claimed that the lack of visual reminders of the truth of God in Protestant churches betrays a lack of a sense of beauty. Does it, rather, betray that the objector has failed to understand the progress between the Testaments from inanimate reminders to living ones?

4. Do we actually fulfil that role of reminders which the Scripture requires of us?

7: *The Lord is among Us: Exodus 17*

The key issue in the earlier part of the book of Exodus may be put as a question: Who is Lord? Are Israel to serve Pharaoh or are they to be free to serve the Lord their God?

Once Israel had been released from the tyranny of Pharaoh, the key issue changed. It now revolved around the presence of God. In this text it was posed as the question: Is the Lord among us or not? It was posed in another way in Moses' statement to God in 33:15, 16. If God is not present with Israel, then Israel are nothing. The presence of God explains the elaborate laws concerning the tabernacle, its service and its sacrifices. If the holy God is to live in the midst of a sinful people, then there have to be elaborate precautions to preserve his holiness and to atone for their sin.

So we have these two issues. Who is Lord? and, Is God among us or not? If you can remember back to the time before you became a Christian, you may remember your own struggle with that first question. Who was to be your lord? Were you going to be dominated by people and be afraid to stand up against them? Were you going to live selfishly as your own boss? Or, was the true Lord the Creator to be your master?

If you are a believer, you will most likely also understand

something of the second question. Is God present with his power and mercy, or is he not? The question is particularly pressing in adversity, which is when the question arose for Israel. We see their complaints and doubts several times before these incidents, notably in Exodus 14:10–12 and 16:1–3.

In Exodus, God's presence is symbolised and expressed by one particular thing: the staff of Moses. It is first mentioned when God commissioned Moses in 4:1–5. Moses used it a number of times in bringing the plagues upon Egypt.

The staff is mentioned twice in this chapter. The first time, Moses was commanded to strike the rock in order to bring forth water for Israel. The second is a little more difficult to interpret. Moses stationed himself on the top of the hill, with the staff in his hand, while Israel were fighting Amalek. He then held up his hands. What was he doing? The common interpretation is that he was praying. I am not sure, though certainly standing with hands held up is a biblical position for prayer. We also read, in connection with the crossing of the sea, that Moses lifted up the staff, stretched it over the waters, and the waters were divided. He stretched it out again and the waters came back, and over the Egyptians. Thus, the staff seems to be the means by which God's power acts through Moses. I therefore wonder whether Moses' upraised hands at the battle against Amalek were a placing of the power of God, through the staff, against Amalek.

There may be questions raised in your mind at this point at this whole mention of the staff. Because people stay people, a lot of things in the Old Testament are somewhat similar to things today. The Israelites complained, and people still complain and groan. However, the way in which God deals with people has changed. We have no staff of God and it is rather difficult to think of anything really equivalent to that staff today. Indeed, in Old Testament times such use of a staff seems restricted to Moses, apart from one or two mentions of Elisha's staff. That is a problem we will leave to one side for now but come back to later.

What do we learn from this chapter? First, and most important, doubting the presence of the Lord is putting God to the test. It is saying that we do not believe God is present among us unless he actually demonstrates that presence. 'God, you must do something to prove you are present.' When we complain and grumble about our circumstances, and when we say that God has to prove he is really with us by changing our circumstances for better; when we see such changes as what is needed to prove God's presence and love, then we put God to the test. Indeed, when we grumble we have already gone a step further than that. We say that these things would not have happened to us if God were really among us. God graciously showed himself to be present by giving Israel water, just as he often blesses us in spite of our grumbling. Nevertheless, to grumble and complain is to test God.

It was not only Israel who doubted the presence of God. If we judge from their actions, it would seem that Amalek also doubted God's presence. They came to fight against Israel.

There was once a man who went into the bush on the upper Clarence River and found a snake. It was not one of the known poisonous varieties and he thought it was a carpet snake. Carpet snakes are not poisonous, and though it may not be your, or my, idea of a pet, many people think differently and keep them either as pets or to keep the rats down around barns. So the man put the snake into a bag and took it to Sydney, where he went into a hotel bar. Some people like to show off once they have taken a few beers on board, so he took the snake out of the bag to scare the others and to show his bravery. The snake bit him and he died very quickly. It certainly was not a carpet snake, but a rare variety not known at that time to be dangerous to humans. That man had been carrying danger and death in his bag. He thought that he could use it for his own ends, but that was not the case. His confidence and arrogance were misplaced, just like Amalek's confidence in its attack upon Israel. They were without true appreciation of the power that resided in Israel, though the power was not in Israel itself, but in the God who was present in Israel.

Once again, it is not easy to find equivalents in our age, the New Testament age. Perhaps the closest equivalent which I can find is not really all that close. It is the story of Ananias and Sapphira, who thought they could deceive the church. They lied, saying that they had given all the money they obtained for their land when really they had not. They did not recognise the presence of God in the church, and thought they lied only to mere man. Peter accused them of putting the Spirit of the Lord to the test (*Acts* 5:9). They had doubted God's presence, and had thus put God to the test as to whether he really was present in the church or not. Of course, God is present through his Holy Spirit, as Ananias and Sapphira found out.

I mentioned earlier that I found it difficult to find a modern equivalent to the staff of Moses. The closest I can think of is the Holy Spirit, because the staff seems to be the outward expression of God's presence in power amongst his people. God is present amongst his people today as his Spirit in their midst.

When people attack the church today, they are acting like Amalek. They do not recognise what power lies in the church. Certainly it is not a power at our disposal, for it is God's power. It is not a power that is used immediately, just as God did not immediately use his power to exterminate Amalek. Note however, we have here the first mention in all of Scripture of God commanding somebody to write something. Here is the first mention of Scripture, and the first words to be written down indicate God's firm and unshakeable resolve to deal with the sin of those who attack his people. It is good to be reminded of that. Sometimes we tend to think of the church as defenceless, but it is not. It is better to put your hand in a snake's bag than to attack the church.

My main concern in this passage, however, is with the grumbling, the unbelief and the testing of Israel. That is the real problem which we have, and not the attacks from the outside. We can feel sorry for those who attack the church, but the real problem is with us.

Note very clearly that it is wrong to test, and wrong to complain. Yet God provides for complaining, grumbling Israel the water about which they were nagging. They did not attack God directly, they attacked Moses, but really that was just their way of getting to God, just as it generally is when people complain against faithful servants of God. Yet, God provided water for them!

God has mercy on doubting people, because they are his people and he will not abandon them. Yet, there came a point at which God said that this doubt had to lead to a loss. Remember how Israel doubted whether God could give them the promised land, and God said: 'Right! You doubt my power, so I will not give it to you.'

Do you understand the biblical balance I am trying to portray? I do not say that any doubt as to God's presence, any grumbling, any uncertainty, any putting of God to the test, immediately loses for you what you desire from God. If I were to say that, I would be blind to God's faithfulness to his people. Yet I do say that you cannot continue to doubt and grumble and complain without losing the blessings you most desire from God.

If I were to ask if you have ever grumbled or complained, your answer would have to be 'Yes'. If I were then to say: 'Well, you have had your chips. You won't get anything from God', that would discourage you. If, on the other hand, I were to respond: 'Well, aren't we all grumblers? Israel certainly was, and look how God took care of them. Don't worry about it', then I would encourage presumption and lack of fear of God. Rather, we should look at the passages in the New Testament which reflect upon God's providing water in the wilderness, and see it as a reminder of the grace God offers us through Christ (see John 7:38–39). Look at God using that power he has placed in Israel to give water to his grumbling people. Is not such a God to be both feared and trusted? Is not the right response to such a God to trust him without grumbling or complaining when things do not go the way we would like them to?

There is also warning. God does not tolerate grumbling and doubt forever. Maybe you do not trust in Christ at all? Maybe you doubt his power to save and the real root of that doubt is resentment? Things may not have gone as you wanted, and you may be resentful. You feel as though you should not have been put to the test. You were called upon to trust and you did not, and so you experienced not the power of God, but fear, doubt and uncertainty. You may feel that your complaint is fully justified, but from God's perspective it is an insult! Suppose I were to ask you for a loan of $20 to get through the weekend because I forgot to go to the bank on Friday, and you replied: 'Not on your life; I doubt that you even have a bank account.' You would insult me because you doubt my solvency and my word. So it is that we insult God by doubting his power and his word!

Perhaps you are a believer, but you have not overcome your habit of grumbling. I do not say that you will miss out on all of God's blessings, but you may miss some, and I would not want you to miss any. Leave off grumbling and complaining!

Questions for Discussion

1. The closest equivalent to the staff in our time appears to be the Holy Spirit but we do not have the Spirit at our disposal the way Moses had the staff at his disposal. What is it about Moses' role in the whole plan and work of God that leads to his greater power?

2. It has become popular in some circles to argue for the necessity of miraculous demonstrations of the Holy Spirit in our day in order to convince unbelievers. In the light of Israel's doubt in this passage and the strong tendency of Christians to doubt the presence of God, is it possible that the greater demand for miracles in our day is coming from believers rather than unbelievers?

3. When the psalmist cries, 'Why hast thou forgotten me? Why go I mourning because of the oppression of the enemy?' (*Psa.* 42:9) is he doubting the presence of God?

4. Israel's grumbling and doubt eventually led to punishment, even though God previously showed patience. Can we or should we be able to determine whether we are reaching the limits of God's patience?

5. Why does one display of the powerful presence of God not satisfy men?

8: *Law and Grace at Sinai: Exodus 19:3–20:17; 24:1–11*

Most Christians would be familiar with the words which accompany Jesus' giving of the cup to his disciples in Matthew 26:28. They would probably not be surprised to learn that there is an Old Testament background to these words. When Jesus called the wine 'my blood of the covenant', he was relating to himself the Old Testament term 'the blood of the covenant'. One expects Christians would not be surprised at an Old Testament background because they would be aware that the Lord's Supper has many connections to the Passover. They might also know that the sealing of covenants by blood was part of the Old Testament order, just as it is part of the New Testament.

What may come as more of a surprise is that the words 'blood of the covenant' do not come from the institution of the Passover. They come, rather, from Exodus 24:8, and refer to the covenant at Sinai. In using these words, Jesus was connecting his New Covenant to the covenant at Sinai.

Of course we may be putting too much stress upon a few words, and so must enquire as to whether there are other connections between the meal of the New Covenant and the Sinai covenant making. There is another obvious one: both involved a meal. Further when we think of the Lord's

Supper simply as a replacement for the Passover, there is a detail that does not fit. At the Passover, the stress was on eating the lamb and the unleavened bread. Drinking did not play a role. Yet, in the Lord's Supper, drinking plays a very important part. As Exodus 24:11 tells us, the ratification of the Sinai covenant involved both an eating and drinking in the presence of God. At Sinai, God invited the representatives of his people to eat in his presence, just as he did at the last supper.

Further, understanding this background may help us understand part of the discussion which took place at the supper. In John 14:7 Jesus was concerned to stress that the disciples had seen the Father. One wonders whether part of the reason is because he was thinking of the background in Exodus 24:10, where it is clearly stated that they saw the Lord. (In case you are troubled by the statements elsewhere in Scripture that God does not have a visible, bodily form, note that Deuteronomy 4:15 says that they did not see a bodily form at Sinai, and that in Exodus 24:10, the pavement under God's feet can be described, but not God himself. The fact that the glory of God is visible does not mean that God is visible. Yet God's glory is so much a reflection of God himself, that to see his glory may be described as seeing God.)

Aside from realising these points of connection, is there any addition to our understanding of the Bible if we see that the Lord's Supper is patterned not just upon the Passover, but also upon the covenant made in Sinai? In fact it raises some very basic and important issues. There is a strong tendency among some Christians to make a strict separation between law and gospel as far as the Christian life is concerned. Obviously if it is a separation as far as the way of salvation is concerned, then there is no problem. It is through the gospel that we are saved; not by the keeping of the law. However some Christians want to go beyond that; to say that also in the Christian life the law is a danger. For them, living by grace and not by law means that something like the ten commandments has no relevance to the Christian, and may even be a hindrance to him, in turning his eyes from Jesus and his grace.

A connection between the Lord's Supper and Sinai raises a very important question. Certainly the Lord's Supper is a reminder to us of the mercy and grace of God. Christ used it to explain to his disciples that he was to be offered as a sacrifice for their sins. If Jesus was connecting the Lord's Supper and Sinai, was it because he saw an affinity, or was it only because his death would completely nullify the Sinai law and covenant? If he saw an affinity, then he would be implying that his death and work of salvation was a fulfilment and a completion of what was begun at Sinai. Obviously the way we resolve this question has implications for the way we see our lives as Christians.

By way of answering the question, let us turn first to Exodus. I have been referring to the Sinai covenant, yet taking most of my quotations from Exodus 24. What do we mean by the Sinai covenant? If we read Scripture carefully, we see that the story of the covenant at Sinai stretches from chapters 17 through 24. It is more involved than just the ten commandments! In chapter 19 God reminded Israel of how he had made them his people by a mighty work of salvation. He had a special role for them, but that task demanded obedience, which the people promised to give. The second part of the chapter is concerned with preparation for God's speaking to them. There is a particular stress on the danger of the people approaching God.

In chapter 20 God revealed his will for the people in what the Bible later calls the ten commandments. The reaction to God's speaking is fear (verses 18, 19). Then follows a section of several chapters in which the practical application and consequences of these laws are spelled out in more detail (20:22–23:33).

In chapter 24:37 the people repeated the promise given in 19:8 that they would obey all that the Lord commanded. Following that, there were sacrifices and the sprinkling of the blood on the people. Then followed the eating together as mentioned earlier.

We have a tendency to think of Sinai as meaning the ten commandments and nothing else. If we read the text, we see clearly that the ten commandments are but a part; important, but not everything. The whole section begins with an explanation of God saving his people to bring them into a special relationship, a relationship which required obedience. The ten commandments were a summary of the obedience required in that relationship. A summary needs filling out and explanation and that is what chapters 20–23 do. If the text had stopped at chapter 23, we would have the terms of the relationship, but not the evidence that the relationship had actually been formally established.

When we look at the formal establishment in chapter 24, we see that the element of law is prominent. The people promised to obey all that God had said. However, grace is also prominent. Moses sprinkled the people with the blood of the covenant. When the representatives of the people were allowed into the presence of God and ate and drank in his presence, was that on the basis of their obedience to the law, or on the basis of grace? It cannot be on the basis of obedience, because there had been no time for Israel to demonstrate its obedience. It must therefore be on the basis of the sprinkled blood. The approach that was not permitted in chapter 19 was permitted in chapter 24 because Israel had been sprinkled with the blood of the covenant. If we go back to the beginning of the narrative, we see in 19:4 that the very opportunity of coming to this relationship came from God's gracious acts. Thus, if we take the whole narrative of the Sinai covenant, we find that it contains both grace and law. It is grace that brought Israel into the relationship . Continuance in the relationship depended upon obedience.

This raises a question. If there was grace in the Sinai covenant, why did Paul not deal with those advocating salvation by the works of the law by expounding the Sinai covenant, pointing out the elements of grace in the account? In other words, why does Paul's exposition appear to make Sinai totally opposed to the grace that is expressed through the promise to Abraham (see for example Galatians 4:21–31)? Since Paul did not address himself to that question, any answer we give must be speculative. However, I suspect that there is a simple answer. Within Judaism, there had been a speculative interest in law, which had torn the law loose from its context in Scripture. One symptom of that is that detailed considerations of the application of a particular law could be carried on without concern for the great biblical principles (see for example the issue of the tithing of garden herbs and Jesus' response in Matthew 23:23). Yet, as is so often the case when such things happen, those engaged in this speculation thought they could find biblical support in the law. Sure, they were misreading the Sinai account by picking out the law and ignoring the rest, but their mind-set made them do that. A questioning but open mind can be shown how to read a text more carefully. A closed and determined mind will see only what it has already seen in that context. Paul's answer was not a close reading of Exodus. It was rather to take them to a section of Scripture which they had totally ignored and yet, as Jews, could not ignore: the promises of God to the patriarchs in Genesis. Instead of going to where law and grace were combined together, and thus the recognition of the elements required a willingness to read carefully, he went to where the Scripture spoke in terms of pure grace.

There is one further thing that must be said in this connection. There were both grace and law at Sinai, but Sinai was Old Covenant. The sprinkling of the blood of animals foreshadowed the death of Christ, but it did not have the effectiveness of the death of Christ. Israel was in a relationship that arose from the saving and delivering work of God, but while the Spirit gave gifts to individuals, there was no outpouring of the Spirit upon the people. Consequently, they responded to the demand for obedience not by a willing but flawed discipleship, but rather, by repeated open rebellion. It is wrong to look at Sinai and not see grace, but it would also be wrong to attempt to make Sinai the pattern for the New Testament church. By going to the promise to Abraham, Paul set the church on a foundation of pure grace.

There is a further issue which should be considered here. I have described the section of laws which followed the ten commandments as an explanation of the practical application and consequences of the ten commandments. In that section, we find laws which clearly belong to the Old Covenant (e.g. erection of altars and sacrifices: 20:24–26). If the ten commandments were spelled out in terms of applications which belong exclusively to the Old Covenant, can they be of any value to the New Covenant believer? That is the logic of some people who would like to make a complete severance between the Christian believer and the Old Testament law. They are then considerably embarrassed when the Paul to whom they appeal makes appeal to the law (e.g. Ephesians 6:1–3). There is a dangerous arrogance in thinking that we understand the logic of Paul's position better than the apostle did himself! Once again I believe that a solution is not too difficult. The principles of our relationship to God, such as are expressed in the ten commandments, may have different detailed outworkings in the situation of the Old Covenant as compared to the situation of the New Covenant. Nevertheless, they are valid in both eras. Of course, we also find that in both eras there are detailed consequences which are the same. Being a Christian does not mean we can approve the perjury and gossip that are condemned in Exodus 23:1.

A summary of what I have been saying about Exodus 19–24 is that we must recognise that elements of grace and law occurred together at Sinai. How could it be otherwise when the gracious and holy God came to meet with his people? Certainly, we must recognise that Sinai reflected the weakness of the Old Covenant, not weak from God's side, but made weak by the sinfulness of man. Yet we must also recognise the graciousness of God in gathering and meeting with a sinful people. The two elements show clearly in the contrast between the warnings in chapter 19 concerning the danger of approach by a sinful people to God and the summons to approach after the sprinkling of blood.

Hence, it is not at all inappropriate that the meeting of Jesus with his disciples in the upper room should contain echoes of the meeting of God with his people at Sinai. Note well that where I have found links, those links are to the elements of the covenant ratification ceremony where the grace of God is most evident: the sprinkled blood, eating and drinking in God's presence, seeing God.

That raises a further question. We have seen that it is wrong to obscure the element of grace in the Sinai covenant. Is it also wrong to obscure the element of obedience in the New Covenant? Of course it is, and nowhere is the connection more clearly expressed than in John's account of the meeting in the upper room. We could choose many passages, but John 14:15–21 is quite apt. Jesus talks about keeping his commandments. This stress of itself reminds us of Sinai. It rules out the possibility that Jesus was reminding the disciples of Sinai because he wanted to set his covenant of grace in opposition to the concern for obedience at Sinai.

Yet we may not treat the Old Covenant and the New Covenant as though they were strictly parallel. Notice two emphases in this passage from John: love and the Spirit. The richness of the New Covenant as compared to the Old includes that it is rooted in a love drawn out of us by the far greater display of God's love in giving Jesus. And we are not alone in our struggle against sin and the world: the Spirit has been sent as our helper. Yes, there is obedience in the New Covenant, but, all glory to God, we are made more capable of giving that obedience.

I must close on a note of warning. I have mentioned those who want to make an absolute separation between law and gospel. Certainly that reaction is understandable if legalism is abroad, but I must say that I see laxity rather than legalism as the dominant mood in the church today. Is the tendency to make this absolute opposition, between law and grace in the Christian life, a concession to the spirit of the age? How can we, as believers who have experienced the love of Christ, not want to respond in obedience? How can we respond to the mention of obedience to our Lord as though it were some dangerous doctrine? Israel met God at Sinai, yet fell through rebellion because grace did not meet with the appropriate response. If we rebel against the commandments of God, and use a theology of grace to cloak disobedience, then we also are in great danger!

Questions for Discussion

1. 'To read the New Testament without hearing the echoes of the Old Testament means that we miss its richness and may even misinterpret it seriously.' Do you agree? Are there other passages where one must grasp allusions to Old Testament sayings or events to understand the meaning?

2. If obedience and grace are involved in both the Sinai covenant and the New Covenant, does that mean that there is no essential difference between the two covenants?

3. Read Genesis 17. Does the question of the relation of obedience and law arise, in some respects, also with the Abrahamic covenant?

4. 'If we focus our attention on what is the contrasting predominant element of each covenant (for example promise in the Abrahamic covenant, law in the Sinai covenant), we may say that there are many covenants in Scripture. If we look rather at the way in which covenant reflects the character of God, then we are led to see but one covenant.' Do you agree? Outline the contrasts and similarities between the New Covenant and the various Old Testament covenants.

5. *The terrors of law and of God*
   With me can have nothing to do;
   My Saviour's obedience and blood
   Hide all my transgressions from view.

   Toplady

In what sense is law a threat to a Christian?

9: *Spirituality and a Dead Ox: Exodus 22:1–15*

A passage from the Old Testament law such as this leaves us somewhat confused. It seems strangely dated. Have you looked after anyone's ox lately? In the mass of legislation, there seem to be some matters that might be relevant to us, such as the rules about stealing, and others which seem totally irrelevant to our day.

We then have the problem of what to do about this law as Christians. We are afraid of being Pharisaical. The thing that strikes one about the Old Testament law is its concern for detail. You do this when the animal is stolen, and that when a wild animal has killed it. Now compared to the jargon and official sounding nonsense and loopholes that make up our law, the biblical law is a model of straightforward simplicity. Nevertheless, we expect one sort of language and concern when we read a business contract or some other legal document, and another when we read the Bible.

Law, in a sense, is making fine distinctions – this is right under these circumstances, and wrong under those. That carries with it the danger of becoming lost in concern for detail. Christ did not condemn the Pharisees for concern for detail in itself. He condemned them because they had lost sight of the principle. The statement of Christ in

Luke 11:42 clears up the matter. Christ condemned the Pharisees not because they tithed mint and other herbs. He condemned them for forgetting the weightier principles of the law, such as justice, mercy and faith. They were right to tithe herbs. Jesus positively approved meticulous observance of the law, but attacked any apparently meticulous observance which neglected the real substance and principle of the law.

This we must stress, because the temper of our times is against meticulous and careful attention to anything. Few people want to do anything that takes care, concern and effort. If you look at the things you buy you see that the craftsmanship is lacking – the work is sloppy. What a lack of deep thought characterises news commentary and opinion! How half-baked and half-cooked are the great crusades for national reform! How careless and indifferent to the precise teaching of Scripture is the church! We can claim that we are being motivated by some great overall principle like 'love' or 'being spontaneous' when we are really just being swept along by the mood of the times. Before the Puritans were nicknamed Puritans they were referred to as Precisionists. On being asked why he was so precise and wanted to be so careful to be correct in matters of religion a Precisionist minister answered: 'Because I serve a very precise God.'

At the same time that we stress precise attention to detail we must understand and put into effect the principles. When reading such a passage of Scripture we must discern the principles. I would draw your attention to the laws dealing with the care of animals. A man had been entrusted with an animal. If, when nobody was there to witness or to prevent the event, it died, was hurt or was driven away, then the person looking after it was not responsible. This covers those cases in which he could not reasonably be expected to do something about it. As there are no eye-witnesses, nobody can prove what actually happened to the animal, so the caretaker takes an oath before God that he had not touched it. On the other hand, if the ox was stolen from him, and the implication of the *from him* in distinction from the other case is that here was a situation in which the caretaker was with the animal and therefore was in a position to do something about it and did not, then he was responsible and must make restitution.

Thus in this case somebody had been given an animal to look after for someone else. This is a different situation from the one in which somebody had borrowed something. Borrowing always implies the obligation to return what is borrowed. If it dies or is hurt then, no matter how it happened, the borrower had to make restitution. Even here there is the exception that if the owner was with this animal when the mishap occurred, then it is his loss since he did nothing to prevent the accident. With this exception borrowing implies a duty to return. Safekeeping implies a duty to restore only when a person could have done something to prevent the loss.

Biblical law often omits the obvious. We find no law to cover the situation of an animal given to keep, which dies or is injured while the caretaker is there. The reason for the lack is obvious: it would be the caretaker's responsibility. The law deals with those areas where a question was likely to arise: namely, when the accident to the animal happens when nobody is present or where it is a case of theft and you could argue that the loss was the thief's fault and not yours. It is important to remember the fact that biblical law states the principles and then spells out the application of the principle in those cases where a dispute may arise. In the modern concept of law those areas in which the application is not spelt out would constitute a loophole in the law, and the accused would be acquitted. There is a great array of things which the Bible does not forbid but which are contrary to the principles of Scripture. If your approach is to do everything the Bible does not explicitly condemn then you will act against the principles of Scripture. You can never defend an action by saying: 'The Bible nowhere says I can't.' You must be able to show that what you are doing is in accord with biblical principle and not in conflict with it

So we see that the close interaction of principle and specific precept is evident even at this level in our study of biblical law. Of course we have to be careful of the opposite extreme – that is of taking the principle in such a way that we contradict the specific teaching of the Bible. For example one might take the teaching that one is responsible to take care of an animal left in one's keeping to the point of saying that you are responsible even if you were fifty miles away and could do nothing to prevent the death of the animal. That is far-fetched but you can worry yourself to death with responsibility and guilt for things you were physically unable to prevent. I have seen an old woman die of stroke and old age and her daughter blame herself for that death which she could not by any means have prevented. The Bible sets limits to responsibility in such cases.

We have looked at the interplay of principle and specific commandment, but what is the broader principle? These regulations come in a section which is an elaboration of the principles involved in the commandment against stealing. They illustrate that the commandment has a wider range than the mere negative, involving positive concern for all the goods of one's brethren. An ox has been delivered to you to keep. Can you think: 'Well, I'm doing him a favour by looking after his ox, therefore I don't need to care too much about it'? No, you are responsible for that ox.

If we leave it there, we have a bunch of rules. I have to be careful when I start a fire lest it destroy someone else's field. I have to be careful that my animals do not get into my neighbour's field and eat the grain. I have to be careful for the ox I am taking care of. Behind all this, however, lie principles. Why all this concern? My concern is out of love for my neighbour. My love for him creates a concern for his goods and property. This concern shows itself in all the detailed duties which are spelled out in this passage. Biblical law is thus a system with principles which are spelled out in more and more detail, getting down to the particular instance. The particular illustrations, as I said before, are to deal with those areas in which sinful man would try to wriggle out of his obligations. The specific teachings of the law are thus aimed at man's refusal to apply the principle. I think that this is the sense in which we should understand the difficult statement of Paul in 1 Timothy 1:9–10. The law spells out these crimes which are the failure to apply its general principles. It does this in order to convict the unruly. The truly righteous man will be applying the principle.

I must distinguish what I am saying here from what is called Situation Ethics, or the New Morality. The New Morality says that love is the principle, but you cannot say ahead of time what would be the outworking of the principle in any specific instance. In contrast to that, the Bible tells us the application of the principle in specific instances.

I began by referring to the fact that this law is very particular, very precise. It has a lot of detail, and it searches our hearts. God's law makes us not just our brother's keeper, but the keeper of our brother's ox also. Have you shown such detailed concern for your brother? Love which fails to show itself in practical everyday matters is not really love.

I had the experience some years ago of attending a church which was quite proud of the love and warmth of its congregation. I found that a lot of people gushed over me and were so glad to see me, but only one or two appeared really interested in me and my needs, and in trying to meet those needs. Everybody in that group said: 'Don't go to the church down the road because it is cold and dead and has no love.' Well, I began attending the church down the road (the reason being not the lack of concern, but over a matter of principle). When I went to that church, nobody gushed over me, though they seemed pleased to have me there, but I found people who showed more genuine concern. The second church, I think, knew better than the first the meaning of love.

The church must show love, but it must be the real love which shows itself in concern for detail. It is only real love if there is concern for your brother's ox. Have you had any opportunity to show concern for, or to meet, somebody's needs, or to do something for somebody recently? Did you do it to the limit of your ability? If you answer, 'No', you are a thief! We are selfish people, but we hide that truth from ourselves by saying that we did not actually take anything which was not ours. 'I just look after myself and take what is my due. His problems are his own concern. Why should I go out of my way?' Wherever there is such an attitude, the positive side of the commandment against stealing has been ignored.

God's law condemns us, but it also gives us hope. Where do we see how the law of love should be applied? Where do we see someone with a great concern for our needs? We see it in Christ, and for good reason. Why does God require all of this of us? He requires it because that is his nature, and he demands that we be like him. His Son is like him. The love of God in Christ is a true love, in that he saw us and our failure to imitate him, and he came to meet our need for forgiveness and rescue from sin.

Thus this law either condemns and destroys us, or it gives us hope. Have you been showing love? If you say, 'Yes', then I will throw this law at you. Where is this detailed, precise, constant concern in all the areas of life for the goods, welfare and needs of your brother? If you try to excuse yourself by saying, 'Well, I tried', or 'I try more than some people I know,' then again I would throw this law at you. You are a liar. You don't try. You may be a little better at hypocrisy than some that you know, but I am talking about a deep and genuine attitude of heart which constantly flows out in practical concern for others. I warn you not to get into the habit of making excuses when confronted with your sin by the law of God. Genuine repentance knows no excuses.

If however, you say, 'I have not been trying,' then I would show you this law as a law of hope. It shows the meticulous concern that the Lord has for you, of how he will look after you and all that is yours. It shows his concern for your needs, and especially your greatest need: to have that sinful heart of yours changed.

Questions for Discussion

1. What are some contemporary applications of the laws discussed here?

2. Is the fear in the modern church of being Pharisaical in a concern for detail a genuine concern or a smoke screen for laziness and disobedience?

3. The law says there are certain situations in which people are not responsible for an accident or loss even though the object in question was in their care. What is wrong with the person who sees himself as always to blame, no matter what the circumstances?

4. If there is no law of love to one's neighbour which Christ has not fulfilled, does it then follow that the whole law can be read as a statement of Christ's love to his people?

5. If the law is actually concerned, amongst other things, with establishing limits to responsibility, how can people claim that biblical law is too demanding and rigorous?

PART FOUR

Deuteronomy

1: *Being a Holy People: Deuteronomy 7:1–16; 10:14–17; 14:1, 2*

The purpose of this section is to develop some of the main themes in the book of Deuteronomy. From the passages above, we see that one of those themes is to be a holy people. Holiness is one of the most misunderstood of biblical teachings. People will often use the word with little idea of its meaning, such as in criticism of someone for a 'holier than thou' attitude. Both the Old and New Testaments call for God's people to be holy. What does that mean?

We will see first of all what it meant for the Old Testament people of God, then we will look at the ways in which the requirements for New Testament believers are different.

Holiness meant separation. It meant being set apart, different and distinctive. Israel were not to be fused and absorbed into the pagan nations of the lands they were about to conquer. That separation was to be a political separation. They were to form no alliances with the inhabitants of the land. In fact, they were to go beyond making no alliances: they were to kill all of the Canaanites. It was to be a family separation. They were not to marry any who did not worship the true God. It was to be a religious separation. They were not to worship any gods other than their own God, the true and living God who made the heavens and the earth.

Political, family and religious separation: that was part of what it meant to be holy. That is fairly comprehensive, but there were other things as well. For example, holiness included the body. Because they were holy, they had to treat the body with care and not disfigure it. Their bodies were holy and precious. Apparently some of the surrounding people had a custom of inflicting the body as a sign of grief over a death. God does not allow the body to be treated in this way.

These laws imposed a lot upon Israel. We may not mind a law which forbids us to cut ourselves in mourning as we would not be inclined to do that anyway. However, the law also restricted political options, marriage options, and freedom of worship. People do not like restrictions. What would make them maintain their holiness?

How we act depends upon what we are convinced is true. If you believe that happiness depends upon wealth, and you believe yourself to be smarter than all the bookmakers, (and maybe even smarter than the horses!), then you will play the horses and go broke doing it. So the reasons for Israel's holiness are truths: truths about God and Israel, and it is these truths which give Israel a reason to remain holy. The reasons are given in 7:16ff.

First of all, Israel cannot be fused or merged in with the pagan society all around them because there was something which set them apart. They alone, of all the nations, belonged to God. God had chosen them not because of worth, but because of his own love and faithfulness. The idea of God's choosing, or election, is very important for holiness. God said that there was nothing in all of Israel that caused him to choose her. She was not great, but the least of the nations. Israel owed what she was to God's choice. Love begets love. We see that even amongst sinful men; husbands and wives will respond to the kindness and love of their partners. Children respond to the love of their parents. God had shown love, choosing and electing love, to Israel. Should Israel not cling to him and his ways rather than going the way of the pagan nations?

There is an additional factor in this matter of choosing. Suppose someone were to want me because of my gifts and abilities. Suppose my employer were to say that there was no-one else in the world who could do the job for him that I did? I would then have a certain amount of leverage on my employer. I could ask for a higher wage. I could decide to take the day off, or say, 'No overtime, thanks!' To be chosen for qualities in yourself gives you leverage over your employer. If I had money in the bank, and no debts or likely debts forthcoming, I could spend more freely. I would think: 'I have credit. I do not need to be frugal or careful.' If we were selected by God because God needed and wanted us for our intrinsic qualities, then we would have leverage on God. We could set the terms and conditions under which we would serve him. If God selected us because we were such good people and had such a record of righteousness and good deeds that even God was impressed, then maybe we could afford to spend some of that stock, or diminish it by a little sin.

If, however, we are chosen despite what we are, and not for any ability or righteousness within ourselves, but out of the pure love of the one who has chosen, then we have no leverage on God; no bargaining position and no store of righteousness which we could afford to diminish. It is love and gratitude which binds Israel to God, but also the knowledge that God is free, and not tied to them or dependent upon them. If they disobey him, there is no reason why he should continue to bless them, apart from his own love and patience. It is the knowledge that we are chosen out of God's free love and grace which gives the incentive for holiness.

As I mentioned before, this passage concerns the holiness of Israel in Old Testament times. How does it apply to us as New Testament Christians? In principle there is very little difference. The one crucial difference is best understood in terms of the way the history of Israel foreshadows the history of the church. We can think of Israel's history as a forerunning of the history of the church. Things do not necessarily come in the same order or make exact parallels, but the prefigurings are there. For example, we have in the Old Testament several foretastes of the final judgment to come at the end of the age. One of them is Israel's judgment on the Canaanites, who were to be exterminated because the time of God's patience with them was over and God delegated that judgment to Israel. Naturally there can be no alliances or peace treaties with people who are to face the final judgment of God. We however have not come to this age's time of final judgment. Our time is more like the time of Abraham, who lived amongst the Canaanites and even had an alliance with them for mutual defence of the land against foreign invaders. However, he did not worship their gods, nor would he allow his son to marry one of them.

We are in a situation in which our separation has to be family and religious. It is not political in the sense of being physically at war with the unbelievers around us. Otherwise, the situation of New Testament believers and their holiness is very much like that of Israel under the Old Testament. There is to be a family and religious separation from unbelief. A Christian cannot marry a non-Christian any more than an Israelite could marry a Canaanite. Nor can we worship their gods.

Just as important as that is the fact that our motivation is the same, stemming from the fact that God has chosen us to belong to Christ. Notice the clear connection in Ephesians 1:4. We are chosen that we might be holy and blameless.

Is not that in itself sufficient reason for us to live lives appropriate to our calling? We are chosen for a special relationship to God. Let us live that way. There is an incredible amount of nonsense being written and spoken today about self-esteem. People are supposed to have a very good self-image. They are supposed to like themselves and be happy with themselves. All this is spouted, whilst at the same time the unhappiness and the suicide rates continue to climb, because there is a fundamental fallacy in it all. Sure, people are discouraged with themselves and their problems, but it is no use just telling people to feel good about themselves and all their problems. If my car is all rusted and the engine not working, the tyres bald, and the upholstery in tatters, then you do me no good by saying that I should have a positive attitude about my car. I know what is wrong with it. But suppose an expert who sees all the car's problems far better than I do comes along and says that though the car is ready for the scrap heap he will remake it to become better than new! I would then have a positive attitude to my car. Our self-esteem is not based on what we are, but on the fact that God loves us and chose us to belong to him.

In conclusion, I return to the body. Remember that we saw in the Old Testament that the body shared in that holiness. That is equally true for the New Testament. Note 1 Corinthians 6:15–20. Its teaching has to be stressed because there is such a problem with sexual immorality today. Our world is saying: 'We do not have all the prudish views of the Victorian age about sex and the body. We have a healthy view on such things.' Rubbish! If you commit sexual immorality, it shows that you have a very poor view of your own body. Remember that the Bible does not 'pussy-foot' on the matter of divorce. If you leave your wife or husband for another woman or man, it is adultery. It is sexual immorality. The people who engage in such things have a poor view of their own body. You may say that you have reason for a poor view; that you are ugly or that nobody likes you or wants you. That merely shows your problem. You may not look like Marilyn Monroe and I am certainly no Clark Gable, but it is not what man thinks of us that matters. God has chosen to take up residence in our bodies and to consecrate them as his own temple. Therein lies our value and the value of our bodies. If we know that, then we will keep our bodies separate for pure use, and we will be holy unto God.

Questions for Discussion

1. 'The modern scorn of holiness reflects an age that is so submissive and cowardly in its conformity that it is paranoid about anything which involves a separation from the crowd.' Would you agree?

2. If both the Old Testament and New Testament relate holiness to the election of the believer without any merit of his own, what must the consequence be for the church of a denial of the doctrine of election?

3. It has become common to blame drug and sex problems among adolescents on low self-esteem. Does the Christian have an alternative explanation for why people contaminate their bodies?

4. If our separation in this age is no longer a political one, would it still be legitimate (N.B. legitimate, not practical) to establish an exclusively Christian political party?

2: *Dealing with Fear: Deuteronomy* 7:17–26

In this passage we read of fear, which is a problem we face in various forms. Sometimes we face it as Israel did soon after they came out of Egypt: the immediate fear of violent death (*Exod.* 14:10–14). Sometimes we face it more as Israel faced it here in Deuteronomy. They were looking forward to a situation of danger, having to go into a land where people confronted them with chariots and armies and walled cities. They had to fight on terrain they did not know, against people who had lived there all their lives.

Probably we more often face fear of a future situation where we feel as though we cannot cope: we face something beyond us. It may bring pain, or maybe failure, disgrace or embarrassment. It may bring emotional upheaval and pain. We become anxious and afraid.

God, in this passage, gave Israel an answer to the problem of fear. That answer is in verses 18 and 19. It is the memory of what God has already done. They face a test and danger, but God has already shown his power and his ability to save and give victory. They need not be afraid because they have seen what God has already done. However, we need to read this passage in connection with Deuteronomy 11:2–7. Moses could remind them of what God had done on this and that occasion, and he could argue that they had actually seen these things. How can that be the answer for our fear?

Whilst we have not seen what these people saw, the point made is still valid for us. The answer to fear and anxiety is recollection: remembering the great things God has already done.

We can remember what God has already done in our own experience. Often, the things that are worrying us in the future are far less serious than things we have already escaped through the Lord's mercies. We need to remember what we have already been through. Sometimes we forget. Kefa Sempangi, in a book I would recommend, *A Distant Grief* (or *Reign of Terror, Reign of Love*) tells how, during the Amin years in Uganda, as a pastor of a church, he was suddenly confronted with a man sent to kill him. In that moment, God gave him courage and peace so that he was able to pray for his assassin. The assassin was amazed, having never before seen anybody react like that. He could not go ahead and kill Kefa. Some time later, having escaped from the dangers of Uganda, Kefa was placed in a situation where he needed money which he did not have. He was controlled by his anxiety until he remembered. 'Why am I worried about money? Cannot the God who delivered me from the assassin's gun provide? If I could face death at peace, can I not face this at peace?' So we also need to remind ourselves of what God has already done for us.

Secondly, whilst we were not there when these things happened to Israel, they are still of benefit to us, simply because they happened and our God is the same God. In my years of preaching and teaching, I have made an observation. Sometimes I may be preaching on a well-known story such as Daniel in the lions' den. I wonder to myself how the people will react to a story that they have heard so many times before. Will they switch off? Yet, I have found that people listen, and will often comment that they were blessed and encouraged by something so familiar to them. Why is that? It is because we need to be reminded of something: of the power and ability of God to rescue his people from danger and difficulty. Our own problems and difficulties crowd in upon us and we forget. In God's Word, we have a reminder of the great things God has already done. We see the sort of God he is, and find comfort in knowing that that same God is our God.

That is our reason for reading the Scriptures, including the passages and stories we think that we know. That is why we need to sing the Psalms and sing them intelligently with thought for what we are singing, for frequently the Psalms direct us back to what God has already done. How can we encourage the people of God and help them overcome their fears? By reminding them of what God has done and who he is. That way we praise him and give him the glory which is his due, as well as encouraging his people. In our singing therefore we need to choose hymns which do that.

Whilst not on the same level as Scripture, there is something else we can do too. We can become familiar with the display of God's power in the history of the church. I have also noticed from preaching that people are blessed and encouraged when I use illustrations from church history. Why do they respond? They see that God did it for others, and realise that he can do it for them. There are many fine and edifying books of church history, often with the excitement of a novel, which will strengthen and encourage believers.

None of these instances of God's display of his power are, however, the most impressive; they are not what will really be most effective in calming your fears. What God did when he raised Jesus from the dead was even more important, for fear is often related particularly to the fear of death and the fear of death is related to guilt. There is a very interesting passage in Genesis where Joseph's brothers are frightened. They do not recognise this man who has become a great power in Egypt. They think that he is going to throw them into prison for the rest of their lives, for spying. They then start talking about their past sins. When we face something unpleasant, we have a sense that we deserve it. That is particularly true for the greatest threat we face: the threat of death. But God sent Jesus to die for sin and to rise in order to overcome it. I once heard an account of the death of a man of some fame, or maybe notoriety, in religious circles in Australia earlier this century. He was prominent amongst those who denied the divinity of Jesus, or that there was any aspect of the super-natural in connection with him. He said that Jesus was just a very good man, with wonderful ethical teachings which we should try to follow. Jesus did not do miracles, nor rise from the dead. The man to whom I refer died screaming in fear. In a very sad way, his death was consistent with his beliefs. However, as a matter of fact Jesus has been raised from the dead. God has displayed his power in overcoming death and he did not do it just for Jesus, but also for us. All who belong to Jesus will overcome death through him, and that is also a fact of which we need to be continually reminded. We read the Old Testament history books and the Acts to be reminded of the great things God did in the lives of his people in the history of the church, but we need to read the Gospels and the Epistles to be reminded of the great power he showed in rescuing Christ from the dead. We should sing the psalms to be reminded of God's great deeds of old, and if we sing hymns we should sing hymns which specifically focus on Christ's victory over sin and death. They are an excellent remedy for fear. There come times, where, either through imprisonment or sickness, believers find themselves without the ability to read their Bibles or go to church. At those times, the memorised Bible and memorised songs minister to our souls. If those things are not going into your memory, then you are preparing yourself for more agony and turmoil when you face the difficult patches in life.

This passage in Deuteronomy provides several other antidotes to fear, the first of which is in verse 21. God is in the midst of his people. We do not go alone. Remember the story of Elisha, when he was in the city of Dothan and the king of Aram (or Syria) sent an army to capture him (*2 Kings* 6). They woke up in the morning and the city was surrounded by troops. Elisha's servant was very frightened, so Elisha prayed that God might open his eyes. His eyes were opened and he saw the town full of horses and chariots of fire around Elisha. Elisha's words to the servant were: 'Those who are with us are more than those who are with them.' When John Paton was alone on Tanna in the New Hebrides, one night the cannibal chiefs sent men to kill him, but they found his house surrounded by men, guarding him. They asked Paton: 'Where during the day do you hide your men who guard your house at night?' To be a believer is never to be alone. God may not open our eyes to see the angels of the Lord encamping around us, but they are there. Some time ago I was asked to speak on the topic of 'Angels' and I have repeated that talk at different places. In the course of the talk I have told the story of Paton on Tanna and other such stories. The interesting thing to me is the number of people who have come to me afterwards to recount their experiences of being preserved in amazing ways. If God allows us to face trouble, and even death, it is not because there was nobody there to prevent it, but because it suits his plan and purposes.

That thought leads us on to the other reason given in this passage as to why God may not necessarily do things we would like, and that is in verse 22. There are reasons for God's timings. If I had been there in the camp of Israel, I would have been praying: 'Lord, please clean out those Canaanites before we have to go over and fight, or, if we have to fight them, please can it be short and sweet, rather than a long-drawn-out conflict.' That is how we tend to think and pray. 'Lord, take the problem away so that I do not even have to face it!' God reminded Israel that if he took the Canaanites away, there would just be another enemy to fight. If there were no humans around, the lions and leopards would become a problem, and they would be no further ahead. In a sinful and fallen world, if one problem is removed, the vacuum will be filled by another. That may seem discouraging, but understand what God said to Israel: I am timing things so that your problems and dangers will be minimal. If God does not solve a problem ahead of the crisis, rest assured that it is for good reason.

In conclusion, let me outline some simple steps to follow when trying to help someone who is anxious and fearful, maybe even yourself:

1.   Does the fear spring from having forgotten the great deeds of God in your past, or the past of his people? If so, you may need to refresh their memory.

2.   If that does not help, then we need to ask if it is because you have no reason to hope that God will exert his power on your behalf. In other words, is it because you are not a Christian, or, even though a Christian, you are clinging to some sin in your life, and you fear that God will not be merciful to you because of that. If that is the case, there will be no relief from the fear until the sin is dealt with. If you are not a Christian, then there is nothing surprising in your anxiety. In fact, it is a normal state for an unbeliever, and there will be no relief until you repent and take the one and only powerful God as your guardian.

3.   If that does not seem to be the problem, then it may be because of the strange and twisted 'logic' used by us sinners. Sometimes there are reasons why we actually want to be afraid; maybe to attract sympathy. I do not suggest mere acting, as the fear is often real, but to remove the fear would mean to remove the sympathy we crave. A quite different approach, but another case to illustrate the point, is the person who does not want to do something and uses fear as an excuse for not doing it. If you are building up that sort of an excuse to avoid something, then you would not want your excuse taken away.

All such excuses fall away when we realise that God's word to his people has always been: 'Do not fear, for I am with you to save even as I have in the past.'

Questions for Discussion

1. What are the situations in which you have faced or do face fear?

2. How has God, in the past, delivered you from similar or greater problems?

3. What incidents in the Scripture do you find the best antidotes to the things you tend to fear?

4. Is feeling alone a major component of your tendency to worry?

5. Do we tend to think that the problem we presently face is the only or at least the most concerning problem we are likely to face?

3: *Humbling before Blessing: Deuteronomy 8*

The passage before us says something which we would probably prefer was not true, that God humbled Israel. He gave them a hard time, subjecting them to affliction and hunger. He reduced them to a state of dependence. They had no security, no full barns to tide them over difficult times. They were one day away from utter poverty and abandonment. If the manna did not come that day, they were in real trouble.

Moreover, the Bible tells us that God did this deliberately and purposefully. It was not mere oversight, but a deliberate plan.

Herbert W. Armstrong, the leader of a cult whose magazine, *The Plain Truth,* you may have seen given out at news stands, attracted many people to his cult by promising that if you joined his organisation, and paid a tithe to him, then God would make you rich. Here is a God that is far from the god of Herbert W. Armstrong. Here is a God who reduces his people to poverty.

Why does he do that? He does it because he plans to make them rich, and being rich is a very dangerous condition. We may not think of it that way, but it is, for pride and self-sufficiency very often follow riches. When people become proud and self-sufficient, they forget about God, and they forget about others.

God's concern here was not unreasonable, for the later history of Israel is proof of the very point being made. They did become secure and self-sufficient. They forgot God, and when they forgot God, they ignored his law. Their national life became filled with corruption, and, in turn, God's judgment came upon them.

You will find a similar pattern repeated in the history of the church, and I will give a few examples. The Netherlands received the gospel which broke forth at the time of the Reformation in the sixteenth century. Through war and great affliction, they clung to that gospel. Yet, by the end of the seventeenth century, the church in the Netherlands was in process of turning from the gospel. What is called Arminianism began to take root, teaching that it depended upon man to prepare himself and to make himself fit for the gospel. It became not God who saved, but man who saved. It was not in a time of war, siege or famine that the change took place, but in a time of prosperity and growing riches, as commerce and industry in the Netherlands flourished. The rich merchant did not like to be told that he was needy and unable to help himself.

A very similar situation occurred in America. You may have heard the stories of how the Pilgrim Fathers escaped from religious persecution in England to found godly societies in the American North East. If you go to that area of America today, you find the church probably weaker than in any other part of the U.S. What happened was the same thing that happened in the Netherlands. In cities like Boston, the emerging wealthy turned to a message which flattered them more.

God seeks to prepare the generation which was to enter

Canaan for the wealth and security that were to follow. He tells us why he humbled Israel. It was to teach them their own dependence. They had to learn that God was the source of all. They had to learn to depend upon him and receive everything from him. In doing this, they learned the dependability of God's Word. What God said did come to pass. The promised manna was there day after day after day. They learned more than just the dependability of his Word, for they learned also of God's graciousness in many other ways. When God focuses on a particular humbling or trial, he very often blesses richly in other ways. The trial which Israel faced was focused on food and water, yet in other ways they were not tried, but greatly blessed. More than food and water is needed, and especially in a wilderness: their clothes did not wear out, and their feet did not swell from years of walking. They were humbled and tested in one way, but kept and blessed in another. They learned from this and from the daily supply of manna, how richly God provides for his people. They were poor and humbled, yet lacked no necessary thing.

I mentioned that Herbert W. Armstrong attracted people to his cult by promising them riches. That is the sort of Christianity that many would like, but is it real Christianity? Or, is what we see in Deuteronomy 8 true for our lives as well, that God humbles us and makes us needy, in order to teach us very clearly that he is the one who provides for all our needs?

We find a verse from this chapter quoted in a very interesting context in the New Testament. Jesus, at the very beginning of his ministry, was led out into the wilderness by the Spirit. He was there for forty days, which of course is to remind us of Israel's forty years in the wilderness. At the end of that time he was hungry. Why did he have to endure hunger? There are many reasons. Israel had failed God. They had grumbled and complained when tried. In the wilderness, they grumbled and rebelled at difficulties. Where Israel failed, Jesus succeeded. He showed that sin could be beaten, and by doing that, he became the only man who did not have to suffer punishment for his own sin. Notice too, that he did not just succeed when offered a temptation arising out of poverty and need. He succeeded also against the temptation of riches. Satan offered him all the kingdoms of the world and their riches, and Jesus turned him down (*Matt.* 4:8–10).

As we look at the dialogue between Jesus and Satan, a question arises in our minds. Jesus was the Son of God. He himself could have turned stones into bread. Why would it have been wrong for him to do so? If he had, he would not have succeeded where Israel failed. He would have aborted the test. He would not have demonstrated that calm dependence upon God which God had tried to teach Israel. That is why he answers with these words. He came to be one who learned all the lessons God had been teaching Israel. Our children may complain at how hard school work is, to which we may respond that we do not think that it is really as hard as they make out. Will they believe us? They may respond: 'Right, Dad, if you think it is so easy, you go to school and do my exams for me tomorrow.' Would they believe us if we said that we did not need to do examinations because we know it all anyway? Jesus did not avoid the test. He demonstrated that he knew all that God had to teach man.

We can go a step further. As the one who has learned all

the lessons of God, Jesus is the pattern we seek to follow. Note how Hebrews takes this up in Hebrews 5:7, 8 with specific reference to Jesus' suffering. I wonder whether the writer had in mind Deuteronomy 8:5. Jesus was also trained by the Father. See how the author of Hebrews develops these ideas in 12:1–11.

Jesus endured humiliation and suffering, so he is the model for us. For we also are being trained by the Father through suffering and hardships. Israel were disciplined and trained by privation. Jesus, demonstrating what Israel should have done, accepted discipline in obedient submission. Jesus is our model in these things. The conclusion cannot be escaped. God will also deal with us as he dealt with Israel. He will humble us. If God dealt so with his own Son Jesus, we have no right to expect anything else!

We can look at the way God has dealt with so many of his saints in order to prepare them for the blessing to follow. Joseph was prepared to be prime minister of Egypt by being a slave and a convict. David was a fugitive and an outlaw. Ruth lost her husband and moved to a foreign country to live in poverty. We could find many in the history of the church. John Knox was a galley slave before he became the mighty Reformer of Scotland. In the 1950s there was a powerful movement of the Spirit of God in Indonesia. One of the people used in that movement, which brought many Muslims to Jesus, had been trained by adversity. He grew up in a Christian village and became a pastor but without any experience of bringing the gospel to unbelievers. During the Japanese occupation, as a Christian pastor, he was imprisoned and nearly died. After the war he resumed his work but was falsely accused by his own congregation and once more found himself in prison.

There he found himself sharing a cell with a Muslim. For the first time he faced the issue of bringing the gospel to a Muslim. Finally vindicated of the false charges he was used by God to bring the gospel to many.

When we are humbled, therefore, and when we undergo times of discipline, we should not react as though some terrible thing were happening to us. God is preparing us for the blessing to follow. I have used a number of anecdotes but I would stress that what I am saying is not based on my own experience. It was Jesus who said: Blessed are the poor and the meek and those who hunger and thirst for righteousness because of the blessing to come later. It was Jesus who lived through affliction, and without riches or ease or comfort for this life. In due time, of course, God exalted him to be a rich and splendid king, but only at the other side of death. Often God does give blessing in this life, but if he does not, we cannot complain, for he did not give it to his own Son in this life.

Humbling is therefore not a theological problem, though there are people who say that they cannot understand why God would humble this or that believer. They fail to see that God has a goal: that God is preparing each of us to enter the promised land. If humbling continues for years, the results will be deeper. Remember that Israel had forty years of humbling, and the generation which came through that training were one of the mightiest in Israel's history. They were the ones who took Canaan.

So when the times of riches come, and when we are blessed beyond measure, let us not forget what God taught us in those times of affliction. It is he who gives us strength for wealth and peace. Whether rich or poor, we must remain dependent on and thankful to him.

Questions for Discussion

1. What is it about man that makes success such a snare?

2. 'The man who regards humbling as unfair is already infected by pride.' Would you agree?

3. Jesus was tempted in all points like us. Was his humbling also so comprehensive as to include any humbling which men must undergo?

4. Is our society raising a generation who believe they deserve success? What would be the consequence for the church of such attitudes?

4: *Israel's Failure and Ours: Deuteronomy 9:1– 10:5, 12–16*

When we think back over our lives, sometimes the failures rise up to hit us. We messed up on this, or failed at that. Maybe there is one particular thing we have tried and tried to do without success. As we think over these things, it is very discouraging. Sometimes, if we are feeling a little 'blue', it discourages us even further when we think back over past events.

Thinking about our past failures is a generally discouraging thing. Sometimes the memory of them stays, and becomes a problem in our Christian life. We want to succeed, and this is a message to us that we cannot succeed, because of our past failure. What hope is there for doing better in the future? It is because of this generally discouraging influence of our past that I want to look at this passage from Deuteronomy, for here we have a record of sin and failure used as an encouragement. When Moses wanted to encourage Israel, he went back through the history of their sin.

To understand this use of history, we need to look at the beginning of the section, for the concern of the passage is the impending war against the Canaanites. There are dangers both before and after the conflict with the Canaanites. Before the battle, there is the danger that Israel will become afraid. God therefore reassures them of his presence and power. He does not deny the reality of enemy power. The Anakim were giants. Remember Goliath was one of the descendants of the Anakim. After the battle and victory there is the danger of Israel's victory going to their heads. They might become convinced of their own goodness, righteousness and worth. Before the battle the danger is fear; and after the battle it is pride. It is to the danger of pride that this passage is particularly directed.

In any Old Testament historical narrative, we need to look for repetitions. Moses does not tell us the point of the story, yet the point is made reasonably obvious by the selection of highlights and repeats. We look for the things which occupy the centre of the story, and there are two such highlights. One is the tablets, which were made, broken and remade. There are many other parts of the story of the golden calf which could have been emphasised, but Moses chose to focus on the tablets. The second point of emphasis is the role of Moses as intercessor. He was the one to stand in the breach when the anger of God threatened to destroy Israel. It was in response to Moses' prayer that God turned his anger away from Israel.

These two elements say something very important to Israel. Israel were once in relationship to God. He was their God and they were his people. The tablets were the concrete sign of that relationship. On them would have been written things like God's great declaration: 'I am the Lord your God, who brought you out of the land of Egypt, out of the house of slavery.' On them would have been written Israel's duty. Israel, however, destroyed that relationship. Israel disobeyed one of the most important commandments, and therefore broke the covenant relationship. Moses' smashing the tablets was a concrete illustration of the breaking of Israel's relationship to God, just as the existence of the tablets was proof of the relationship.

If you have ever taken a plane flight, you may have had the fear that I always have: that I will forget my tickets. Suppose you were to arrive at the airport, join the queue, and hear a person in front of you being told: 'There is a problem on this flight due to a computer malfunction. The flight is overbooked and we do not know who we can take and who will have to wait for the next flight.' You really have to catch that flight. You have connections and arrangements. As your turn comes up, you prepare your arguments and reach into your pocket for your tickets. They are not there! You go through your pockets frantically, and then you remember. You had them in your hand when your wife had trouble shutting the window, so you put them down to help her. What of all your arguments, and your special reason for catching this flight, when you have no tickets? Israel had just thrown away their tickets to their relationship with God. They were not just mislaid, but destroyed, used to light the fire of their own sin and rebellion.

Yet, God gave them new tickets! He graciously remade the tablets and took Israel back into relationship. Israel stood in relationship to God not because of their own righteousness, but because of God's grace. They were no better than the Canaanites. They too had been idolaters. If God showed favour to them and went with them to give them victory, it was only out of his grace.

The same truth is brought out by the record of Moses'

intercession. Israel had sinned, even having done the very thing the law just given them had warned against. They deserved the punishment threatened to disobedient sinners. Moses could make no plea on the basis of Israel's worth or goodness, so he based his plea on God's faithfulness. He appealed to God to remember his promise to Abraham, Isaac and Jacob. So Israel's being helped by God to overcome the Canaanites was not because Israel was any better. It was because God had promised that land to Abraham, Isaac and Jacob, and because God would fulfil that promise. Once again, Israel experienced victory, not because they were good, but because God in his mercy listened to the arguments of an intercessor. They stood through grace alone.

If the record of past failures can be used as an incentive to righteousness and faithfulness, why do we find our failures so discouraging? Why does the mere memory of them so incline us to feel that the service of God is beyond us? Let us look at what is involved in that discouraging recollection of our own failures.

First of all, we have guilt. We look back, and our consciences rise up to accuse us. They may accuse us now with even greater intensity than they did at the time of our sin. We then need to remember that we too have an intercessor. The Lord Jesus brings to his Father not just the argument from God's promises of old, but the fact that he himself did not argue away the anger of God, but took it. Moses provided God with reasons why he should not destroy Israel. Jesus bore, and absorbed in himself, the destruction we deserve. If God heard Moses, how much more will he hear Christ? If Israel, who, almost immediately after receiving the laws, turned to breaking them, can be forgiven, can we not also be forgiven? If that truth does not comfort your guilt, then I will follow on with two more questions. Does your conscience bother you because it knows of sin which you are not yet willing to face or confess? Second, Scripture tells us that when we sin against man, we are to confess to God and be reconciled to man. If you stole somebody's $5, you do not just confess to God, but you also need to give back the $5! If you spoke unkindly to somebody, do not just confess that to God, but also ask forgiveness of the person you hurt.

The second thing which makes our memories so miserable is pride. It hurts to remember that in the moment of testing, we were not as good as we thought we were. It shatters our whole confidence in ourselves to know that we have failed. There, I am afraid our memory is right, and we are wrong. We are not as good as we think we are. But does that matter? It was on failures, on Israel, that God set his love. It was with such people that he went to victory over the Canaanites. Does it matter that you are a failure when God gives his people such victories?

There are those who think that only by building up people's pride, can we get them to perform at their peak. School pupils, salesmen and athletes are fed confidence-building nonsense. No wonder that such people can become insufferable in their pride. The greater their success with their chosen task, very often the less their success with people and with God. And the greater the fall when God proves that they are failures.

Our memories of failure, if used correctly, will do something very important for us. They will prove to us that we are not as good as we thought we were. Why do we have to pretend to be perfect, when our history is proof that we are not? Yet keep remembering that it was to failures that God promised victory over the Canaanites. Being a failure, and knowing it, does not remove the hope of success, but rather, is the very basis of success. Only the Christian can both live without pretension and pride, and yet go ahead to success, knowing that the Lord is with him.

When people look back to their failures, there may be a third factor, beside guilt and wounded pride. There may also be resentment, because in their minds it was not their failure. There are some people who can never admit that they failed or did anything wrong. It is always the other person's fault! When you think that way, then there will be bitterness and resentment against other people, and sadly, it is frequently a bitterness against people who should be the closest: husbands to wives, children to parents.

The antidote lies in two things. When we acknowledge the fact that we also fail, it is harder to resent another person's failure. Remember the parable Jesus told about forgiving your debtors (*Matt.* 18:21–35). The second factor is remembering the biblical command to pray for our enemies and do good to those who hurt us (*Matt.* 5:44). You may ask how you can be expected to ask God to bless someone you hate, and really want to get back at. Read Moses' prayer in Deuteronomy 9:26–28. His dominating concern was the glory and reputation of God. Take that person whom you feel, out of your own bitter experience, to be so very hurtful and malicious. Would not God be glorified by the conversion of such a person? Would not his grace be magnified by his willingness to bless such a person? Moses might have had all sorts of human reasons to feel angry at the people who had let him down. Instead, he prayed for them, trying to turn God's anger from them, for the glory and reputation of God was his main concern.

If we learn from these lessons, then there is another time when the memory of our failures will be a great blessing, and that is when we succeed because of God's blessing. Then we also face the danger of pride. We also can think that we have success because we are so good. Let our failures remind us that we succeed only by the grace of God!

Questions for Discussion

1. 'Failure is the thing people cannot talk about. Even in Christian circles we have built a cult of success and tried to escape the hurtful reality.' Would you agree that the problem is that serious?

2. Why are Christians troubled by problems of guilt?

3. Is the threat of Christ in Revelation 2:5 that the church's lampstand will be removed from its place the equivalent of the broken tablets?

4. Have you known in your own experience the grace of God that turns failure into success?

5: *Thinking Like a Refugee: Deuteronomy*
10:12–22; 24:10–15, 17–22

If you measure the importance of a teaching by the number of times it is mentioned in Scripture, then concern for the poor is certainly an important teaching. Scripture, when it talks about the poor, commonly links together the widow, the orphan and the alien. 'Alien' may need some explanation. You can be an alien in another country for many reasons. You might be a tourist, a student or a businessman. All of those can return to their own country. There is another class of foreigners however: those who are forced to live in another country and cannot return to their own. They therefore tend to be poor and subject to exploitation. Today we call them refugees. So the passages of Scripture we are considering are concerned with the poor and specifically with groups likely to end up in poverty like widows, orphans and refugees.

We have a number of passages in Scripture which are expositions of the ten commandments. They take the general summary statements we find in the commandments and turn them into more detailed rules. They show what those commandments mean in practical detail. We find one case of this immediately after the ten commandments in Exodus 22 and 23. We find another case in Leviticus

19. In both of these expansions of the ten commandments we find laws devoted to the poor. Note the following: Exodus 22:21–27; 23:8, 9; Leviticus 19:9, 10, 13.

What is the law concerning the poor warning Israel against? What sort of behaviour is excluded by the law? There are a number of things.

1.   It is against any sort of favouritism or corruption. You must not take bribes. Note the connection in Deuteronomy 10:17, 18 and 19. God is incorruptible. He cannot be influenced. He does not take a bribe. Hence he shows justice to the needy. Note also in Exodus 23:8–9 that a prohibition on bribes is followed immediately once more by a concern for justice to the poor. Who is hurt when a country is corrupt? Generally it is the poor rather than the rich. The rich can pay the bribes, whereas the poor cannot. So concern for the poor is concern for a legal system which is not corrupt.

2.   It is concerned for the dignity of the poor. Note the method of poor relief set up in these passages. It is a method whereby the poor can glean in the fields, picking the grain, grapes or olives which have not been harvested. That is work. They have to work for their keep. Being in a situation of dependency is a discouraging and soul-destroying situation. Many of us grumble about what is taken out of our pay to give to those out of work; but have you thought about how much worse it is for the person who receives it? 'Of what worth am I?', he thinks, 'I am not even good enough to earn my own keep!' But this law provided a way by which they could earn their own livelihood.

This concern for the poor shows also in the law about the pledge. Loans to the needy had to be without interest. The person who made the loan received nothing from it, and he risked not getting his money back. Therefore he could ask for a pledge whereby the debtor had to give him something which would be returned as soon as the loan was repaid. Note however that you could not walk into his home and take whatever suited your fancy. How would you feel if someone could walk into your home and march off with your prized possession? You would be humiliated. So, even while holding the poor responsible to pay their debts, we must not humiliate them.

3.   Another concern of the law is that we be sensitive to the misery and problems of poverty. For example, what can a poor man give as his pledge? He does not have surplus things to pawn. Apparently it was common to give their outer garment, their overcoat as it were. That is fine during the day, but what about at night? The poor usually do not have both an overcoat and a blanket. The overcoat would serve as a blanket at night. You cannot say 'Well, he has to give a pledge. Too bad if he's cold at night!' You must return the pledge at night. Another problem of the poor is their lack of usable cash or credit. They have no reserves. They cannot wait until next day for their pay. If they were not paid that day, they could not buy food that night. So labourers were to be paid at the end of each day. The employer was not to keep the pay overnight for the labourer to come back the next morning. The labourer was to be paid that day. I suspect that the law about not being able to take a widow's garment in pledge has a similar motivation. You must be sensitive to her dignity and

modesty. Being poor should not also mean being exposed to embarrassment.

We turn now from what the law requires to the motivation for keeping the law. There are two basic motivations. The first is clear in Deuteronomy 10:17–19. It is the character of God in his justice and mercy. Corruption in the legal system is a contradiction of the character of God. You cannot be like God and take bribes or be pressured into wrong decisions. God is absolutely impartial. Further, he shows mercy to the poor and needy. If we are to be like God, we must have similar compassion.

The second reason occurs again and again in the passages we read. It is Israel's own experience of being an oppressed alien. They were exploited foreigners in Egypt. They should know what it feels like.

We note here another way in which Deuteronomy appeals to the past experiences of the people of God. We have seen the appeal to their experience of God's greatness, to their experience of being humbled and disciplined, and to their experience of failure. Now the appeal is to their memory of slavery.

Since most people have known experiences of difficulty and sorrow, you might think that would make them compassionate. I do not think that any group of people who came to Australia found it easy in the early days. We might therefore expect Australians to be very compassionate. Obviously they are not. What has gone wrong? Why do people fail to recall their own difficulties? Several reasons can be suggested. One is that we want to forget those origins. We are embarrassed about our past. In a world in which success is seen in terms of material prosperity, to be poor is a sign of failure. We bury that evidence as quickly as we can. In the course of discussions and debates on Christian school uniform, I have sometimes reflected aloud on my own experience. I grew up in a town in northern New South Wales where it was hot, and being in a river valley there was not a stone for miles. Most of the people of the town and surrounding farms were not well-off, and so it was the 'norm' for primary school children to go without shoes. I have sometimes commented that it is a pity students have to wear shoes to school, with the suggestion causing horror to parents. I am sure that the image of their sending their children to school barefooted was too much for their ideal of what a good parent does. So with us, views of our own proper dignity, our responsibility as parents and providers, are bound up with our financial status. The image of being poor is an attack on our own dignity and worth. It is hard for us to say, 'Yes, I was poor. My parents, or my grandparents, were very poor people.'

A second reason why people, even though their background was one of poverty, may be unsympathetic to the poor, is because they feel that they had to struggle hard to get out of poverty, and that it is not fair for others to get out of it the easy way. In answer to that, I would say two things:

First, it is not our struggles which released us from our poverty, but the goodness of God. It is the Lord 'who gives you power to make wealth' (*Deut.* 8:18). If God chooses to make another poor man wealthy, who are you to complain?

Second, I would emphasise that the biblical way is so planned as to allow for both generosity and work. All the laws we have seen, like not gleaning the fields or the grapevines, or not cutting the corners of fields, allow opportunity for the poor, but still require work. A beautiful example is found in the book of Ruth. Ruth qualified as poor on many counts. She was a foreigner. She was a widow. She was the only support of her widowed mother-in-law. So she went to glean in Boaz' field. Note Ruth 2:14–16. Boaz was being generous. That particular way of helping the poor is not mentioned in the laws we have read, but is certainly in the spirit of the laws. Ruth had to work. This is an example of grace and works. Boaz could go to bed knowing that he had done right, and Ruth could go to bed with the dignity of having earned what she had.

Somebody may object: What about the person who was born rich, and is from a long line of wealthy people? How can he know what it feels like to be poor?

To deal with that problem, and maybe with the problem of a lot of people who have effectively shut out any memory of poverty, we have to go deeper. Scripture exposes the poverty of us all. James 1:10–11 puts it well. In reality the rich man is in poverty, for he has nothing of lasting wealth. That is why one must be 'poor in spirit' to be blessed. It is only those who know their poverty who can enjoy the blessings of the kingdom.

Further, every believer is an alien. He is a foreigner in this world. Have you ever known what it is to be in the midst of people who do not speak your language, or who do not sympathise with your feelings or values? If not, then I must ask if you have ever lived as a Christian in the midst of this world.

Finally, all of us have a very close connection with a poor person. If you are a Christian, your Lord was a pauper. 'Foxes have holes, the birds of the air have nests, but the Son of Man has no place to lay his head.' If you have no feeling for misery, poverty and injustice, where is your feeling for the Lord's misery?

So what is required of us? As individuals we are to have sensitivity to the needs and dignity of the poor. As a church we are to have an openness to the poor and the alien. We need to show more wisdom in our political life than is currently shown. We really can have no sympathy with the attitude of so many on the political Right, which says that these people are poor just because they are too lazy to do anything about it. That ignores the reality of injustice and corruption. But we can also have little sympathy with a welfare system that destroys dignity by controlling people's lives and giving them no way to earn their livelihood. We must work not to feed people with handouts, but to provide them with work.

Questions for Discussion

1. Have you known what it is to be poor? Do you tend to be ashamed of that part of your life?

2. Are we indifferent to corruption in society because we are more immune to its effects than some other sections of society?

3. What forms of help for the poor today preserve their dignity and save them from embarrassment?

4. Why do we lack a Christian political presence which is sensitive to the way both the Right and the Left show indifference to the poor?

6: *Changing Times and Changing Laws: Deuteronomy 12:1–28*

You will often hear people say that what the Bible says on a certain subject is not applicable today since it was intended only for the time when the Bible was written. They say that since times have changed, so that teaching of Scripture is no longer relevant today. This teaching tends to cause Christians quite a deal of confusion. For one thing, it is quite clear that some things commanded in the Bible are no longer commanded today. For example, we no longer offer the sacrifices which were once commanded, because Christ has been offered for us. Further, is it not the case that there have been great changes since biblical times? Yet carried through consistently this teaching would imply that no commandment of biblical times is still relevant for our time. If that were the case, then Christianity would be no more!

If you think through this dilemma, I think you will realise that there has to be some way to distinguish things which are no longer commanded from those which remain valid. Generally, those who would set aside a biblical commandment as outdated do not worry as to whether that commandment can be distinguished from the commandments which are always valid. They say, 'Oh, that was just because of such and such a situation in Bible times.'

The way to make the essential distinction is surely to go to Scripture itself and to see what principles it uses in making distinctions.

When Israel came to Mount Sinai, God gave them laws. We tend to think in terms of the ten commandments, but they were just the basic principles. There were many more detailed commandments. Of all the commandments given at Sinai, I know of only one which was changed during the period of the Old Testament, but that change is very informative.

In Leviticus 17:3–7, we have a commandment given with the purpose of preventing the slaughter of an animal killed for food becoming opportunity for the worship of demons. Any animal killed for food had to be made a peace offering. It was to be brought into the tent of meeting and sacrificed, with certain parts offered on the altar (the fat parts) and the rest then being available to the worshipper as food.

When this commandment was given, the Israelites were in the wilderness, living in tents around the tent of meeting. When Israel had conquered Canaan and settled in it, that was no longer the case. Deuteronomy is the book which looks forward to the new situation to apply after Israel have entered the promised land. For our purpose, Deuteronomy 12:20–28 is the significant law. This law looks forward to the situation in which Israel, settled throughout the land, would be too far from the altar to bring every animal they wanted to eat. Hence, the law was changed, and the reason given for this change is most significant. It is that God has extended Israel's borders, in fulfilment of a promise.

The Israelites were brought into a new situation by God

when he fulfilled his promise of bringing them into the promised land. This new situation required a new law, but we must remember that the new situation was one created by God himself. It is not just that customs and beliefs had changed so that the law was outmoded. God was the one who changed the situation. Change of law followed God's fulfilment of promise.

Let us return to Sinai, and the great period of law giving in the Old Testament. When were the laws given? They were given when God had fulfilled his promise to bring Israel out of Egypt. He had brought them out to be his peculiar people. They were thus in a new situation; hence there had to be a new law to regulate and guide them in their new situation. Sinai was thus also a case in which God first acted, in creating a new situation, then gave laws to direct in that new situation.

Another thing to remember is that when Israel went into the promised land, only this one commandment changed. The situation was not so changed that they no longer had to refrain from murder, adultery or theft! Was it so changed that they no longer needed to bring sacrifices for sin? No, in fact the change that needed to be made to the law was quite restricted. Suppose you left your present work for other employment. Many things about the way you work might change, yet your approach to work would not be different in every respect. We can imagine more drastic changes, such as from school to work, or from work to retirement. The changes are there, but they are not total changes.

Let us leave the Old Testament and go to the New Testament. There we see far greater changes. For one thing, sacrifice ceased; and all sacrifices – not just one instance. However, I think we can still understand this change in the same way as the change we previously considered. God fulfilled his promise and brought his people into a new situation. For that new situation, new laws are appropriate. Now, because Christ has been sacrificed, we no longer need to offer sacrifices. But are we in a situation where it does not matter any more whether we murder, commit adultery, or steal? Of course not! In that respect, our situation has not changed.

Once again, we see the connection between God acting, and his creating a new situation and a new law. Why is there this connection? One reason I have already given: because in a new situation you need a new law. There is another reason: Christ, our Saviour, is also our Lord. As our Saviour he deserves our obedience and has a right to determine the rules under which we live. We cannot set the rules, because we did not save ourselves.

There are two points of possible confusion which I would like here to clear up. The first of these arises when Paul is misinterpreted. Paul puts grace in contrast to law. We are saved by grace, and not by the keeping of the law, says Paul. From that, it is sometimes said that Christians should not be under any law. Most who would say that do not take it to the lengths that their logic implies. They do not say that we are free to commit whatever possible sin. Nevertheless, they do spread a lot of confusion. The whole biblical pattern is not that salvation and law giving are opposed in every way. On the contrary, new law giving follows salvation. When Paul puts law in contrast to grace, it is very clear in the context that he is talking about the way of salvation. We are saved by grace not because we have kept God's law. The Israel that God brought out of Egypt was similarly saved by grace. Rather, being in the new situation of being saved, we need to know how we should then live, and that is where the law comes in.

The second confusion occurs when trying to work out which laws are appropriate for the new situation, and which are not, or, which Old Testament laws remain binding and which do not. People generally say that moral laws are still binding, but ceremonial law is not. That is to say that the ten commandments are still in force, but laws on sacrifice and temples are not. That distinction generally works, but it is a little simplistic, and can cause confusion in some particular cases. Take a look at Ephesians 6:1–3, where Paul quotes the sixth commandment, though not as it was originally given. The original promise was 'that your days may be prolonged in the land which the Lord your God gives you'. Paul changed that to: 'that you may live long on the earth'. Why the change from the 'promised land' to 'the whole earth'? The people of God in the New Testament era do not just live in Palestine, and the special status of Palestine and Jerusalem are done away with, and believers are scattered throughout the whole earth. The point I want to make here is that the great change brought about by Christ impacts upon even the ten commandments. Why did the New Testament church with a background of the synagogue practice of meeting on the seventh day begin to meet on the first? I believe that it was because, in that regard also, there was a change: Christ's resurrection was an anticipation of the new creation. We therefore look to that new creation and celebrate its first stage. The position of Seventh Day Adventists, who say that God's law can never change, really ignores how much God has changed our situation and brought in a new law.

With this foundational understanding, the question of male/female roles becomes much more straightforward. Those who say that the biblical roles of men and women are no longer relevant, say that the Bible was merely reflecting the view of its time, and that we who are in different times, where the roles are different, no longer need to apply the biblical teaching. Put very bluntly, it seems to say that the Bible is man's work and not God's, reflecting the views of its time. The position might be somewhat modified to say that the writers of the Bible did not want to give offence, so they conformed to the expectations of the time, even while stating principles which, in our time, have led to the abolition of distinct male and female roles. But the question still arises, even with that position: How do we know that the Bible writers were merely condescending to the views of the time? How do we know that in this part of the Bible there is a sort of planned obsolescence? Could you not then say the same thing about many of the other things which the New Testament teaches?

May I emphasise that the Bible, as we have seen, is not a modern motor car. The design does not change just because regular design changes are fashionable. It is God who changes the design when he puts his church on a new road. The real question is: has God intervened and fulfilled his promise so as to bring us into a new situation where new rules are needed? No! On the contrary, the push against distinct male/female roles has come from unbelievers.

We are not left to rely upon that sort of hypothetical argument alone, however. The key passages that deal with roles in the church take us all the way back to creation: 1 Corinthians 11:8–9 and 1 Timothy 2:11–14. Remember that we are in no new situation regarding murder or theft since the coming of Christ. What Paul is saying is that the distinction between man and woman was set at creation and nothing has happened to change it! The distinction that goes back to creation continues to exist!

Some people fret at that, finding it very restrictive. Why should my freedom be limited by God's creation? And so they reject Christianity. That is very foolish. Yes, we are limited here; we are restricted. Our real restriction is not creation, however, but sin, and all that sin has caused. My wife and I attended a funeral of two sisters killed in a car accident, one of whom had been a student of mine. In one way it was a study in contrasts. The sister who had been my student seemed to be superabundantly blessed with gifts: an honours university student, brilliant at music, loving and caring. Her sister was so retarded that the parents were told when she was born that she might never be able to do anything. Through the family's love and care, she did make some accomplishments, yet she was retarded and difficult, as retarded children can be. Yet, as was said at the funeral: 'Now the difference is done away.' There is going to be a time in the future, when God, once more, will fulfil his promises, and bring his people into a new situation where new rules will apply. Anybody who for freedom now forfeits his chance of that future is nothing more than a fool!

Questions for Discussion

1. The Bible says that law changes when God creates something new. The world says that law changes when fashions change. What different assumptions about the nature of law and the authority to make law lie behind those two positions?

2. Some will say that changes in fashions and ideas in the course of human history are under God's control. Therefore they warrant change in divine law. What are the differences between changes such as were brought about by the exodus, the conquest and the death and resurrection of Christ and the changes in human fashions?

3. How is God's role as law giver connected to his role as Saviour?

4. What changes in law do we expect when Christ returns? Do those changes fit the pattern we have already seen?

7: *The Narrow Gate: Deuteronomy 12:1–32; 14:22–27*

When we read the book of Deuteronomy, there are things which we can fairly readily see as applicable to our situation, such as the warning not to be afraid, or the concern for the poor. We recognise those things as problems in our day, and teaching on those issues is immediately relevant to us. There are other things which do not appear so immediately relevant to us, such as are found in this passage and a number of others throughout Deuteronomy: the concern that Israel come to one place for their sacrifices and festivals. They were not to offer them, or celebrate them just anywhere, but in one place alone: the place the Lord their God chose.

We, as Christians, are very used to the idea that we may worship God anywhere. It does not require a holy building nor does it have to be a particular city with all sorts of holy associations or a long history of God's dealings, like Jerusalem. It can be anywhere. When we meet this Old Testament concern, we are likely to pass it by as having no relevance or message for us.

Yet we should not treat any part of God's Word in that way. It does have a message for us. To understand the message for us, we must first understand the message for Israel. Why did God say this?

If we look at chapter 12, first of all we see that this command is placed in clear contrast to pagan practice. The pagans worship their gods everywhere. They have their holy places, their altars everywhere: on every high hill, under every green tree. Every place that has even a little bit special about it is a pagan place of sacrifice. You may say that in one sense it was easy to be a pagan. You did not have to go anywhere special to sacrifice. It was close to where you lived, like a petrol station on every corner: very convenient and accessible.

Furthermore, if it was not convenient, or if you thought the tree down the road was a little more impressive, there was nothing to prevent you from sacrificing there. You could make another shrine. You were in fact free to make as many shrines as you liked: no limitation on your industry or imagination in that regard! Thus we might say that pagan worship had no restrictions. God was freely accessible, however and whenever you chose to approach him.

In contrast, in Israel, God himself sets the rules for approach. Only in the way he chooses may man approach him.

This attitude of paganism is still very much with us. What is one of the greatest offences of Christianity in our day? It is that it is exclusive. It does not say that there are many ways to God. It does not say that you can approach God just however you like. It is faithful to the words of Jesus, when he said: 'I am the way, and the truth, and the life; no one comes to the Father, but through Me' (*John* 14:6). There is a New Testament equivalent to this concentration upon the one place of access to God. It is Jesus as the only way of access to God. In both Old Testament and New Testament God determines how man may approach him. He determines the way; man does not. As mentioned earlier, this is part of the offence of the gospel. Yet this is also the glory of the gospel. We do not follow the figments of men's imagination, the self-appointed religious leader who comes along and says: 'Since everybody is free to make his own way to God, I will establish my way. I think this would be a nice place to worship God. I think this would be a good idea for a religion.' It is God himself who chooses the way of access. If we go that way, we can be confident of having found the right way.

In Deuteronomy 14, we have this focus upon the one place of worship set in a slightly different context, with a different emphasis. The subject at the beginning of the chapter is the animals Israel were allowed to eat. You cannot find just one principle to explain the Old Testament food laws. Partly it was to teach Israel to make distinctions; partly also to teach the unnaturalness of death. Note 14:21. While there are some exceptions, carnivores, that is, animals which eat other animals and animals which will eat carrion, are on the list of unclean animals. Thus, in Israel's food laws, there is a separation between the clean and the unclean, between life and death.

Following this, we have teaching on eating at the chosen place. Israel were to come and eat and drink with rejoicing. The note of rejoicing is in contrast to what we read earlier in the chapter. There is an eating that is not connected to death and uncleanness. There is an eating that is connected to life and joy; a rejoicing at all the bounty which God had provided for Israel.

In John 7:37, Jesus stood up at the festival and called

men to come to him and drink. I think that the place is significant. Anybody who knows Deuteronomy should understand the significance of what Jesus said. Here, Jews had come up to Jerusalem, to the place God chose for the festival. Why had they come up to this place? They came to eat and drink in the presence of God. Then Jesus stood up and said: 'I am the one. It is to me you have come to drink!' He thus claims to be the fulfilment of the Old Testament pilgrimage to Jerusalem.

In John 6, there is a long discourse in which Jesus compared himself to the Old Testament manna, and urged men to feed from him. The main passage of the Old Testament alluded to by Jesus was the story of the manna. However we need to consider a broader Old Testament background if we are to understand all that Jesus was saying. He spoke of eating his flesh and drinking his blood. When that caused some of his followers to turn away, Jesus explained to the genuine disciples that he did not mean it in a very literalistic sense. Yet, where did Jesus get that picture and why did he speak of eating his flesh? To understand we have to remember the two aspects of Old Testament sacrifices and tithes. One aspect was that of dedication to God. Thus in the whole burnt offering the whole animal was dedicated to God and destroyed in the flame. In the peace offering, something different happened: it was only part of the animal that was burnt up, and the rest was for the worshippers to eat in the presence of God. That eating symbolised fellowship with God. Very often those two sacrifices went together: first the whole burnt offering to symbolise the venting of God's anger upon the sacrifice destroyed in the fire; and then the peace offering to symbolise that the person was restored to fellowship with

God. Eating the sacrifice is the action of one whose sins have been forgiven and who now enjoys communion with God, which is why Jesus invited them to come and fellowship with God through himself. He is the sacrifice. Through his body and blood we come into fellowship with God, so Jesus used the picture of our eating his flesh. As he pointed out to the genuine disciples in John 6:63, this blessing comes not from a physical eating of the flesh, but through the Holy Spirit. The Old Testament worshipper got a physical benefit: a physical benefit which symbolised much more, but nevertheless, a physical benefit. He ate the meat or bread or whatever and was nourished in his body. That is not what Jesus was talking about here. This is spiritual nourishment, and hence quite appropriately conveyed to us by the Holy Spirit. It is however still true that the source of this nourishment is Jesus. He is the sacrifice from which we all may obtain life and joy.

So the Old Testament emphasis on one place of sacrifice fits into the whole biblical framework. Our way of access to God is laid down by God himself.

Therefore I would ask you: are you a pagan at heart? I do not mean – do you run around beating tom-toms and eating people? Those are things which have resulted from paganism. I am talking, rather, about the beginning, the basis, of paganism: the belief that man can find God whenever and wherever he chooses; the belief that it is man who determines the way and not God.

That leads to a further question. Have you come to God in the way he has chosen? Have you come to Jesus as the sacrifice that opens the way to life and rejoicing for us? The year of the believing Israelites focused on that approach to God, when they could go up to wherever the ark was, to Shiloh, or later to Jerusalem, to meet with fellow believers, to eat and to rejoice, and to have there the sort of party that leaves no bitter taste or sorrow. They did it at the great festivals three times a year because they could not be at Jerusalem and away from their fields all the time. When the New Testament came, it abolished the festivals, calling them a mere shadow of the reality to come, namely Christ. The question is not: Do you go to a temple on a particular day of the year? or, Do you look forward to it? The question is: Have you approached God, and do you daily approach God, through Jesus the sacrifice and the temple? If not, you are a pagan, and like the pagans of Canaan, the time will eventually come for God to destroy you too.

There are several other passages of Deuteronomy that make reference to this going to the special place. Looking at them is like a review of much that we have already seen in earlier studies of Deuteronomy.

In 16:11, where it describes the way they were to rejoice and enjoy the offerings brought at the time of the feast of weeks, it includes the poor and the needy in the celebration. When Israel rejoiced they were to see that others had reason for rejoicing also. It was not to be a feast for the rich, with nothing for the rest.

So also the whole logic of the New Testament is that we should include others in our joy. We who have known what it is to be fed, nourished and filled by Jesus should bring others into that circle of blessing. Sometimes people say that the Old Testament was uninterested in evangelism. That is not true. Notice the way that the alien is expected to be present and to be included. It was not that the Old Testament was uninterested in the outsider, but rather, that its aim was to bring the outsider into the joy and blessing of approach to God in the way he had chosen. Israel did not go out to establish churches everywhere. They called the Gentile in to come to God at the place where he had caused his name to be remembered.

In 26:1–11, we read what Israel were to do with the first-fruits of their land. As they came with their riches and abundance, they were to be reminded of all God had done for them. They had not received out of their own efforts, but all by divine grace. Rather, they had been poor and starving. It was God who delivered them from starvation and oppression and brought them to this land. Here we see coming together more of the themes of Deuteronomy: that gratitude which springs from a memory of what God in his mercy has done for us, that realisation that we did not succeed by our own efforts, that inclusion of others. What better model could we ask for a Christian; full of a sense of gratitude for what God has done for him, and reaching out to include others in the blessing?

Questions for Discussion

1. If Jesus replaces the Old Testament central shrine, is it an insult to Jesus to treat any building or place today as holy?

2. 'Western secular views of paganism generally picture it in two different ways. Sometimes they see it as primitive and superstitious. They do not recognise the pride of the worshippers in being able to choose their own way to God. At other times they view it with relativistic tolerance and argue that they should be free to worship as they like. They do not see it as an expression of ignorance of the true way.' How do you regard paganism?

3. Do you think there might, just possibly, be another way to God except via Jesus?

4. The Old Testament commanded Israel to include the poor and the needy in their celebrations. The Gospel parables picture God as the host who invites people, especially the poor, to the feast. How is the Christian to act as a host?

8: *The Seriousness of the First Commandment: Deuteronomy 12*

When we read a chapter like this, our first reaction may be a sense that this does not fit into what we are used to doing. We do not expect prophets to arise. We do not expect to be seduced to idolatry. We do not stone people, and certainly not family members. We do not unite as a people against particular villages and towns. Thus, our initial reaction may be to read on to see if we can find something more directly relevant to us in Deuteronomy.

However, if we believe that all Scripture is profitable for instruction, we will return to this passage. What is it saying? To discover the answer to that, we need to ask: what is the major thrust, or concern, of the passage? The main point is the first commandment and the way the first commandment is to be kept; as well as some of the ways in which Israel might be tempted to weaken their devotion to that basic commandment and what they are to do to meet those threats.

How do we translate that concern into things more familiar to us? How do we put it into language, turn it into commandments, to which we can relate? Let me put those questions another way: what is the New Testament equivalent of the first commandment? In asking that question I am not suggesting that the first commandment is not valid for New Testament times, for it most certainly is! I am asking how it might have been expressed had it been written in New Testament times.

Such hypothetical questions are almost impossible to answer. I ask it merely to draw your attention to the fact that there are New Testament commandments which express the basic concerns of the first commandment.

Take 1 Corinthians 16:22: 'If anyone does not love the Lord, let him be accursed.' That is very strong language, bringing the curse of God down upon a man. Some in the church of Corinth were going in the wrong direction. Their very commitment to the Lord was brought into question. If they were not sincere in their love and devotion, then they were out!

We could also take 2 John 9. If anybody leaves behind the teaching of Christ, he has no relationship to God. You cannot mess around with this interesting idea, that new theory which leads away from the teaching of Christ. To do that would mean to forsake God. 1 John 2:23 says the same thing. Note also John 14:6.

There is an Old Testament exclusivism which says: there is only one God. There is an equivalent New Testament exclusivism which says: there is only one way to God. It is by Jesus. Do not try any other way. Do not think that you can depart one iota from the teaching of Jesus. If you forsake him, you are under a curse!

The next step in translating this passage into New Testament terms is to ask what is the New Testament equivalent of stoning. It is all very well to know that we are required to be as unswerving in our devotion to Jesus as Israel were to be in their devotion to God in Old Testament times. But what if somebody does deviate: what do you do about it? Suppose somebody in the church were to say: 'Jesus is not the only way to God. He is not the sole and perfect sacrifice for the sins of his people. You have to leave those ideas behind you.' 2 John is very clear (verses 9–11). You cut him off and have no fellowship with him. We commonly call that *excommunication*. It is a cutting off of the oneness, or communion, we have had with that person. We declare that we no longer share his ideas or projects.

This Old Testament passage is certainly very strong. There is an absolute determination behind those laws. Israel are not to be swayed from their devotion to God. The threat is serious, and therefore the counter-measures are serious. Often, when the subject of church discipline and excommunication is raised, the reaction is: Isn't that going a little too far? Sometimes that reaction is prompted by a wrong use of discipline; by a use of discipline to maintain one group in power, or to settle theological differences about matters which really are only trivial. If that is the source of the reaction, we should say: Just because something has been misused does not mean that it should not be properly used.

The more serious situation is when people are opposed to discipline as such. Because there is such an opposition to discipline abroad in Christian circles today, we have to ask ourselves: How seriously do we take devotion to Jesus and his teaching? How much does it mean to you that your church remains devoted to Jesus? What unpleasantness will you endure; what steps will you take; what mental and emotional trials will you face, in order to keep this church, this church which teaches you and your children, faithful with exclusive loyalty to Jesus, and Jesus alone?

The Old Testament remedy was not mild, and neither is the New Testament remedy, for excommunication is a death sentence. It says to a man that he is outside of the fellowship in which life exists. Now mind you, he has to show that he is spiritually dead before the church takes such action. He has to show that he will not heed the words of Christ. Nevertheless, it says to a man that whatever he thinks about his ideas or what he is doing, it is the way of death. The church will not allow him to spread that putrefaction of death within its ranks.

Is there another way to God except by Jesus? Is there another way to have our sins forgiven except by Jesus as the atoning sacrifice for our sins? If there is no other way to God, then faithfulness to Jesus is a serious matter.

Without Jesus, you and your children will go to hell and damnation. No, 'perhaps', no 'maybe', but certainty! You end up just like the idolater.

When the church refuses to discipline, it does not just face the danger that false doctrine and wrong life will take over. In a way they already have done so, for the seriousness of the first commandment has been lost.

Hence we approach this passage not as something which breathes a totally different spirit to our enlightened age. We recognise that God has not given to the church the power physically to punish false teachers. Nevertheless, the intent is an intent with which we sympathise.

Many pacifists today have a great problem for their theory in the Second World War. When asked: 'Did men do wrong in fighting to stop the cruelty and barbarism of the Nazis?', they do not know how to answer, for they sense how wrong that whole movement was, how it threatened so much of what was good and worthwhile in the world. God did not put first in his commandments: You shall not murder. He did not condemn gas chambers and concentration camps as worst of all sins, horrible though they may be, but he condemned first of all any departure from himself as the one and only God and Saviour. If you could not sit by and support the Nazis; if your conscience tells you they should have been stopped, how much more the man who would turn us to false gods?

The passage treats three ways in which the threat may come to Israel. It deals particularly with three sources of seduction which will be particularly difficult to resist.

The first is provided by the false prophet. What he predicts actually comes to pass. Bear in mind that one of the marks given by which Israel were to discern a true prophet was the accuracy of his predictions (*Deut.* 18:22). Here is a prophet who seems to have the badge of the true prophet. Not only that: ability to predict the future accurately is impressive. If anybody should have some knowledge of God, it is the man who knows the future.

We are coming out of an age in which people denied the very possibility of prophecy. The world was a world in which there was nothing beyond what we could see and feel. There was no God and there were no spirits. There are still people who believe that, or at least say that they do. As the increase in interest in the occult shows, people are turning away from that world and that belief. They are looking for a power beyond physical experience. In other words, we are moving into an age which is open to false prophets. We should not be surprised at that change, for the book of Revelation pictures false prophets and wonder workers as amongst the major allies of Satan in the period before Christ returns (13:11–13; 19:20).

If a man were able to give you a sign and it came to pass, such as saying: 'Tomorrow you will have a car accident, or your mother will die suddenly and unexpectedly,' how would you respond to him? Would you trust him? Would you think him to be close to God? What if he told you to change your mind about Jesus? You may say: 'Surely nobody would change their faith just for that.' Consider what we have seen in the last hundred years or so. Those who have told men to change their views about Jesus were not miracle workers. They could not predict the future. All they could say was: 'We are the scholars and the experts. Believe us.' So men have believed them, changing their views about the Bible and hence about Jesus. They did it for men who could only parade degrees, not miracles; for men who could only claim to have a better knowledge of the past rather than a knowledge of the future. If men will change their views for such unimpressive persuaders, how much more will they be susceptible to men who seem to have power and knowledge? This threat is not, therefore, to be underestimated.

The second threat is created by members of one's own family and intimate companions. Who would do anything against their own relatives, even if they were to entice you to forsake the Lord? But then there is a choice: who is more valuable to you, God, or your closest human loved one? Is the Old Testament harsh and un-Christian in setting that choice before us, and making us choose? What does Jesus say? 'He who loves father or mother more than me is not worthy of me; and he who loves son or daughter more than me is not worthy of me' *(Matt.* 10:37). It is the same choice, is it not?

If the fact that relatives were commanded to be foremost

in the stoning bothers you, then look at Deuteronomy 17:6-7. The Old Testament law did not allow you to accuse a man and then have someone else put him to death. If you accused him, then you started the execution. In other words, you had better be really sure that they did what you claimed, or their death would be doubly on your conscience. It is a consequence of this law that the one who has been enticed by a relative or friend should bring testimony and therefore participate in their execution.

A man turned himself into a New York mental hospital, screaming: 'I am going to kill! Stop me!' They locked him away for a few days, but did nothing really to investigate his case. A staff psychiatrist said: 'He is really very harmless.' So, they let him go, and he went out and killed several people. Then there was public indignation. The same indifference goes on in churches. We see in people the obvious signs that they are losing the battle against their own sinfulness, yet nothing is done. The friends and relatives say: 'Don't do anything. Don't do anything. We taught them that they must love and serve Jesus, but when they don't, please don't talk to them. Do not rebuke them. They are our friends and family after all. If they spurn Jesus, that does not matter. We do not want to do anything that might hurt them or make them upset.' Is it real love for our friends and relatives when we do not want them dealt with in the way that God has set forth for the correction of sinners?

The final problem is somewhat different. It is not a person so close to you that you do not want to take action. It is a person so distant that you can wash your hands and say, 'That is really not my responsibility.' The situation is that the evil begins in a particular village. The people and elders of that village do not take action. Soon the whole village is corrupt. Then what do you do? The natural reaction is to say: 'Sorry to hear about it, but it is not my sin. It is not my department. It was the responsibility of the people and elders of that town and they blew it. Nothing much that I can do.'

Well, God says there is something you can do. You are to punish the whole city that has embraced, protected and supported evil. The whole biblical teaching is clear. When you fail to deal with sin you make yourself guilty. The town that did not deal with sin is now equally guilty.

A good example of this principle in action is the Benjamite war recounted at the end of the book of Judges. The tribe of Benjamin refused to act against murderers and rapists in their midst. So the whole nation of Israel acted against the whole tribe of Benjamin, and it is made quite clear in the text that they were acting with God's full approval.

There have been cases in churches where a pastor or a professor has been teaching heresy. The assembly or synod of that church has then said: 'We do not agree with what the minister is teaching, but discipline is the task of the local church and its officers, and they are not doing anything, so what can we do?' The biblical answer is surely very clear. That local church is then guilty and should be disciplined. If you do not carry through at that level, then you are not following the biblical principle. Hence, you can expect corruption to spread further.

We have already seen that basic to this section of Scripture is a conviction about God. He, and he alone, is God. There can be no deviation from that truth. Under-lying the practical measures commanded is a conviction about man. Man is easily seduced and corrupted. Dislike for that biblical teaching also lies behind the opposition to discipline. 'Really, do we good, upstanding, pure, moral individuals need to be warned and punished so that we do not deviate from the truth?' Yes, we do, because we are not good and upstanding and moral! It is interesting that Scripture singles out the case of punishment of family members and close friends as the case to serve as warning to all Israel. If the whole community fears departure from God more than it loves its closest friends or family members, imagine the impact of that on the community. Here is a people that loves God and fears sin that much. You cannot get away with sin in such a community. Is that not something we desire for ourselves, our children and our church?

Questions for Discussion

1. Why does the unbeliever raise the medieval burning of witches as an argument against discipline in the church but does not conclude from political purges under tyrants that the state should be without any power to punish?

2. Is your attitude to excommunication shaped by experiences and stories or by Scripture?

3. This chapter has concentrated upon church discipline for denial that Jesus is the only way to God. Should discipline be used in response to other sins also?

4. Would you find it hard to argue that a close relative should be put out of the church?

9: *Knowing the True Prophet: Deuteronomy 18:9–22*

A number of years ago a nuclear reactor in the Ukraine went out of control. Those trying to contain it faced a very simple problem. How do you get close to something that is dangerous? That is an apt comparison for the problem of man's relationship to God.

You often hear the question raised: 'Why does God not make himself known to everybody?' Those who ask the question may not realise it, but they might as well ask: 'Why don't they ask people to bring their toasters and radiators and whatever, and plug them into the unshielded core of a nuclear reactor?'

The passage we are considering refers to what is probably the most public and open revelation of God in all biblical history. There, in front of the millions of Israel, God came down and revealed himself. It may not be what some people would want. It may not have been God revealing himself personally and individually to every person on the earth, but it was a revelation to millions.

What was their reaction? It was one of fear. It brought the request: 'Please do not do that again. Your glory is sufficient to kill me.'

Those who ask why God does not reveal himself more openly to man have overlooked who God is and who man is. At this point, my comparison with the nuclear reactor breaks down. A nuclear reactor is dangerous because it has power and force and energy. God has power, but not wild, uncontrolled power. There is something more than just power. The Bible calls that something more 'holiness'. Holiness is power aimed against whatever is sinful and defiling. Man is certainly sinful and defiling!

The Bible tells us that a day is going to come when God will reveal himself to everyone. We call that day the day of judgment, and the Bible says that man's reaction will be to flee in fear. How does the criminal react to the policeman? How does the man condemned to die react to the sound of the executioner approaching? So sinful man reacts in fear to the sight of the glorious judge. How can man have contact with God? Can God reveal himself and man not be destroyed?

The passage we read tells us that God has a solution for this problem. God's word and revelation do not come directly to man, but through another man, a prophet. When Israel responded in fear to God's speaking on Mount Sinai, God had pity on them. He arranged to communicate not directly to them, but through a mediator, Moses. God promised to Israel that he would continue to communicate to them that way even after Moses was dead. There would be other prophets to act as Moses did.

God will not reveal himself publicly until the day of judgment. That gives the unbeliever a problem. He desires information because he does not know the secret things that are hidden in the plan of God. So mediums appear as a non-Christian substitute for the prophet. The non-Christian uses diviners, fortune tellers, and people who claim to communicate with the spirits of the dead. All these things are attempts to put something in the place of what God has planned, and that is why they are wrong. That is why they are an abomination to God. Do not ever have anything to do with them. You will not meet God in that way, and nor will you get reliable information. On the contrary, you would meet a particularly angry God on the day of judgment!

It follows from what I have been saying that the prophet himself has to be a special person. He has to have a holiness so that God may speak to him, yet not destroy him. Many prophets found that a problem. Some were disobedient and suffered for it, like the prophet in 1 Kings 13. Even Moses had a problem. He disobeyed God and was punished for it by not being able to lead Israel into the promised land of Canaan.

The prophet thus occupied a very special place in God's plan. There is much importance in being a prophet, hence it is not surprising that impostors attempt to play the roles of prophets. Naturally, the impostor does not have the required holiness, but since sinful men often seem unable to recognise true holiness and to distinguish it from acting, they succeed in fooling people for a while. There are many charlatans who can do tricks or who can speak in an impressive way. They will fool people. God however, sets a standard by which Israel could distinguish the true prophet. He had to be able to tell what was going to happen and not be wrong. If he was wrong, he was a false prophet and was to be put to death.

There are many people who claim, or have claimed for them, an ability to predict the future. Nostradamus and Jean Dixon are two examples. Do they qualify as prophets? The biblical law says that if a prophet predicted something and it did not come to pass, he was a false prophet and was to be put to death. It does not say: 'If his predictions are correct much of the time'! It does not say: 'If they are half right, he is probably a psychic.' It says: 'If he is ever wrong, he is a false prophet, not to be followed, but to be rejected.' For a true prophet is a mediator, speaking the words of God. God is never wrong. If God says it will happen, then it will! Somebody who claims to predict the future, but makes mistakes, is not speaking from God. Even if he is right about some predictions, but tries to turn people from the true God, he is a false prophet.

Scripture does not go into a debate about how psychics make predictions. It does not discuss whether those who claim to call up the dead really do so, though from the rest of what Scripture tells us about the dead, I would think it unlikely. Instead, it tells us that these people are not the means of God's communication with men. They are to be shunned. We are to listen to God's messengers and to them alone.

I have already mentioned the problem the prophets had. They had a role which brought them close to God, yet they themselves were not completely holy. That did not make their message wrong, for after all they were still simple spokesmen. God put the words into their mouth for them to speak, yet they were not perfect intermediaries to reveal God's plan to men.

Jesus is that perfect intermediary, the one who completely fulfils the prophecy here of a prophet. He is the perfect one to reveal God's words to man because he knows what is in the mind of God the Father. See John 7:29: 'I know Him; because I am from Him, and He sent Me,' and Matthew 11:27: 'All things have been handed over to Me by My Father; and no one knows the Son, except the Father; nor does anyone know the Father, except the Son, and anyone to whom the Son wills to reveal Him.' Jesus is more than a prophet, that is, one who spoke the words of God without necessarily understanding all that was involved in those words. He is the one who knows the Father intimately and completely.

Further, he became a man able to speak the language of men, both in a literal sense and in the sense of knowing what men need to hear. There can be things that are true and yet irrelevant. I once had a teacher who would deduct marks for anything irrelevant in an answer. He used to delight in writing across the paper 'true, but irrelevant'! You would have to agree with him that what you wrote was not directly and absolutely on the topic of the question. Truth that is irrelevant, that does not seek to address the problem at hand, is of no use. Jesus not only knows the answer as God, but he also knows the problem as man. He is therefore qualified to play the role of the one who conveys the truth from God to sinful man.

As a second main qualification, we could list the fact that he was holy. He alone, of all messengers of God, did not need to be afraid in God's presence, because he alone had not sinned. When we read in Scripture of God coming to men and commissioning them to be prophets, then very often the first words of God are: 'Do not be afraid.' God did not speak that way with Jesus, because their fellowship was continual and constant and not marred by the fear that results from sin.

In the third place, he has satisfied the test of Deuteronomy 18:22. What he said has come true. He came predicting that he would die by crucifixion, betrayed by his own people. The disciples rejected that. The multitude did not understand it because it did not fit into their expectation of what the Messiah should do. Yet he was right! He claimed that by his death, he would draw men from throughout the world to himself. Present believers are proof of the truth of that prophecy. He foretold that Jerusalem would reject the gospel and be destroyed. The Jews rejected the gospel and the Romans destroyed the city and the temple in A.D. 70. He himself has foretold that, at the final judgment, we shall all stand before him to be judged. That prophecy has not yet been fulfilled, but it will be. He showed the mark of a true prophet in that he did not seek to turn men to false gods, but back to the true God alone. If you read the Gospels, you will be struck by how often Jesus directs people to God the Father. He constantly quoted from the Old Testament to show that what he taught was not a contradiction of it.

Given all that, there are two interesting things about the revelation of Jesus. In one way it was also a restricted revelation; that is, not a general and indiscriminate revelation to everybody in general.

Jesus taught publicly, and yet the full explanation of his teaching was reserved for his small band of disciples. The other Judas (not Judas Iscariot) asked Jesus why he would reveal himself to the disciples, but not to the world in general. Jesus' answer is very interesting. In effect, he says that he and the Father will fellowship with the one who loves Jesus and his Word, but not with those who do not want to keep his Word (*John* 14:22–24). It comes back to the question of human sin. Jesus does not parade his precious words before men who despise them and scoff at them. The same is true after his resurrection. He revealed himself alive to his disciples, though, as mentioned earlier, that does not indicate an unwillingness to show himself to men. He will do so on the day of judgment.

Yet, there is also a sense in which Jesus' revelation is public and available to all. He came to reveal the Father to all who wanted to know. He came to reveal the message of God in language men could understand. He commissioned disciples with a task to carry that message throughout the world. We have the Bible. It is not frightening, not terrifying. You can read it. The revelation of God has come in two forms. One is the revelation of his glory which no sinner can abide. The other is the non-threatening revelation mediated by men, above all in the man Christ Jesus. If you will not obey the revelation which does not terrify you by its mere appearance, you will be more than terrified when God is revealed in the last day in all his glory.

Questions for Discussion

1. Do we tend to carry on philosophical discussions about revelation which ignore God's holiness?

2. Contrast occult communication with biblical revelation.

3. Present-day prophecy has become a topic of major interest in some churches. Should a present day 'prophet' be judged by a standard as strict as that set out in Deuteronomy 18:20-22?

4. How would you answer somebody who argued that biblical revelation lacks the wonderful and impressive characteristics which one would expect in a divine revelation?

10: *How to Fight a War: Deuteronomy 20:1–8*

Some people say that the Old Testament, by comparison with the New Testament, is a rather worldly book. The New Testament is spiritual. The Old Testament is full of the concerns of the sinful world; hatred, wars and murders. Its laws are harsh and legalistic.

I wonder if those people have ever read this chapter. Certainly it is about war, yet it shows a contrast to the way the world fights its wars. Some of you reading this may have been in the army or the navy. When you were conscripted, or when you signed up, were you asked whether you had a sweetheart at home, or whether you had any ideas of marriage? And if so, were you told to go home? If that had been the case, many of you may have married a lot earlier than you did! Did they ask you: 'Have you just started your own business? We could not take you away before you have begun to see some profits.'? Or, were you asked: 'Do you have a block of land on which you plan to build? Away you go then. We do not want to take you away before you have begun to enjoy your own home.' Or: 'You are not afraid of going to war, are you? If you are, you are free to go.'! That is not the way that the world fights its wars!

Note the way this is presented. Israel were going out to war. They saw horses and chariots and a lot more soldiers than they had. The officers had spoken to the soldiers telling first this group and then that group to go home. Imagine that you were left standing there. You were not engaged, nor had you just planted a vineyard or built a house. You could not go home, yet you saw your army dwindling away, with the other side getting more and more! The officer kept saying: 'You might get killed.' Finally, when all the frightened people were sent home, might you have been one of them?

When your sporting team is playing the best team in the competition, what does your coach say? If it is football, does he say: 'Any of you doing anything this week that you need two good legs for? This is a pretty tough team we're playing, and we may well end up with some broken legs. If you need two good legs this week, you had better not play!' If it is cricket, does he say: 'Are any of you afraid of being hit in the face with a cricket ball? This team has some pretty fast bowlers. If you are afraid, you had better not play!' If he were to say those things, you would be so scared, you would never play your best. So, instead he might say: 'You can beat them! They are really a soft team.' It is called psychology, or morale boosting, the power of positive thinking. You are to think only of how easy something will be.

The Bible does not do that however. Did Jesus say to his disciples: 'It will be a piece of cake. You will be popular. People will fall over themselves to become Christians.'? No! Rather, he said: 'They will hate you. They will beat you. They will ridicule you. They will cast you out of the synagogues.'

We see in this passage very different concerns, which I will take up one by one:

1. There is a fundamental concern for a sort of justice. A man should enjoy the fruits of his labour. Have you worked for something? Then you deserve to enjoy the result. That principle, because it is a principle of God's justice, has precedence over any pragmatic considerations of what will help to win a war. If that principle were to rule our economic system, we would have such a better system. If bosses treated their workmen, and paid them not out of some grudging obedience to some industrial award, but out of respect for the workers' right to enjoy fruit from their labour, then we would have a lot less industrial strife. If workmen wanted the bosses to see the fruits of the work they had put into the enterprise, there would be a lot more harmony on the job.

Yet, this principle applies to much more than our employment. It is also the principle which God applies to all who serve him. Paul says: 'Let us not lose heart in doing good, for in due time we shall reap if we do not grow weary' (*Gal.* 6:9). How can he say that with certainty? It is because God applies this principle, and rules the world according to this principle of his justice. Have you seen little fruit for your labour in the service of the Lord? Is there a certain discouragement because you expected a lot more? Well, know this; God will not deny his own law. Do not grow weary. Persevere and you will see the fruit of your labours.

We can go a step further. Your labour, if labour in the Lord, is carried out to extend the kingdom and rule of the Lord Jesus Christ. How do we know that his kingdom will be extended? We know it because God himself has applied this very same rule to Jesus. Remember that verse towards the end of the description of Christ's sufferings in Isaiah 53 (verse 11): 'As a result of the anguish (or perhaps we should translate the "hard toil") of his soul he shall see and be satisfied.' Jesus also laboured, and far more than any of us. Abundant fruit, fruit which would satisfy him, is promised to him. We may at this time be discouraged by the yield, wishing it were far greater. We may wonder, given the hardness of men's hearts, whether it will ever be greater. But we know this, that it will be a yield which will be to Jesus an adequate satisfaction for all his anguish and labour. Is that not in itself sufficient reason for us to expect abundant fruit in the future?

2.   The main problem facing the army was not lack of numbers, but fear. Israel is told not to be afraid because God, the God who brought them up from Egypt, is with them. When you know that, then numbers are not important. Perhaps it is even far better to have a small and trusting group, than a large one containing men who are afraid, for those men serve to make their companions afraid also. A man panicking, or talking about how large the enemy army is, or running away, are all things which would spread panic through the army, destroying the will to fight.

One can see the effects of such people today. There is a group of people who seem to delight in demoralising the people of God. You expect that sort of thing from people outside the church, but not from those inside. There are people who delight in pointing out that respect for the church is declining, that church attendance is dwindling, that we live in a post-Christian age, when most people are uninterested in the gospel. I know a man who produces books of statistics to illustrate the decline of the church in Australia today. If he said, as is an obvious fact, that the churches which are declining are those which have abandoned the Bible, then he may be able to draw some useful conclusions. But no! He just seems to get satisfaction from painting the gloomy picture.

There are others who point out that all good churches ultimately go bad. They spread a demoralisation by saying: History proves that your church will go bad eventually. So, why try? Why do anything about it if you see the rot beginning?

It is true that the enemies of the church are numerous. Israel were outnumbered on many occasions. It is true that there have been churches that have turned from the truth and suffered decline and loss of membership. The decline in overall church attendance in Australia is an instance of that. In numerical terms, there is a preponderance of those who do not obey the gospel. However, Scripture tells us not to look to the numbers, but rather, to look to God. It tells us not to look to the things which indicate how hard the battle is, but rather, to look at who is on our side: the Lord!

So we need to say to those who are spreading demoralisation, to those who, because they themselves lack confidence in God and his Word, are spreading uncertainty and panic: Why don't you just go home? If you have no confidence for the fight, then we do not need you. The battle will be a lot easier without you.

We need to go back to the point I made earlier about Christ being satisfied with the fruit of his labour. There is no assurance here that nobody will get hurt, or even killed. All there is, is the assurance of victory. I give you no comforting doctrine that you will not fight hard and difficult battles, battles that may hurt. All the Word says is that Christ will ultimately be victorious.

3.   The fundamental perspective behind this passage is one found throughout Scripture. Man is fundamentally irrelevant when it comes to winning the Lord's battles. Remember how God decreased the numbers in Gideon's army just to make the point that statistics are irrelevant to the battles of Israel.

You may then ask why God asks us to engage in the battle at all. David and his sling prove that one inexperienced, but trusting, Israelite was all that was needed to defeat Goliath and the Philistines. But why David? God could have thrown the stone himself!

There are many possible answers to this problem. I will take one aspect of a complex truth. It is by these experiences that faith is tried and faith grows. When we look at the men who, in the history of the church, succeeded against tremendous odds: the Pauls, Luthers, Whitefields and Patons, then we say: 'What faith! What courage those men had.' True! They did have faith. Why? Because they faced so many adversaries. Because they had no human hope of success. Therefore, they trusted in God and achieved the victory. Because man is irrelevant and God is everything, we have great men of faith.

That may sound like a paradox, and yet it is true. The more you depreciate the significance of man, the more you emphasise the importance of God, the greater the men you produce.

That is quite contrary to the wisdom of the world which so often infiltrates the church. People say: 'We need to put more emphasis on the human side,' and we see the results in the statistics of emptying churches.

In short, the Bible fights wars as it does anything else. Put God first and trust in him, and the rest will take care of itself.

Questions for Discussion

1. Is the modern church too reluctant to tell inquirers to count the cost?

2. Is the contemporary antipathy to hard work, both in society in general and in the church, a consequence of ignorance of God's attitudes to work and its rewards?

3. Tabulate the ways in which contemporary motivational techniques are foreign to the Bible.

4. If we live in a 'post-Christian' age and things are, supposedly, much harder for the church, why do we seem to produce so few men of faith?

11: *Blessing, Curse and Restoration: Deuteronomy 28:1–10, 15–26; 30:1–10*

If I were to ask you: 'Are you blessed, or are you cursed?', you would probably respond with a very blank look. We are not used to thinking in those terms. At the most we might think about being lucky or unlucky, or, realising that talking about luck is superstitious, we might say: 'I am having a relatively easy time at the moment' or 'I am having a hard time'; but we would not be as likely to use the terms 'blessed' or 'cursed'.

Those are the terms in which God looked at the history of Israel. They will have a future of blessing, abundant blessing, overflowing blessing; or they will have a future of curse, frightening curse.

These passages are a problem to people for reasons other than the fact that we do not think of ourselves as 'blessed' or 'cursed'. There are two common objections raised to what the Old Testament says about blessing.

The common objection is that the Old Testament teaching on blessing is very materialistic. The blessings promised are things like wealth and prosperity, health, and defeat of enemies in battle. This is claimed to be unspiritual, in contrast to New Testament teaching, where the blessings we receive are spiritual: sins forgiven, and peace with God.

We cannot deny that the New Testament has a much stronger emphasis upon the work of the Holy Spirit than the Old Testament. The Spirit is poured out in far greater abundance as a result of Jesus' death, resurrection and ascension. Nevertheless, we cannot draw an absolute contrast, because that would be untrue to Scripture. For example, the Christian looks forward to a new heaven and a new earth. The blessings we shall experience in that new creation will include some very material blessings, for example, we look forward to the end of pain and weeping and death. We will be in a world where there is no darkness. We will have food without shortage. There will no longer be strife and killing in the animal kingdom, but rather peace. Are we unspiritual because we look forward with anticipation to those things?

On the contrary, you would be very unspiritual if you said: 'Well, as for this no pain and no weeping bit, I can take it or leave it! People's suffering does not really bother me.'

This comparison to our anticipation of the new heavens and the new earth is important, because Israel was to experience these blessings in the land of Canaan, the promised land. In the outworking of God's plan for man, there is a relationship between Canaan and the new heavens and new earth. Canaan was a forerunner, a foreshadowing, or to use the language Scripture uses for such things, a 'type', of the new heavens and the new earth. It was not a perfect duplicate. Even though long life was promised for obedience in Canaan, the Israelites still died. Even though there was assurance of victory over enemies, they still had to fight. There was, as this passage shows, a prospect of losing that inheritance. The New Testament often takes the Old Testament term 'inheritance', used for the inheritance in Canaan, and uses it to refer to our hope of a future inheritance. 1 Peter 1:4 is a good example. Notice that the inheritance to which we look forward is an imperishable one, one that will not be lost. Nevertheless, as there is a relationship between our future inheritance and Israel's inheritance in Canaan, it is not surprising that Israel experienced, in Canaan, many of the blessings to which we look forward.

Finally, this contrast between the Old Testament as a book of material blessings and the New Testament as a book of spiritual blessings makes an unbiblical separation. God created man body and soul. Man cannot be fully blessed without bodily material blessings simply because he has a body. Our situation now parallels the situation of Israel on the way to Canaan. Israel had their need for food in the wilderness met by manna. So we also pray for our daily bread. Yet the diet of manna was not so rich, varied and exciting as they would enjoy in Canaan, and nor was it as varied and tasty as what Egypt had offered. Hence, the rebellions which said: 'Let us go back to Egypt.' Similarly, we may be tempted to give up our hope of future blessings, including those of diet, for greater riches now. It is that temptation which poses for us the danger of thinking materially and not spiritually. If we really read the Old Testament for what it says, it will not be a source of temptation to materialism, because it tells us that these material blessings will be ours if we are obedient. Our temptation is not to seek material blessings by way of obedience, but through the way of disobedience. If we know that we await the return of Christ to receive our full material blessings, so we will also realise that we cannot simply take over these Old Testament promises of material prosperity and expect them to be fulfilled for us here and now. That will no more happen than Israel in the wilderness could expect abundant harvests before it was God's time to take them into the promised land.

The second argument raised against the teaching of blessing in this text is that it is a doctrine of works: that Israel were to be blessed in reward for obedience. It is claimed that, in contrast, the New Testament doctrine is one of grace: that God's blessing comes to us sinners who have done nothing to deserve it.

The answer lies, once more, in seeing where we are and where Israel were in God's plan. The Israelites to whom these promises were addressed were already redeemed; for the Old Testament redemption, which corresponds to our deliverance through Christ, is the exodus, the deliverance from bondage in Egypt. It is to a redeemed people that God gave such promises. Israel were not delivered from Egypt for their goodness, but in spite of their sinfulness. There is grace in the Old Testament! We know that they worshipped other gods in Egypt. We know that their ancestors served other gods. Nevertheless, God redeemed them from Egypt and made them his people. Once they were redeemed, they were to live as a redeemed people. If they did not, then they could not continue to enjoy the blessings of redemption. The teaching here is really no different from the teaching in the New Testament, such as in 1 Corinthians 5:11–13. Nobody who continues a life of sexual immorality, crime or greed and such like can receive the blessings of God. That does not mean that a Christian may not once have lived that way, but that salvation is salvation to live a new life. So it is for us, and so it was also for Israel.

Perhaps if you remember Deuteronomy 13, this will be clearer. The punishment for seducing people into idolatry was death. A person, a village or a nation could not continue to enjoy the benefits of God whilst they turned to idolatry. So also in the New Testament we enjoy the blessings into which Christ has brought us, whilst we persevere in his service.

These passages have raised questions on another score because they seem so harsh. Do stories of famine and drought, war and pestilence, disease and cannibalism belong in Scripture? Ironically, some people reject Scripture, saying that it is not fit to speak to the harsh realities of the modern world. Actually sudden death from a nuclear blast might be a preferable end to the slow death of starvation during a prolonged siege. You may respond that you would like neither, and nor would I! The point is, simply, that there are some cruel, unpleasant and horrible things in this world. The Bible does not pretend that they are not there: it knows they are there. The Bible is about the realities of our life upon earth.

The Bible can also tell us why they are there: because of the sin of man. You cannot find a one-to-one correspondence between sin and calamity, saying, for instance, that a particular drought was for any particular sin. Nor can you say that a country experiencing drought has worse sinners than those countries receiving adequate rain. God's blessings and punishments always retain the character of sovereign mystery. Nevertheless, as this and many other passages of Scripture make clear, God's judgments are judgments upon disobedience. You cannot continue to know the rich and full blessings of God while you live in disobedience. The history of Israel knew prosperity, but they turned from the one who gave that prosperity, so experiencing all the consequences listed here. So also have many other nations and individuals experienced God's wrath. As we slide from prosperity, we also will know the consequences of disobedience until, and unless, we repent.

One of the interesting notes made in these chapters is the fact that blessings and curse cannot be kept secret. Look at 28:10, 37. If you are blessed, people will notice. If you are under curse, people will know.

There are many different recipes for creating a church that is growing, evangelistic, and attracting others in. One of the most interesting is simply to go to work to build up the members of the church, to help them overcome their needs and their problems. It is not an infallible recipe, but it very often works, whilst the more elaborate and seemingly explicitly evangelistic strategies fail. Why is that? It is simply because, if you are being blessed, you cannot hide it. Conversely, if you have personal problems, or if the church has problems, you cannot hide it, and you attract only those who want to share your misery.

We have here blessing and curse, prosperity and calamity. You may think that that is about all there is to be said; that it sums up everything, but there is more. Blessing and curse was not the whole story. In particular, curse was not to be the end of history for Israel, a point made very clear in 30:1-10. Beyond the terror of the curses, there was still hope. Scripture does not treat the curses as something hypothetical, which might possibly happen but will not really happen. It knows the sinfulness and unfaithfulness of man. Nevertheless, it says: when these things have happened, yet there is hope. After Israel seem to have lost everything, even their land, they can still be restored.

I raised the question earlier of whether these passages, especially those about blessing, teach a salvation by works. To put your mind at rest on this, take note of what the text says about restoration. After Israel have so acted as to forfeit all right to God's blessing, God received them to be his people again, restored them, and returned them to their own land, to enjoy prosperity once more. That was an act of pure grace.

The whole history of the people of God has been one long fulfilment of this promise. Take the period of the judges. Again and again God's people turned away. God took away their prosperity and gave them into the hand of their enemies. Yet, that was not the end. They sought the Lord, and he delivered them. During the monarchy there were also periods of apostasy. You may remember the apostasy which led to Judah being delivered into the hands of the Assyrians, but God raised up prophets like Micah and Isaiah, and a king like Hezekiah. Again, after the curses had been fulfilled, and Judah had been taken from their land by the Babylonians, God brought them back.

Then again, even in their land they were subjected to Roman bondage and the domination of false teachers, but God did not leave them there. He sent Jesus to deliver them from their spiritual bondage.

You might think that the story of restoration would stop there. Would God do anything about the men who have spurned the grace that is in Jesus, and turned to a religion in which man is his own saviour? Could his grace extend thus far? The Reformation is proof that it did. Can it continue? After the Reformation, the church was corrupted by those who placed their own wisdom above God's, and declared the Word to be no longer their authority. God did not abandon his church, but sent revival through people like Whitefield, and through the separation movements of last century and this century.

No logic demands that God again and again restore his wayward people. He owes them nothing after they have rejected him. Yet, out of his grace and mercy, he again and again restores them to himself.

There is one particular case of such mercy that we need to consider: Paul, in Romans 9–11, talks about his Jewish contemporaries, who have rejected Jesus. They are in a state of rebellion, and that rebellion was to lead to their being delivered into the hands of the Romans, and the destruction of the temple in A.D. 70, which resulted in the exile of many Jews and then again, in the next century, when the Second Jewish Revolt was crushed, the exile of many more. Israel was in revolt against God. Israel was being given over to the curse. Could there be hope for Israel? Yes! Paul is confident that God will again gather his people. Here, the structure we have seen in the Old Testament is again at work. Rebellion and curse are not to be the end for Israel.

There is a school of biblical interpretation called Dispensationalism, which makes much of the idea of the restoration of Israel. I do not want to take time to go into the details, but there is one point of importance which flows directly from the text we have been considering. Most Dispensationalists see the creation of the modern state of Israel as part of this gracious working of God.

Modern Israel, they say, is God fulfilling Deuteronomy. He is bringing Israel out of their exile and back into their own land. If that sounds convincing, I suggest you read what the text actually says (*Deut.* 30:1–3). First, Israel recalled God's word and repented in their land of captivity. Then, God brought them back. There is no restoration without repentance. The curse continues until people turn back to the Lord.

The modern state of Israel is not a nation that has turned back to the Lord. It was established by very secular, proud men. There may be people in Israel who have now become Christians, but that is after the fact. If the state of Israel should collapse or be destroyed, the faith of many Christians who have accepted Dispensationalism, would be shaken. It need not be, for modern Israel is not a case of people who have recalled the Lord's goodness and returned to him. That does not mean that other Jews, or masses of Jewry, may not in the future turn to God.

Finally, what about you? As you look back at your life, does it seem as though you are under curse? You may well be. However, curse is not the end. Beyond the punishment that your sin and rebellion have brought upon you, there lies hope of restoration. So call this promise to mind, turn to the Lord, and he will have mercy and restore you.

Questions for Discussion

1. The blessings and curses described in this passage are directed to Israel as a whole. Can individuals also know blessing or curse?

2. Why is it not possible to be neither blessed or cursed but somewhere in between?

3. Is the lack of concern for the material blessings of the new heavens and new earth among Western Christians a symptom of our satisfaction with our material prosperity?

4. Some say that anybody who once professes Christ has eternal security no matter what the nature of their later life. What are the implications of this passage for that idea?

5. If one would not gain the impression that the contemporary church is blessed, what then is its state and why?